E-Learning in the 21st Century

The third edition of *E-Learning in the 21st Century* provides a coherent, comprehensive, and empirically based framework for understanding e-learning in higher education. Garrison draws on his decades of experience and extensive research in the field to explore technological, pedagogical, and organizational implications. The third edition has been fully updated throughout and includes new material on learning technologies, MOOCs, blended learning, leadership, and the importance and role of social connections in thinking and learning, highlighting the transformative and disruptive impact that e-learning has recently had on education.

D. Randy Garrison is Professor Emeritus at the University of Calgary, Canada.

E-Learning in the 21st Century

A Community of Inquiry Framework for Research and Practice

Third Edition

D. Randy Garrison

Routledge
Taylor & Francis Group

NEW YORK AND LONDON

Third edition published 2017
by Routledge
711 Third Avenue, New York, NY 10017

and by Routledge
2 Park Square, Milton Park, Abingdon, Oxon OX14 4RN

Routledge is an imprint of the Taylor & Francis Group, an informa business

© 2017 Taylor & Francis

Library of Congress Cataloging-in-Publication Data
Names: Garrison, D. R. (D. Randy), 1945- author.
Title: E-learning in the 21st century : a community of inquiry framework for
research and practice / D. Randy Garrison.
Description: Third edition. | New York : Routledge, 2017. | Includes
bibliographical references and index.
Identifiers: LCCN 2016014252| ISBN 9781138953550 (hardback) |
ISBN 9781138953567 (pbk.) | ISBN 9781315667263 (ebook)
Subjects: LCSH: Education, Higher–Computer network resources. |
Education, Higher–Effect of technological innovations on. | Internet in
higher education. | Distance education.
Classification: LCC LB2395.7 .G37 2017 | DDC 378/.00285--dc23
LC record available at https://lccn.loc.gov/2016014252

ISBN: 978-1-138-95355-0 (hbk)
ISBN: 978-1-138-95356-7 (pbk)
ISBN: 978-1-315-66726-3 (ebk)

Typeset in Sabon
by Taylor & Francis Books

Contents

Illustrations

Figures

Tables

Preface to the Third Edition

First, let me say how fortunate I am to have the opportunity to revisit *E-Learning in the 21st Century*. Research and practice of online and blended learning have expanded exponentially in the last five years. These developments warrant a close examination and assessment of e-learning during this time. Considering the acceptance of online and blended learning in mainstream educational practice as well as pervasive technological innovation, there is a need to highlight the transformative and disruptive impact that e-learning has had on education. The affordances of e-learning have made possible new approaches to thinking and learning and caused considerable reflection on traditional information transmission approaches to education. With the pace of change, there is a need for a re-examination of e-learning reflected in the form of online and blended learning.

From the beginning, *E-Learning in the 21st Century* was fundamentally shaped by the Community of Inquiry (CoI) framework. However, the original title did not explicitly reflect the influence of this framework in the shaping of the first editions. For this reason, the subtitle has been changed to more accurately reflect the structure and focus of the third edition. The use of the CoI framework to guide the exploration of e-learning is also warranted by the reality that collaborative approaches to thinking and learning have become an educational focus. The change in the subtitle is further reinforced with the growth of the popularity of CoI framework as the conceptual guide to the study and practice of online and blended learning. More community of inquiry research has been published in the last five years than was published the first ten years since the seminal publication of the CoI framework (Garrison, Anderson & Archer, 2000).

Changes and additional contributions to the third edition begin with a significant rewrite of each of the chapters to reflect new research and practices associated with online and blended learning. In addition to updating and expanding each of the chapters, a number of new topics and sections have been added. Emerging theoretical issues of the CoI framework are explored which reinforces the frameworks validity and value in understanding and applying the complexities of e-learning.

Even as I finish this third edition, I need to remind myself that e-learning in the form of online and blended learning has been with us for only a couple of decades. Remarkable things have occurred in this short period of time. What is most remarkable is the shift in how educators conceptualize and approach educational experiences and what we now imagine as best practice. There is a growing consensus that we must provide more active, engaged and collaborative learning experiences if we are to achieve our educational goals to develop critical and creative thinkers and learners. Individuals who can thrive in a connected and rapidly changing knowledge society will have learned to think, learn and work in collaborative learning environments.

As always, I am indebted to my colleagues and all those who have contributed to the interest in e-learning and the development of the CoI framework. I have always found it remarkable how these collaborations have modeled communities of inquiry. Certainly this community of researchers has motivated me to continue to explore new ideas and attempt to resolve emerging anomalies. It gives me great satisfaction to see the insightful and rigorous research that has provided credibility to this increasingly important area of educational research—most of which was achieved through collaborative inquiry.

Preface to the Second Edition

The goal of the second edition of *E-Learning in the 21st Century* is to provide an update based on a decade of research since the first publication of the CoI framework (Garrison, Anderson & Archer, 2000). The first edition essentially compiled the original set of articles authored by the principle researchers. In the second edition, chapters one, four and twelve have been completely rewritten, a new chapter has been added (chapter eight) and the remaining chapters have undergone significant revision to incorporate the considerable research of an e-learning community of inquiry since the first publication. The revisions provide new perspectives and understanding that enhance considerably the CoI framework as a theoretical and practical guide.

This book is an inquiry into e-learning in higher education. By inquiry, we mean the process of transforming an "indeterminate situation" into one that is unified and coherent—to paraphrase Dewey (1938, p. 117). The primary product of this inquiry has been the CoI theoretical framework. The framework has also provided guidance in the subsequent inquiry into e-learning. While this may sound like a closed loop, true inquiry is open to new evidence and insights; and there have been many insights over the years that we will explore in this new edition.

I do want to express how grateful and indebted I am to all those who believed in and contributed to the development of the CoI framework since the publication of the original articles. There is a core group of researchers who have formed a very productive community, provided important insights, and have been instrumental in moving the CoI framework to becoming a credible theory for e-learning. In this regard, I wish to acknowledge and sincerely thank the following for their support, ideas and belief in this work: Zehra Akyol, Ben Arbaugh, Marti Cleveland-Innes, Sebastian Diaz, Phil Ice, Jennifer Richardson, Peter Shea, Karen Swan and Norm Vaughan. In particular, I want to thank former doctoral students of mine, Norm Vaughan and Zehra Akyol, for their friendship and keeping me immersed in research associated with the CoI framework. Finally, I must also acknowledge the many other researchers and graduate students that have used and contributed to the development of the CoI framework and the acceptance of online and blended learning in higher education.

It has been an exciting and fulfilling journey, and I hope there will be further adventures as we move into the second decade of this research. I feel we have just begun to take flight as e-learning and the CoI theoretical framework enters the mainstream of higher education.

D. Randy Garrison
January 2011

Preface to the First Edition

The goal of *E-Learning in the Twentieth-Century* is to provide a framework for understanding the application of e-learning in higher education. We view e-learning as that learning facilitated online through network technologies. This does not preclude any number of other technologies or approaches, including components of face-to-face educational experiences. However, we will confine our discussion to those learning activities conducted through electronic means online.

Various authors have described the growth of e-learning as explosive, unprecedented, amazing and disruptive. In fact, there are those who argue that we are experiencing a revolution in higher education (Report of a University of Illinois Faculty Seminar, 1999). Others suggest that e-learning technology is unique (Harasim, 1989) and represents a new era of distance education (Garrison, 1997). Regardless of the rhetoric, what has changed is the "speed and power of communications and the expanded capacity to send, receive, and use information" (Ikenberry, 1999, p. 57) and the capacity to bridge time and space for educational purposes.

While lifelong learning has become an imperative and communications technologies are transforming higher education, in most instances "the revolution proceeds without any clear vision or master plan" (Ikenberry, 1999, p. 58). Considering the massive adoption of e-learning, what is surprising is that we have much to learn about the use of this approach to learning. To date, published research and guides consist of innumerable case studies and personal descriptions and prescriptions but little in the way of rigorous, research-based constructs that lead to an in-depth understanding of e-learning in higher education.

Considering the ubiquity of e-learning, and the enormous opportunities and risks that it presents for higher education, we need more than a fragmented approach to studying and understanding this phenomenon. Is e-learning to be used simply to enhance inherently deficient existing practices (e.g. lecturing)? Or does this technology have the potential to transform the educational transaction towards the ideal of a community of inquiry? Such questions can only be addressed and explored through empirically based research frameworks such as those presented in this book.

How the Book Came to Be

The authors will provide educators with a deep understanding of the characteristics of e-learning. This in-depth understanding will give direction and guidance to educators who wish to facilitate critical discourse and higher-order learning through the use of electronic technologies in a networked learning context. Every university and college now has large numbers of faculty members using e-learning to enhance their campus-based and distance-education programming. Some of the most innovative technological e-learning approaches are being built in corporations to improve performance and retain competitive advantages.

The first part of this book describes a coherent and comprehensive theoretical framework that has been used to guide research on e-learning. In the second part of the book, the technological, pedagogical and organizational implications of this technology will be explored.

The book demonstrates that e-learning can create asynchronous communities of inquiry which have the potential to support the development of collaborative communities of learning, while still allowing "anytime–anywhere" access by students. We are convinced that such technology, when combined with effective pedagogy and reflective teaching, will transform higher education. In the later chapters of the book, this potential is translated into practical models intended to be used by educators working to realize the full potential of e-learning.

This book contributes a meaningful framework and approach to the understanding of the fundamentals of e-learning and explains why it is proliferating throughout a rapidly evolving learning society. This is the first comprehensive and coherent framework to guide our understanding of e-learning in higher education and society.

To this point, communications technologies have been driving the unprecedented growth of e-learning. The focus in this book is less on the specifics of the ever-evolving technologies used for e-learning, and more on the search for a deep understanding of these technologies from an educational perspective. It is to the purpose of mapping the territory of e-learning, then providing directional choices for higher education and specific guidelines to reach worthwhile destinations, that this book makes its contribution.

This book will appeal to a broad audience interested in e-learning. The primary audiences, however, are researchers, practitioners and senior administrators in higher education who must guide the adoption in their institutions of this unique and rapidly proliferating technology. This book is of particular relevance to those who are less impressed with technological gadgetry but who have been waiting for a strong pedagogical reason to participate in the paradigm shift in teaching and learning that e-learning represents.

This book can be used as a basic research framework and tool to study and understand the characteristics of e-learning and to explore its optimal educational applications. It will also be useful as a textbook for adult education and training as well as any number of instructional-technology and distance-education courses. Finally, it will be a valuable reference and guide for senior decision-makers in higher education.

Acknowledgments

The research on which this book is based originated most directly from a major research grant which allowed the authors to study the characteristics and qualities of e-learning, with specific reference to the ability of e-learning to foster higher-order learning. It also represented the culmination of years of experience in this field by the original researchers who have brought to the project a broad range of different but complementary perspectives and expertise gained through their teaching and learning experiences and original research.

Chapter I

Introduction

Information and communication technologies have socially and economically reshaped society. These same innovations, however, have not had a commensurate influence in the educational domain. Notwithstanding the many inroads that information and communication technologies have made in education, passive information transfer still dominates the educational enterprise. Moreover, there is a growing recognition that we are not taking full advantage of connectivity opportunities for the development of critical thinking and inquiry that has become the foundation of a knowledge-based society. Rethinking conventional education in light of technological developments and the need for higher-order educational outcomes is shaking the foundation of the educational enterprise. E-learning is the nexus of technological and pedagogical developments which has led to insights into deep and meaningful learning.

The emergence of e-learning with its sustained connectivity has demonstrated that deep and meaningful learning is not limited to the face-to-face classroom experience. E-learning is transformational in how we think about educational experiences in terms of sustained communication and collaboration. Ubiquitous communication technologies that can sustain the connection of learners and instantly access information have significantly shifted our conception and acceptance of e-learning. At the educational core is an awareness that students need to be engaged in sustainable learning communities that support reflective discourse and deep approaches to learning. The affordances of ubiquitous and powerful communications technologies with their ability to create and sustain communities of learners have brought e-learning into the mainstream of educational thought and practice.

Education is being transformed as a result of pedagogical advances made possible by e-learning. Educational approaches in the form of sustained e-learning communities are having us reflect on what are worthwhile and relevant educational experiences.

> E-learning is pushing teaching and learning design to evolve and reflect a more authentic and accurate representation of how we as humans,

actually learn. What appears to be a "new" era of knowledge delivery, actually reflects how humans have traded in knowledge for millions of years. Our individualistic educational culture is beginning to recognise the wisdom of collective principles in learning and knowledge.

(Wright, 2015, p. 26)

While it may seem surprising to mainstream education, e-learning is not a radical new innovation but a return to traditional values associated with discourse and collaborative inquiry that distinguishes human development. Innovative e-learning practices represent authentic approaches to teaching and learning based on collaboratively constructing meaning through critical reflection and discourse.

It is this convergence of technological developments and a rethinking of effective educational experiences that has driven e-learning innovation to the point we are today. This book provides a coherent understanding of e-learning and how this innovation is transforming how educators are approaching teaching and learning. E-learning as described here focuses on its potential to create and sustain communities of inquiry. In the context of a rapidly changing knowledge society, the need is to evolve the learning experience in a way that models and prepares students for an increasingly connected knowledge society. However, e-learning will fail if we merely add on to or simply repackage passive educational designs. This challenge requires a roadmap in the form of a coherent framework to guide our understanding and development of e-learning experiences. We begin with understanding what we mean by e-learning.

E-Learning Described

In its essence, e-learning is the utilization of electronically mediated asynchronous and synchronous communication for the purpose of thinking and learning collaboratively. This definition is an explicit recognition of the technological foundation of e-learning in the form of the Internet and associated communication technologies whose distinguishing characteristic is to not only connect individuals at a distance but to create virtual communities. The term e-learning came into use in the mid-1990s along with developments in the World Wide Web and interest in asynchronous discussion groups. The goal of e-learning was to explore the creation of communities of learners who could remain connected independent of time and location through the use of information and communication technologies. These groups of learners quickly evolved into educational communities of inquiry whose goal was to collaboratively engage in discourse and reflection with the intent to construct personal meaning and confirm mutual understanding. This perspective reflects an educational approach that is being increasingly adopted with the emerging possibilities of communication technologies that can cost-effectively build and sustain learning communities over time.

Beyond the definition and origins of e-learning, the two primary applications that constitute e-learning are online and blended learning. Fully online learning is a form of distance education that had its genesis in the field of computer conferencing with its focus on thinking and learning collaboratively (Garrison, 2016). Because of its collaborative nature, online learning is very different from traditional distance education that had its focus on content delivery and autonomous approaches to learning. Moreover, blended learning has become the most prevalent application of e-learning in traditional educational institutions. Paradoxically, the reality is that much of "e-learning innovation has taken place on-campus" (Richard, 2005, p. 69). E-learning in the context of blended learning has shifted the thinking of educators in terms of transformative course and program redesign.

E-learning diverges fundamentally from the autonomous industrialized form of traditional distance education where the educational approach was shaped by the available technology of the times. E-learning is first and foremost directed to providing an accessible and collaborative educational experience. While e-learning can make education accessible at a distance, it represents very different educational characteristics and possibilities. Today, distance has become but a relatively minor structural constraint in providing a quality collaborative thinking and learning experience. E-learning represents a true paradigm shift from a traditional distance education perspective. It represents a shift from the industrial production of prepackaged study materials to educationally shaping the learning experience through the thoughtful application for thinking and learning collaboratively.

E-learning is a distinct educational branch that has its roots in computer conferencing. The distinguishing feature of e-learning is its unique capability to support discourse over time and distance. To focus only on access to information would simply ignore the distinguishing characteristic and innovative possibilities of e-learning to engage participants in open communication. As such, e-learning is not a commodity that is pre-produced and downloaded electronically to be assimilated in whole by an autonomous learner. For these reasons we address independent study only to provide historical context and conceptual understanding of what distinguishes e-learning. The holistic view of the educational transaction emphasizes that we cannot separate the personal and the social. In reality personal reflection and shared discourse are only separated in the abstract. In this way, the potential of e-learning reflects our educational ideals by using advances in information and communication technologies to support the collaborative advantages of human cognition. It is these collaborative characteristics and possibilities that are the central themes of this book.

The theory and practice of e-learning, with its focus on traditional collaborative assumptions and approaches, reflect the digital era of thinking and learning. The digital era of education associated with e-learning approaches is marked by a return to a craft model of designing collaborative educational experiences (Garrison & Cleveland-Innes, 2010). The digital era reflects a connected society whose success is dependent upon collaborative approaches to thinking and learning. At the same time, for e-learning to be fully integrated in the mainstream of higher education, we must not undermine or discount the value of face-to-face educational experiences. In this regard, an important corollary and caveat is that e-learning must not be viewed as replacing the enormous advantages of face-to-face discourse. E-learning must be seen as a means to integrate the strengths of face-to-face and online learning experiences. The potential of e-learning to merge verbal and written discourse, unconstrained by time, has caused educators to rethink the possibilities for engaging campus-based students.

For these reasons, e-learning is described here in terms of both online and blended learning. It has also been noted that e-learning is not a synonym for distance education. With the proliferation of information and communication technologies, distance has become a minor constraint. In an e-learning scenario, communities of learners are able to sustain themselves productively across time and space and be enriched immeasurably through the content of the Internet. The Internet can be a useful source of ideas to complement the direct injection of ideas associated with the defined content of the course. But this does not just happen by mindlessly adopting information and communication technologies. Our educational ideals must drive the vision. These ideals are captured in the Community of Inquiry (CoI) framework that provides the principles and guidelines that make e-learning a viable reality in mainstream education.

A New Reality

It has become apparent that e-learning is not simply another technological innovation that ultimately has little impact on the educational experience. The reason is that e-learning has the potential to offer an open system that blends access to information and purposeful communication into a dynamic and intellectually challenging learning community. E-learning transforms education in ways that extend beyond the delivery of content. Surfing the Internet is not much better than wandering through a library; neither provide opportunities for discourse and purposeful educational experiences. Thinking and learning collaboratively, however, provide opportunities for deep and meaningful learning experiences.

Not long ago, the provision of increased learner independence meant a corresponding loss of collaboration and increased isolation. Before e-learning, independence and interaction were contradictory in an educational context—more of one inherently meant less of the other. From an educational perspective, the "e" in e-learning stands for more than electronic; it can also stand for extending and enhancing the learning experience. It is how we take advantage of e-learning's possibilities that is of educational importance. To realize the potential of e-learning is to see the educational experience as an open but purposely cohesive communication system.

Education is about ideas not isolated bits of information. E-learning's transformative power and capacity to add value is based upon the means to cope with and make sense of the proliferation of information. While e-learning can support passive information acquisition approaches to learning, the real impact is to precipitate new approaches that recognize and seize e-learning's collaborative possibilities. In reality, this may well be a back-to-the-future scenario as we return to historical collaborative educational ideals and practices associated with communities of learners engaged in critical discourse. These communities are where individual experiences and ideas are recognized and discussed in light of societal knowledge, norms and values. These are communities of inquiry where independence and collaboration are not contradictory ideas but the essential elements of a unified process and qualitative shift in how we approach a deep and meaningful educational experience.

E-learning in the form of online and blended approaches to learning has attracted much attention. However, its value is not faster access to information, or even connecting people in continuous ways. The value of e-learning is as a catalyst to rethink its capacity to stimulate and guide the quest to personally construct meaning and collaboratively confirm knowledge. Upon reflection, it should be no surprise that most research into using technology for educational purposes has shown no significant differences in learning outcomes between traditional and technically advanced media. The explanation of this well-known "no significant difference" (NSD) phenomenon is that we should not expect to find significant differences if we only measure simple recall of information. This can be accomplished regardless of how that information is transmitted. Changing the medium of transmission without changing the expectations and learning experience does not address the quality of learning outcomes. It is the recognition of the potential of e-learning to create and sustain purposeful learning communities engaged in critical discourse that is transforming higher education.

In the mid-1980s, the personal computer became accessible to a large and growing number of people. Today, it is personal computing that is the interface of the Internet and the means to connect entire societies setting the stage for the emergence of e-learning. With the help of community of inquiry research and practice we are beginning to understand the extent to which e-learning can be made to meet the needs of learners in the digital era. With the ubiquity of information and communication technologies that offer multiple forms of communication, we are currently rethinking the educational experience in terms of communities of inquiry unrestricted by time and distance.

Conclusion

Information and communication technologies, with their multiple media (text, visual, voice) and their capacity to sustain interaction, have made possible e-learning developments. However, this is not happening based exclusively on the technology. While adoption of e-learning approaches has been accompanied by an understanding of communication technologies, the acceptance in mainstream education is based on the educational deliverables. That is, a collaborative thinking and learning approach sustainable over time and space. At the same time, the complexities of collaboration, context and technology characteristics do not lend themselves to easy or simplistic best practices. There are no simple rules or recipes for designing and delivering an effective e-learning experience grounded in collaborative constructivist ideals. A collaborative educational experience demands the experience and insight of reflective, flexible and knowledgeable educators to translate principles and guidelines to the ever changing contingencies and exigencies of their particular environments.

In realistically addressing the complexities of e-learning, the goal is to provide conceptual order along with corresponding principles and guidelines that will have value for educators. Therefore, the challenge for the reader is to make sense of the ideas presented here by translating the concepts and ideas and applying them pragmatically to their unique educational environment. To do this, we need to ask what e-learning will allow us to do to create a worthwhile educational experience that meets the demands of a knowledge society. It is not about entrenching anachronistic and deficient approaches such as lecturing by using technologies to access more disjoint and incomprehensible information. Nor is it about simply having students experience the same passive learning experience through a different medium.

Increasingly, higher education is returning to its roots by focusing on the values and practices associated with collaborative approaches to learning. This is a reaction to the dominant individual and isolating approaches to learning that have evolved over the decades largely due to expanded access to education and the need for efficiency. This has meant the model of small seminars and opportunities for discussion and debate become increasingly limited. However, it is now time to recast the educational dinosaur and utilize the technologies of learning to move away from the large lecture hall and transmission model. Education is but an illusion if it simply disseminates information without actively supporting critical thinking and discourse with the goal to construct meaningful knowledge. Our purpose is not simply to advocate or promote the use of e-learning. The intent and benefit is to understand the need and nature of learning in a connected world; and to explore the implications of a collaborative and constructive educational experience for a knowledge society.

Part I

The Conceptual Framework

The goal of this book is to provide a framework for understanding the application of e-learning in higher education. This understanding will serve to guide e-learning research and practice for purposes of facilitating higher-order learning. However, before we can construct a coherent theoretical framework, we must explicate the foundational assumptions and perspectives upon which this book is based. Evidence and insights are explored in each chapter.

Chapter 2

Theoretical Foundations

A theoretical framework for teaching and learning will reflect fundamental values and beliefs about a worthwhile educational experience. It is by making explicit the philosophical assumptions and theoretical elements that we reveal our educational ideals. Only then can a framework have pragmatic value to reveal and guide how to approach purposeful thinking and learning. Such a framework is of paramount importance when adopting new communication technologies that can fundamentally alter the teaching and learning transaction. In this regard, e-learning has become the protagonist for change in higher education, but the plot needs purpose and direction. It is our theoretical ideals that ultimately guide the transformation of how we approach thinking and learning in an increasingly connected world.

The goal of this chapter is to outline the assumptions, concepts and principles that underpin a theoretical framework for e-learning. The fundamental questions addressed are associated with the nature of a worthwhile educational experience whose boundaries have been expanded with the adoption of information and communication technologies.

Philosophical Perspective

While new and emerging communication technologies will most certainly be central in the support of new approaches to teaching and learning, sound educational principles must inevitably guide the implementation of these innovations if we are to realize meaningful and worthwhile learning experiences and outcomes. However, before exploring specific concepts and principles, we must be clear as to the assumptions that shape this framework.

The foundational perspective of the theoretical framework that shapes this book reflects a "collaborative constructivist" view of teaching and learning. It is a recognition of the inseparable relationship between the social environment and personal meaning making. This dynamic reflects the interplay between socially redeeming knowledge and individual meaning. More specifically, collaboration and constructivism correspond respectively to the teaching and learning responsibilities of an educational experience.

The teaching and learning transaction described here is a coherent representation and translation of the dynamics of a collaborative and constructive educational experience. The recognition of these two interdependent interests is crucial in constructing a theoretical framework through which we can understand and apply e-learning approaches for educational purposes.

Philosophically, this collaborative constructivist perspective is associated with the work of John Dewey. Dewey (1938) identified the principle of "interaction" which unified the subjective (personal) and objective (social) worlds in an immediate timeframe. Through this interaction, ideas are generated that illuminate the external world. That is, meaning is constructed through repeated sharing of thoughts and ideas. Through purposeful collaboration, ideas are communicated and knowledge is constructed and confirmed. Dewey rejected all dualistic thinking—particularly with regard to the individual and society. For Dewey, society and the individual cannot exist separately, nor can one be subordinated to the other (Dewey & Childs, 1981). Therefore, to appreciate an educational experience is to understand this interplay between personal interests and experience infused with societal values, norms and knowledge. This creates a constructive tension between individual interests and social norms whose dynamic must be monitored and managed to maintain an educationally productive balance. Educationally, this collaborative constructivist approach is realized in the teacher and student transaction.

Dewey's (1938) concept of an activity-based education describes an educational experience as a "transaction taking place between an individual and what, at the time, constitutes his environment..." (p. 43). For Dewey (1916), transactional communication is the defining component of the educational experience when students transform the inert information passed to them from another and construct it into knowledge with personal application and value. Another contributor to this socially situated transactional view of learning was Vygotsky. Vygotsky believed that "both individuals and society are mutually produced and reproduced" (Wells, 2000, p. 55) and by extension in "the notion of learning as a process of inquiry" (Lee & Smagorinsky, 2000, p. 6). Consistent with the view here, Vygotsky (1978) saw high level cognitive functioning (critical thinking and discourse) as being manifested interpersonally from which the individual then constructs personal meaning.

Collaboration must be distinguished from cooperation that essentially lacks the shared influence and contribution to the task. In a cooperative enterprise, participants independently offer their ideas or solution. Collaboration on the other hand is dependent upon open communication and a cohesion of purpose directed to critiquing and constructing shared solutions. This shared approach expands personal construction of meaning to critically consider other thoughts and possibilities. Furthermore, this commitment to collaborative thinking and learning in an educational context requires a sense of community and cohesion. Education is a social enterprise dependent on creating a sense of purpose and belonging. The inseparability between the individual and the group draws our attention to the nature of an educational community that can support deep and meaningful learning experiences that have meaning for the individual and value to society.

There is an enormous gap between connection and community (Garrison, 2013). Community is defined by purpose, collaboration and trust. Moreover, an educational community is greatly influenced by societal knowledge and expectations that must be balanced by open communication that encourages critical and creative thinking and learning. This process of inquiry provides a roadmap of how thinking is distributed across a community of learners. From this perspective, the core dynamic of a community of inquiry is the integration of personal reflection and discourse where meaning can be critiqued and understanding realized. Shared responsibility creates an environment for thinking and learning collaboratively.

Thinking and Learning Collaboratively

We never learn in isolation. It is an illusion, a mistaken belief, which makes us think that we are self-directed learners—that we think and learn as individuals. The reality is that we cannot avoid being influenced by our environment. We are influenced directly through our experiences whether that is with our physical world or through communication with others. Thinking and learning occurs as we receive input through all our senses. A child learns not simply by seeing and hearing. Inevitably they want to touch and taste. Only through multiple inputs do we learn in deep and meaningful ways. We are constantly testing our thoughts through action. In educational contexts this is first done through expression, and if the environment will allow it, by applying ideas and getting feedback as to the outcome of specific actions. This is referred to as practical inquiry by Dewey.

Practical inquiry speaks to the inseparability of the individual and the community. It is to the fusion of the personal and social that is the essence of a community of inquiry. A community of inquiry is a collaborative approach to thinking and learning. What has brought attention to collaborative educational approaches is information and communication technologies that have connected the world and cost-effectively attenuated space and time. Individuals can remain in formal and informal contact long after the classroom experience. This holds the possibility to deepen the learning experience through sustained contact that allows individuals to share and test ideas. Previous to the Internet revolution and online learning, information was scarce and communication severely limited. This created the necessity for the face-to-face classroom, but ironically, meaningful communication was not enhanced appreciably. Communication was largely a one-way process which often made the quality of the academic engagement questionable.

Advances in information and communication technologies have drawn our attention to transactional conditions with regard to learning and have raised serious questions about the nature and quality of the educational experience. New and emerging communication technologies open new transactional possibilities and raise questions about the implications of open and sustained communication. Enter awareness and interest in e-learning. When fully conceived e-learning is more than simply accessing information and connecting with others where and when it is convenient. There is the increasing realization that mediated interaction is not sufficient in and of itself for meaningful discourse. The distinguishing feature of e-learning is in connecting and collaborating with others in purposeful and meaningful ways. Moreover, it is becoming clear that thinking and learning collaboratively is a pragmatic reality and necessity in today's connected knowledge society. The interdependent social and economic demands of society necessitate that we learn to collaborate and collaborate to learn.

Thinking and learning collaboratively is an inherent human characteristic and central to our evolution. In fact, it has been shown that collaboration is linked to the origin of human intelligence and evolution (Wilson, 2012). The human instinct is to collaborate. The reason is the strength of the group over the individual. While individual self-interest certainly exists, there is also a genetic need to belong and collaborate that has been the central feature of human achievement. However, maintaining a healthy balance of the success of the individual and the group is key to continuous learning and growth. Sport teams are perhaps the clearest example of where the individual gets personal satisfaction by collaboratively supporting others and, thereby, contributing to the success of the team. There is an inherent feeling of justice when a win-win outcome can be achieved within the group. The individual interests and the common good become one—the ultimate social form and means for success.

Thinking and learning collaboratively is fundamental to human nature if not always the educational norm. To learn independently is genetically abnormal. The normal functioning of the brain is social, which is why it is so effective and satisfying to learn collaboratively. We need each other to learn in meaningful and worthwhile ways. Interpersonal relationships are the greatest influence on our thinking and learning. This is in contrast to the fallacy of the isolated creative thinker. Thinking and learning is not a private experience. It is dependent upon open communication. We don't know what we don't know until we are confronted with conflicting facts and arguments. Critical thinking really emerges through iterative discourse and reflection – each reinforcing the other. Ideas do not emerge from a vacuum. Ideas are advanced when they are shared with others and exposed to alternative perspectives and explanations. We must approach existing beliefs and new ideas with skepticism which sets the stage to question ourselves and others. This then allows us to actively and collaboratively consider alternate hypotheses that are open to testing.

Collaborative thinking and learning in a purposeful community of learners creates an environment where participants can explore and examine ideas while challenging personal biases. However, we must not underestimate the ability of individuals to reinforce existing beliefs by selectively filtering information and trusting unfounded intuition. In general, humans are not particularly rational and reflective. Too often we rely on quick intuitive thinking that includes cognitive bias, unrepresentative personal experience, preference to maintain status quo and peer pressure (Thaler & Sunstein, 2008). There is a legitimate role for intuition when followed by reflective and rational thinking. Intuition not followed by rational reflection is wishful thinking disguised as grounded intuition—this is simply delusional. As we shall see in chapter five, practical inquiry accounts for intuition and insight as part of a process of thinking and learning rationally through reflection and discourse.

This inherent human bias to confirm widely held ideas creates a cognitive straightjacket if we do not engage in critical discourse that considers alternative perspectives. Educators must create the conditions that encourage diversity of thought by breaking down intellectual boundaries and barriers. Being exposed to multidisciplinary perspectives and ideas will cause individuals to pause and reflect. Learners need to be challenged if they are to move out of their intellectual comfort zone. Personal reflection without critical feedback and diagnosis of misconceptions is subject to simply confirming existing beliefs. Being exposed to a diversity of thinking and opportunities to engage in thoughtful discourse is central to the process of inquiry and deep and meaningful thinking and learning. One of the great dangers in deep and meaningful thinking and learning is a false sense of certainty by confining thinking to a particular set of unexamined assumptions and framework. With paradigmatic certainty comes a disregard of alternative ideas and innovative thinking. All ideas must be seen as transitory/tentative, only waiting for improvement or being proven wrong.

Consistent with previous discussion, human evolution clearly favoured cooperation and collaboration over competition. However, competition (self-interest) can and does occur in a sphere of cooperation and collaboration if we provide opportunities to express disagreement and consider alternative perspectives through constructive discourse. Discourse is a good example for the fusion of collaboration and competition, but constructive discourse requires a delicate balance between competition and collaboration. As much as collaboration and competition tension can be constructive, without an open and trusting environment we undermine collaboration. Competition must emerge in the process of exploring and challenging assumptions and ideas and not be perceived as personally challenging. The only way to make this happen is a climate that encourages and supports curiosity through open communication where learners feel safe to share thoughts, critically explore connections, challenge perspectives and resolve dilemmas. This is where leadership is required to encourage and support cognitive engagement.

With regard to context and climate, we must be clear that social media is primarily what it states—social communication. The social nature of this form of communication can create barriers to deep and meaningful thinking and learning that is predicated upon critical discourse and respectfully challenging assumptions and ideas. Social media are characterized by weak interpersonal connections and content that is not intended for deep and meaningful exploration. Social media content is intended for consumption and entertainment—not for critical analysis. Social media are susceptible to "group-think" where participants follow the mindless mantra of the group (Garrison, 2016). This lack of critical discourse is a form of non-thinking. In other words, "group pressure to conform are major barriers to thinking collaboratively" (Garrison, 2016, p. 112). So the question becomes how can thinking and learning be distributed across a group such that it can overcome the risks of individual confirmation bias and the pressures of group-think?

Skepticism is necessitated by the uncertainty and randomness in all aspects of social existence (Mlodinow, 2008). Uncertainty can cause individuals to make poor judgements without the discipline of critical and collaborative thinking. To avoid and overcome misconceptions requires both personal reflection and shared discourse to create a questioning mindset and openness to external challenge. Too much emphasis on acquiring information can create an over-confidence and a false sense of certainty that prematurely shuts down thinking. In this way, intuition can also be a source of false confidence. While intuition can be a source of inspiration, it must be tested with rigorous inquiry and a skeptical mind. Similarly, emotion can be a great motivating force and even essential in making decisions but it can also be a source of irrationality unless accompanied by healthy skepticism and sense of uncertainty.

Conventional educational approaches have largely treated thinking and learning as an individual activity. While thinking collaboratively to many may seem counterintuitive (thinking is an internal cognitive experience), it is essential if we are to critically examine our thoughts and beliefs. The path to deep and meaningful thinking and learning is through practical inquiry as advocated by Dewey (1933); a process based on a generalized form of the scientific method and embedded in a purposeful community of learners. Thinking and learning collaboratively is the essence of a sustained community of inquiry made practicable by the affordances of e-learning.

A Transactional View

While knowledge is a social artifact and learning in an educational context is a social endeavor, it is ultimately the individual who must grasp its meaning and put it to the test through discourse and application. As important as the group is, we cannot defer to the group in terms of critical and creative thinking. Thinking and learning collaboratively does not diminish the ultimate responsibility of the individual learner to reflect and consider possible misconceptions. Notwithstanding individual cognitive responsibilities, we cannot separate the cognitive dynamic of the individual and the influences of the group or community. This is consistent with Dewey's (1933) view that we cannot separate the world of ideas from the world of experience. The purposeful process of facilitating an outcome that is both socially worthwhile and personally meaningful goes to the heart of the teaching and learning transaction. This transaction is common to all educational experiences, including e-learning.

An educational experience has a dual purpose. The first is to construct personal meaning through reconstruction of experience. The second is to refine meaning and confirm understanding collaboratively within a community of learners. At first glance, this dual purpose would seem to reflect, respectively, the distinct perspectives of the student focused primarily on constructing personal meaning and the teacher who has the responsibility to confirm understanding. Thinking and learning is shared and shaped through the dynamic of a community of learners (Garrison, 2013). However, closer consideration of this transaction reveals the inseparability of traditional educational roles and the importance of viewing the educational process as a unified transaction. That is, teachers are learners and learners are teachers. We are simply viewing the same process from two different perspectives. They both are responsible for constructing meaning and collaboratively confirming understanding. This perspective raises fundamental questions concerning issues of responsibility for learning and control of the educational process.

Responsibility and Control

In an educational transaction, issues of responsibility and control apply to both teaching and learning. The responsibilities of the teacher are complex in that they have a special role in creating and shaping the evolving learning environment. This responsibility becomes more daunting and focused on the educator when communication technologies are introduced. These technologies make possible sustainable cognitive and social conditions where students can stay connected to a learning community. This demands subject matter as well as pedagogical and technological expertise on the part of the educator. On the other hand, the learner must accept responsibility for constructing personal meaning. For this to be successful, control must be commensurate with the abilities of the learner. The complex collaborative nature of an educational transaction should be apparent.

The point is that issues of control apply to both teaching and learning. As Dewey stated clearly, education is fundamentally an interactive or transactional process. The challenges and confusion surrounding control issues go to the traditional normative role and leadership responsibility afforded the teacher. It is the teacher who has the initial responsibility to define the curriculum and design educational activities. Unfortunately, in traditional educational contexts there has been little opportunity for learner input or collaboration in the planning process. That is, the learner has little influence in defining expected outcomes or the nature of the educational transaction. This creates the contradictory situation where the student is expected to assume responsibility for activities and an outcome over which they have little input or transactional control. This is a crucial issue considering "that a student's perceived control over his or her academic performance is strongly predictive of academic achievement" (Yeh, 2009, p. 229). In other words, responsibility with control reinforces effort and engagement.

This transactional perspective on teaching and learning reflects a dynamic balance of responsibility and control issues congruent with the educational purpose and the abilities of the learners. The access and sustained connectivity of e-learning draws attention to the issues of responsibility and control. Understanding the implications that e-learning information and communication technologies are having on educational transactions is the subject of subsequent chapters.

Theoretical Concepts

One way to understanding worthwhile educational practices is to work back from desired learning outcomes. In higher education, these outcomes are first associated with higher-order cognitive processes (i.e. critical and creative thinking and learning) and not with specific content acquisitions. More recently, abilities such as metacognition have also been added to reflect the important ability and disposition to continue to learn in deep and meaningful ways. These abilities and dispositions (critical thinking and metacognition) must be developed if students are to assume increasing responsibility for their learning in a constantly changing knowledge society and economy.

The impermanence of public knowledge, along with the personal challenge of accommodating new ideas, necessitates an ability to think critically and be able to monitor and manage higher-order thinking and learning. Critical thinking is a holistic activity incorporating both reflective and shared activities. Moreover, it is argued here that the most productive environment for critical and creative thinking and learning is "the pedagogy of the 'community of inquiry'" (Lipman, 2003). Critical reflection and discourse is central to the Community of Inquiry (CoI) theoretical framework that shapes this book.

In a community of inquiry, critical reflection and discourse are inseparable and reciprocal. At the same time, it is necessary to clarify misconceptions as to the role of reflection and discourse in a community of inquiry. Discourse is more than casual conversation. It is the external manifestation of reflective thinking and learning and is central to inquiry and a collaborative constructivist approach to thinking and learning. However, discourse is a complex and multidimensional process. Burbules (1993) points this out when he describes four types of dialogue (i.e. discourse) for different orientations and purposes. The four types are conversation, inquiry, debate and instruction.

These dialogues overlap and all are present in an education transaction. As Burbules (1993) states, "a degree of flexibility and pluralism in dialogical approach is essential" (p. 129). There is a place and need at various times in a community of inquiry for a particular type of dialogue or discourse. For example, dialogue for conversation (feeling of trust, respect and concern) is directly associated with the need to create social presence. On the other hand, dialogue for inquiry and debate speak to cognitive presence dynamic and the exploratory and confirmatory aspects of the Practical Inquiry model (see Chapter 5). Dialogue for instructional purposes speaks to the teaching presence element of the CoI framework. The challenge is how we design and deliver educational experiences in an e-learning environment that integrates the four types of discourse through synchronous verbal and asynchronous written discourse.

Approaches to Learning

The judgement of this author is that the most promising research and knowledge base for understanding the educational experience was pioneered by Marton (1988) (Marton & Saljo, 1976) and confirmed by Entwistle (Entwistle & Ramsden, 1983) among others (Biggs, 1987). In its simplest form, this research described two distinct levels of information processing or understanding: surface-level processing, where the student has a reproductive or rote conception of learning and a corresponding learning strategy; and deep-level processing, where the intention is to comprehend and order the significance of the information as well as integrate it with existing knowledge.

It is clear that this intentional approach to learning is greatly influenced by the learning environment. That is, learners adapt to the expectations and characteristics of the environment. The construct is that context strongly influences the strategies they adopt in approaching learning (Ramsden, 2003). A deep or surface approach to learning is a rational adaptation to contextual demands on the part of the student in order to successfully meet expectations. Ramsden (1988) argues that there are three domains that influence perception and subsequent approaches to learning—assessment, curriculum and teaching. There is, of course, considerable overlap among the domains.

Assessment (i.e. testing and grading) has a pervasive influence in shaping intentions and how students approach an educational experience. In fact, it may well be the most "critical situational influence on learning strategies" (Ramsden, 1988, p. 164). How students are assessed sends a very strong signal as to what is important and how they should approach learning. If the examination system is information recall, then students will, rationally, prepare for "recall of factual information to the detriment of a deeper level of understanding" (Marton & Saljo, 1976, p. 125). Obviously, the overwhelming concern of the vast majority of students is to successfully pass the examination. In most cases, this is an overwhelming influence that shapes how students approach learning and ultimately have a significant impact on the quality of the learning experience. Therefore, assessment must be congruent with intended learning outcomes.

The second domain is associated with curriculum, in particular, workload or the quantity of material to be assimilated in a defined period of time. Regardless of the student's inherent preference or intelligence, excessive curriculum demands will encourage a surface approach to learning. With regard to content coverage "there is mounting evidence that less is more" (Lombardi, 2008, p. 4). It is not hard to see the negative influence on deep approaches to learning of excessive content assimilation demands on the student. The challenge facing students and teachers in the age of the Internet is that "the world of knowledge is overwhelming, a vast ocean, horizonless, plunging to impossible depths" (Achenbach, 1999, p. A23). With the increasing access to more and more information this challenge only increases. Learning must be designed to manage excessive content if we are to encourage deep and meaningful approaches to learning.

The third domain, teaching presence, directly addresses the challenges of assessment and information overload by clarifying and influencing deep approaches. The teacher has the greatest influence in creating and shaping the learning environment and learning outcomes. With the proliferation of knowledge and the access to information, a way must be charted and order provided if we are to create the conditions that encourage deep approaches to thinking and learning. This includes higher-order thinking and learning that includes critical and creative thinking along with metacognitive awareness. Perhaps the most pragmatic means is to establish a community of inquiry where students are encouraged and supported to develop the thinking and learning that will ensure deep and meaningful processes and outcomes.

The transactional perspective for effective teaching means moving beyond simple presentation methods. The transmission or presentational approach to teaching is highly prescriptive. This is best exemplified by the large lecture; or in traditional distance education, a mass produced independent study package. The presentational approach is a one-way transmission of information, be it by lecture or independent study materials. Effective presentation depends on organization, clarity and enthusiasm but this has not been shown to be sufficient in and of themselves to encourage or support deep approaches to learning.

As implied in the phrase itself, the missing element in a presentation approach is critical discourse that is central to the transactional perspective and a community of inquiry. A transactional approach to teaching is based on the ideal of a critical community of learners. A transactional approach is balanced with flexibility regarding content, a supportive climate, and an opportunity to critically and collaboratively explore ideas and construct knowledge. The transactional nature of a deep and meaningful approach allows student participation in setting goals, selecting content and methods of assessment, and collaboratively confirming understanding. This demands considerable educational judgment in terms of issues of responsibility and control.

Success in creating an educational community of inquiry requires preparation, sustained presence and considerable pedagogic and content expertise. As we shall see, this kind of teaching presence will ensure the full participation of learners and the achievement of deep approaches to learning, regardless whether communication is face-to-face or mediated. However, in an e-learning context, there are exogenous technical variables that also must be considered in concert with these principles if we are to create and sustain an online or blended community of inquiry. Particular communications technology characteristics must be understood as they provide practical constraints in terms of creating and sustaining a community of inquiry.

Text-Based Communication

It is only in recent decades that linguists and members of other disciplines dealing with language have regarded speech as clearly the primary form of human language. Writing was seen as the direct transfer of the information conveyed by speech into a visible medium. This equivalency assumption is beginning to be considered more closely, particularly within the body of literature on the use of text-based, computer-mediated communication for educational purposes (Feenberg, 1999; Garrison, 1997; Garrison, Anderson & Archer, 2000; Peters, 2000).

We argue that the differences between spoken and written communication are, in fact, a key to understanding the effective use of mediated communication and, specifically, e-learning and communities of inquiry (Archer, Garrison & Anderson, 1999). While e-learning is dependent upon mediated communication, serious questions have been raised concerning the extent and degree to which text-based communication alters the "flow and structure" of educational discourse, as compared to the more familiar environment of speech-based communication. A full discussion of the characteristics of text-based communication will not be attempted here; however, we note that there is sufficient evidence to suggest that writing has some inherent and demonstrable advantages over speech in terms of critical discourse and reflection. One obvious advantage is the permanent record afforded learners. This contrasts with the ephemeral nature of discussions in face-to-face classroom environments. Furthermore, face-to-face conversation is generally less systematic, more exploratory, and less attentive to others' views.

Writing has long been used as both a process and product of rigorous critical thinking. The written word serves best to mediate recall and reflection, while the spoken word functions most effectively to mediate action (Wells,

2000). Ong (1982) argues that speech is a context which all humans are born into and that speech is critical to the development of individual consciousness; however, "writing intensifies the sense of self and fosters more conscious interaction between persons" (p. 179). The characteristics of written, as compared to spoken, language would appear to affect the value of the former in facilitating deep and meaningful learning. This, of course, has a particular application in text-based media.

The apparent advantage of the written word in higher-order learning is supported in a study of questioning and cognitive functioning. It was found "that interaction in this on-line context was more intellectually demanding than that found in face-to-face" (Blanchette, 2001, p. 48). That is, the questions and responses were at a higher cognitive level than in a face-to-face verbal context. A possible (and probable) explanation is the asynchronous nature of written communication. It would appear that because students have more time to reflect, to be more explicit, and to order the importance of issues, teachers were able to conduct high-level questioning. Also, in an online written environment, administrative questions and issues can be separated from academic discourse. That is, students could focus and reflect on higher-order cognitive questions and their responses.

This increased academic focus resulting from a separation of tasks introduces the issue of cognitive load. It is argued that cognitive load can be reduced by shifting from verbally transmitting information to providing information through written communication. This represents a move away from "transient" information communicated verbally and allowing the learner to focus on the task using permanently recorded information. This has been referred to as the modality effect which reduces cognitive load and facilitates learning "when the instructional procedure reduces extraneous working memory load" (Sweller, 2016, p. 7). While there is a place for transient verbal communication as we shall see in chapter eight, there can be clear advantages for written communication with regard to complex academic challenges.

At the same time text-based communication does not have the advantages of non-verbal cues available in face-to-face environments. Potentially this raises social presence challenges in online learning environments. Communities of inquiry are highly dependent upon establishing trust and group cohesion through communication that does not have the non-verbal visual cues. However, it has been repeatedly shown that social-emotional and personality characteristics can be projected through written communication. Characteristics of oral discourse can be represented in written communication through the use of linguistics and paralinguistic signals. In this regard, Gutiérrez-Santiuste and Gallego-Arrufat (2016) have shown that the use of "emoticons can lend support, complement written communication, and facilitate social presence in virtual learning environments" (p. 2). The conclusion here is that written communication can create a collaborative learning environment and meaningful discourse.

Written communication has always been the preferred means of storing and sharing knowledge. This form of communication is central to e-learning and its use can only strengthen the educational experience through sustained online discourse and reflection. In short, text-based communication has considerable potential to facilitate critical discourse and reflection. There is every reason to believe that text-based communication in an e-learning context would have advantages to support collaborative approaches to thinking and learning. The importance of written communication in e-learning has begun to assert itself in higher education and offer new and more effective collaborative educational experiences.

Conclusion

The information age and a networked world have forced educators to rethink educational approaches. It has become clear that the need in a connected knowledge based society will be an environment that develops and encourages the ability to think and learn collaboratively (Garrison, 2016). The inevitable evolution of higher education capitalizing on the potential of e-learning in terms of collaborative approaches to thinking and learning is also a call for a rededication to traditional higher education ideals. These ideals are being brought back through the technological developments associated with e-learning.

Educators are particularly challenged when information and communication technologies are inserted into the equation. The reality is that "digital technologies [e-learning] require radically new and different notions of pedagogy" (Privateer, 1999, p. 70). In this regard, e-learning is altering the nature of the educational transaction by challenging the effectiveness of large and passive lectures. Educators are recognizing that e-learning is a disruptive technology that is currently transforming how learning is approached in an educational context. E-learning becomes an opportunity to examine and realize the ideals of the educational transaction in terms of collaborative and sustained thinking and learning.

It is the potential of e-learning to support and sustain learning communities to which we turn our attention. The challenge is to understand how we create and sustain communities of inquiry that will facilitate developing deep and meaningful approaches to learning. The transactional perspective of e-learning adopted here is embedded in a critical community of inquiry where both reflection and discourse are utilized to facilitate the construction of personally meaningful and socially valid knowledge. How to face the complexity and uncertainty in modern society can be best understood through a community of inquiry framework. It is to the CoI theoretical framework we turn our attention to next.

Chapter 3

Community of Inquiry

Realizing the potential of e-learning does not mean that traditional educational values and practices will be declared obsolete. In fact, because of online and blended learning capabilities to support asynchronous, collaborative communication in a dynamic and sustainable educational context, there is a resurgence of traditional educational ideals associated with rational discourse. Re-valuing the ideal of a community of learners engaged in critical thinking and discourse is at the heart of the e-learning transformation. The framework we describe here is based upon the premise (supported by research and experience) that a community of learners is an essential element of a deep and meaningful educational experience. The necessity of a community of learners becomes apparent with the demands of an evolving knowledge society that creates expectations for individuals to be independent thinkers and interdependent collaborative learners. It is within such a community of learners that the potential of e-learning is fully realized.

However, it is communication technologies that make possible sustainable communities of learners. It is the technological infrastructure that makes possible sustained access to learning communities. The challenge is to use e-learning in ways that support new and more effective collaborative approaches to learning that engages learners in purposeful and meaningful discourse. The technology of online and blended learning has the capability to support and sustain private reflection and public discourse simultaneously. This unprecedented capability has created e-learning approaches that are fundamentally changing teaching and learning in all contexts. The potential of e-learning is found in the framework of an open and critical community of inquiry.

A Theoretical Framework

From both theoretical and empirical perspectives, the effectiveness of thinking and learning collaboratively is seen as indispensable in achieving deep and meaningful learning outcomes. The basic premise is that "the teaching of high-level concepts inevitably involves a considerable amount of discourse"

(Bereiter, 1992, p. 352). Research in both face-to-face and mediated educational environments confirm the benefits of thinking and engaging collaboratively in the support of deep and meaningful learning experiences (Cecez-Kecmanovic & Webb 2000; Garrison, 2016; Garrison & Archer, 2000; Johnson & Johnson, 2009). With the advances in information and communication technologies and the adoption of collaborative approaches to thinking and learning, we gain a deeper understanding of worthwhile educational experiences in highly connected knowledge societies.

A community of learners is composed of participants who assume the roles of both teacher and learner while engaging in discourse with the specific purposes of facilitating inquiry, constructing meaning, and validating understanding that in turn metacognitively develop the ability and predisposition for further learning. Learning communities provide the means to integrate personal reflection and shared discourse. It is the fusion of reflection and discourse that ignites a deep and meaningful educational experience that has personal value and socially worthwhile outcomes. Education is a purposeful and guided activity in which the individual is making sense of societal knowledge and reconciling this with personal experiences. The learning community is the ideal fusion of individual and shared worlds.

From the perspective of a learning community, online and blended learning must be judged from the perspective of the transaction between and among educator and learners. The success depends on the ability to create and sustain learning environments that engages learners in meaningful and worthwhile learning activities. It is counterproductive to artificially polarize teacher and student roles and responsibilities. Roles must be shared with a shifting balance as needs change throughout a dynamic and collaborative educational experience. In this regard, learning communities are no more inherently learner-centered than traditional face-to-face learning is inherently teacher-centered. To capitalize on the possibilities of online and blended learning, this discrete depiction of roles must be rejected and the unity of learning communities adopted.

We have previously alluded to the importance of context and specifically argued for the creation of a community of learners to facilitate critical discourse and reflection. For this reason, we emphasize that individual knowledge construction is very much shaped by the social environment. That is, an environment with choice and a diversity of perspectives that will encourage critical reflection and inquiry. Dewey (1933) considered such an environment for reflection and inquiry as indispensable for a worthwhile education transaction. Lipman (2003) popularized the term "community of inquiry" to describe an educational experience. Lipman (2003) argued for the community of inquiry to operationalize critical or reflective thinking as an educational methodology. This is a community where societal knowledge is revealed in an equivocal, multidisciplinary manner whose goal is to structure relationships (create order) to facilitate "rationality tempered by judgment"

(Lipman, 2003, p. 11). Citing Dewey, Lipman (2003) notes the great mistake of mainstream education is "to neglect the process and fixate upon the product" (p. 20). A community of inquiry is crucial in precipitating and maintaining reflection and discourse and the development of judgment in constructing and testing meaning. Inquiry is the process of actively searching for personal meaning and shared understanding. With the collaboration of the group, the individual assumes responsibility to construct meaning but to collaboratively confirm shared understanding.

In a community of inquiry, there is both rationality and freedom. Lipman (2003) states, a community of inquiry is where "students listen to one another with respect, build on one another's ideas, challenge one another to supply reasons for otherwise unsupported opinions, assist each other in drawing inferences from what has been said, and seek to identify one another's assumptions" (p. 20). In other words, a community of inquiry provides the environment in which students can take responsibility and control of their learning by negotiating meaning, diagnosing misconceptions, and challenging accepted beliefs. As Schrage (1989) notes, creating a shared understanding is simply a different task than exchanging information. It's the difference between being deeply involved in a conversation and lecturing to a group (p. 5).

The Community of Inquiry Framework

The Community of Inquiry (CoI) theoretical framework is a generic and coherent structure of a transactional educational experience whose core function is to manage and monitor the dynamic for thinking and learning collaboratively. The CoI framework has received broad empirical support in the literature (Akyol, Ice, Garrison & Mitchell, 2010; Arbaugh, Cleveland-Innes, Diaz, Garrison, Ice, Richardson, Shea & Swan, 2008; Diaz, Swan, Ice & Kupczynski, 2010; Garrison, Cleveland-Innes & Fung, 2010; Shea & Bidjerano, 2009a). This was reinforced in a study that explored current trends in the seven leading distance and online learning journals (Bozkurt, Akgun-Ozbek, Yilmazel, Erdogdu, Ucar, Guler, Sezgin, Karadeniz, Sen-Ersoy, Goksel-Canbek, Dincer, Ari & Aydin, 2015). Descriptive analysis of publications during the period of 2009 to 2013 revealed the most frequently used theoretical perspective was the community of inquiry theory of knowledge formation. The same study also reported the CoI seminal article (by Garrison, Anderson & Archer, 2000) as the most cited in the studies of this period. This is evidence of the popularity and influence that the CoI framework has and is having with regard to e-learning.

More specifically, the CoI framework establishes procedures for critical inquiry and the collaborative construction of personal meaningful and shared understanding. It represents a process of designing and delivering deep and meaningful learning experiences through the development of three interdependent elements—social presence, cognitive presence and teaching

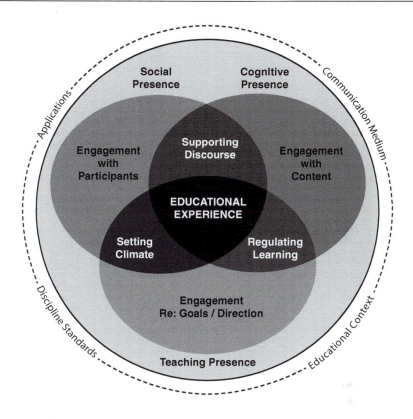

Figure 3.1 Community of Inquiry Framework

presence. These presences create a sense of being or identity through purposeful communication and distributed teaching and learning responsibilities. To begin to understand the complexities of a community of inquiry we begin with a brief description of each presence. The structural relationships among the three presences are provided in Figure 3.1. However, more detailed analyses of the presences and discussion of the complex dynamics is found in subsequent chapters.

Social Presence

Social presence is the ability of participants to identify with a group, communicate openly in a trusting environment, and develop personal and affective relationships progressively by way of projecting their individual personalities (Garrison, 2009b). However, when the communication medium is the written word, establishing social presence presents a particular challenge. The shift from spoken communication to written communication in an online learning environment presents a special challenge to establish social presence. Written communication lacks a sense of immediacy that builds interpersonal relationships. Immediacy is important to a supportive and secure learning environment as it reduces personal risk and increases acceptance, particularly during critical discourse that purposefully questions ideas and understanding.

Socio-emotional communication in text-based communication is possible through the use of compensating strategies, such as the adaptation of textual behaviors to reveal social and relational messages and paralinguistic signals (Gutiérrez-Santiuste & Gallego-Arrufat, in press; Walther, 1992). Compensating redundancies benefit communication that carries potential for misunderstanding. Attention must be given to establishing and sustaining appropriate social presence if the full potential of a community of inquiry is to be realized. Not only is acquiring higher-order learning more successful when cooperatively based (Resnick, 1987), cognitive presence is also enhanced and sustained when social presence is established (Akyol & Garrison, 2011a; Fabro and Garrison, 1998; Gunawardena, 1995; Gutiérrez-Santiuste & Gallego-Arrufat, 2016; Liu, Gomez & Yen, 2009).

Cognitive Presence

Education is a formally constructed type of social learning defined by the specific parameters of purpose, process and product. To this end, cognitive presence speaks to intent, transaction and learning outcomes. In this regard, cognitive presence is defined generally "as the extent to which learners are able to construct and confirm meaning through sustained reflection and discourse in a critical community of inquiry" (Garrison, Anderson & Archer, 2001, p. 11). Reflection is consistent with the ability to think critically (rational judgement) while discourse relies on trust, purposeful relationships and communication focused on understanding a dilemma or problem. In essence, cognitive presence is a condition of higher-order thinking and learning focused on critical reflection and discourse.

Cognitive presence is described in the context of a general model of critical thinking and scientific inquiry. The primary source for this model is Garrison and Archer (2000) but is derivative of Dewey's (1933) work on reflective thinking. Cognitive presence is operationalized by the Practical Inquiry (PI) model that consists of four phases of inquiry—triggering event, exploration, integration and resolution. The PI model represents a generic structure of critical inquiry that operationalizes the inseparability of reflection and discourse and the multi-phased process designed to collaboratively construct meaning and confirm understanding.

Teaching Presence

The third mutually reinforcing element in a community of inquiry is teacher presence. The need for leadership became immediately apparent in the early applications of online learning using computer conferencing. The main difficulty with early computer conferencing was sustaining participation and critical discourse (Gunawardena, 1991; Hiltz & Turoff, 1993). Low levels of interest and participation were rooted in a lack of structure and focus resulting from its informal nature and excessively "democratic" approach. While there must be full and open participation in a community of inquiry, there is also an inherent need for an architect and facilitator to design, direct and inform the transaction if it is to be productive and sustainable.

Considering the previous issues, teaching presence is defined as "the design, facilitation and direction of cognitive and social processes for the purpose of realizing personally meaningful and educationally worthwhile learning outcomes" (Anderson, Rourke, Garrison & Archer, 2001). The function of teaching presence is to bring the elements of a community of inquiry together in a balanced and functional relationship congruent with the intended outcomes while respecting the needs and encouraging active engagement of the learners. It must be noted here that teachING and not teachER presence is used to reflect the shared roles and responsibilities of a community of inquiry (see next section). This is, of course, an enormously imposing task and presents new challenges associated with e-learning approaches.

Indicators

For theoretical and practical purposes, a template has been constructed consisting of categories of indicators within each of the three presences that reflect meaningful learning activities. Indicators are key words or phrases that suggest the presence of the three elements. Table 3.1 provides the template that guides our assessment of the nature and quality of a community of inquiry learning experience. These indicators have been used to identify presences and guide the coding of transcripts in the early stages of this research. The template and qualitative coding has been enormously useful in gauging and understanding the dynamics of a community of inquiry. Moreover, this template was crucial in the development and validation of a quantitative survey instrument (see Appendix A).

Theoretical Developments

The CoI framework has been demonstrated to be a credible and prominent theory that has guided numerous online and blended learning studies (Befus, 2016). In this regard it has been noted that the CoI framework "has formed a theoretical backbone for much of blended and distance learning research" (Halverson, Graham, Spring, Drysdale & Jeffery, 2012, p. 393). The primary reason for its widespread adoption is that prior to its publication, few

Table 3.1 Community of Inquiry Categories and Indicators

Elements	Categories	Indicators (examples only)
Social presence	Personal/affective	Self projection/expressing emotions
	Open communcation	Learning climate/risk-free expression
	Group cohesion	Group identity/collaboration
Cognitive presence	Triggering event	Sense of puzzlement
	Exploration	Information exchange
	Integration	Connecting ideas
	Resolution	Appling new ideas
Teaching presence	Design and organization	Setting curriculum and methods
	Facilitating discourse	Shaping constructive exchange
	Direct instruction	Focusing and resolving issues

e-learning studies were grounded in a coherent theoretical framework that addressed a range of e-learning contexts (Zawacki-Richter & Anderson, 2014). A major advantage of grounding research in a comprehensive theoretical framework is to ensure that the learning experience is not defined by the technology. Ultimately, the potential of new and emerging technologies must be judged by the educational transaction and intended learning outcomes. Educationally, the CoI framework focuses on the active and creative engagement of learners to think and learn collaboratively.

The CoI framework was first proposed in an article by Garrison, Anderson and Archer (2000). The original framework was grounded in the higher education teaching and learning literature, a series of seminal studies, and the educational experiences of the research team. Since its inception, the CoI framework has been referenced in hundreds of publications and is the leading theoretical reference point for research in online and blended learning (Befus, 2016). More importantly, studies have consistently demonstrated the stability of the CoI framework and evidence supports the position that collaborative inquiry can be supported in e-learning contexts (Garrison, 2016; Garrison & Arbaugh, 2007). In fact, considering the reflective and explicit nature of the communication, as well as the opportunity to access data sources, there are distinct advantages to creating a community of inquiry in online and blended learning environments. The permanence of text-based communication lends itself to reflection and the ability to challenge thoughts as well as edit text and rewrite positions.

Early validation research created the groundwork to construct a quantitative CoI survey instrument (Arbaugh et al., 2008). Data analysis based on this instrument concluded "that a three factor solution emerged regardless of the underlying socio-epistemological orientation" (Akyol et al., 2010, p. 67). Similarly, another study that used the CoI survey questionnaire concluded, "factor analysis of multiplicative scores [course and importance ratings] … supported the CoI model's tripartite structure" (Diaz et al. 2010, p. 22). More recently and consistent with previous research, a study concluded that the CoI scale was "found to be reliable and valid by the means of Classical Test Theory and Item Response Theory" (Horzum & Uyanik, 2015, p. 206). This supports the CoI questionnaire as a valid instrument that can quantitatively assess the state of a community of inquiry (see Appendix A).

Research using this instrument has consistently confirmed the CoI framework and provided new insights. The CoI instrument has opened up the study of online and blended learning in general and specifically the theoretical structure and dynamics of a community of inquiry. Such a quantitative instrument can be particularly efficient and effective in conducting large scale and multi-institutional studies. The CoI instrument also has a practical application in terms of guiding the development of course and program design as well as assessing the effectiveness of a community of inquiry (Richardson, Arbaugh, Cleveland-Innes, Ice, Swan & Garrison, 2012). It has also been noted that individual items provide design insights with regard to each of the presences and are useful in judging success of implementation (Ice, 2009; Richardson, Ice, Boston, Powell & Gibson, 2011).

It is important to appreciate that each individual in a collaborative constructivist community of inquiry manifests each of the presences. That is, participants must take responsibility for aspects of social, cognitive and teaching presence. The exact nature and the degree to which they assume responsibility for each of the presences will depend on the individual, task and context. To further complicate this dynamic, this balance will shift as the educational experience progresses (for example, students will be expected to assume increased teaching presence as their inquiry ability develops). However, it should be kept in mind that there is no "learner" presence or "teacher" presence per se. Each participant (teacher and students) assume varying degrees of teaching presence (notwithstanding that the instructor will generally exhibit greater teaching presence at various times). The goal is always to have students assume more teaching presence and become increasingly responsible to construct meaning and confirm understanding. Individually and collaboratively, students will assume increasing cognitive responsibility as they become more competent and confident. As well, through shared metacognitive awareness, students will learn to guide purposeful discourse within an environment of trust, communication and cohesion (social presence).

An important development in CoI research was the study of the dynamic relationships among the presences. Understanding the dynamics of a community of inquiry helps to understand the development of the learning community as a whole. While the CoI framework was intended to describe the interdependent and dynamic nature of the presences, much of the early work was focused on defining the structure of the presences. However, learning experiences are a function of the evolving relationships among the presences. The interdependency of the presences has been supported by several studies (Arbaugh, 2008; Bangert, 2009; Garrison et al., 2010; Ke, 2010; Nagel & Kotze, 2010; Shea & Bidjerano, 2009b). Taking this a step further, we see that the presences evolve in concert which reveals the developmental nature of a community of inquiry. In this regard, Akyol and Garrison (2008) found that the presences evolved over time as hypothesized by the CoI theoretical framework. That is, social presence was dominant at the beginning of a course but dropped over time. On the other hand, both cognitive and teaching presence increased gradually throughout the course as would be expected with increased focus on academic requirements and outcomes.

The interdependency of the presences was also demonstrated in two seminal studies that explored the causal relationships among the social, cognitive and teaching presences (Garrison et al., 2010; Shea & Bidjerano, 2009b). In addition, other studies have confirmed the important mediating role of social presence (Gutiérrez-Santiuste, Sabiote-Rodríguez & Gallego-Arrufat, unpublished) and revealed the key role of teaching presence to establish both social and cognitive presence (Archibald, 2010; Daspit & D'Souza, 2012; Joo, Lim & Kim, 2011; Ke, 2010). Kozan and Richardson (2014) have extended this area of study by exploring between presence relationships (focus on each pair of presences) while controlling for the third presence. They concluded, "efforts to increase social presence should not only focus on social interaction but also on encouraging cognitive presence through social interaction" (p. 72). This suggests that participants identify first with academic goals, and social presence must be directed to academic activities (i.e. cognitive presence) and not solely interpersonal relationships.

Another development with regard to the dynamics of the presences is the internal dynamics among the categories of each of the presences. Here it was found that the intra-presence dynamics evolved as theoretically hypothesized (Akyol & Garrison, 2008). For example, with regard to social presence, open communication received greater attention at the outset but gave way to group cohesion as the course evolved. This also held for cognitive presence as activity shifted through each phase of inquiry. However, it was important to note that the final phase responses (resolution) diminished since the assignment was to be submitted individually. Teaching presence categories were clearly distinguishable and revealed the expected change in emphasis from facilitation to direct instruction as students required specific input regarding content and expectations. Among the presences as a whole, it was also revealed that social presence declined over time as cognitive and teaching presence increased.

While most studies have confirmed the structure of the CoI framework, there have been arguments for adding other constructs. One study suggested included a fourth element, individual learner presence, to account for self-regulation (Shea, Hayes, Uzuner-Smith, Gozza-Cohen, Vickers & Bidjerano, 2014). The difficulty of this is that it fundamentally violates the premise of a community of inquiry and creates unnecessary complications. The premise that it violates is the requirement that participants function collaboratively and assume responsibilities as both teacher and student. The suggestion is also unnecessary in that the issue of regulation has been incorporated into the CoI framework through the shared metacognition construct that manifests itself primarily at the intersection of teaching and cognitive presence (Garrison & Akyol, 2015a; Garrison & Akyol, 2015b). Another suggested new construct was to add a distinct emotional presence (Cleveland-Innes & Campbell, 2012). The argument against this is similar to the previous suggestion. Notwithstanding the increased complexity of the framework this would create, the main point is that it is unnecessary as it is largely accounted for in the social presence construct that has a pervasive influence on all aspects of a community of inquiry.

The suggestion to add learner presence raises an important defining characteristic of the CoI framework—that it is a process model. Assigning roles to individuals based on their formal organizational status (e.g. instructor) would undermine the CoI as a collaborative constructivist process. A community of inquiry is about shared learning processes where individual responsibilities are shaped by the collaborative learning experience. Responsibilities are constantly shifting as learning progresses but a focus on individual roles introduces a rigidity that potentially limits participants assuming responsibility for the quality of the learning dynamic. For collaborative learning experiences, it is less of a question *who* than it is *how* ideas are being shared; the emphasis is on the process and responsibilities of collaborative inquiry. The emphasis on individual roles restricts students to take on roles and responsibilities that may have been arbitrarily reserved for the formal instructor typical of a traditional passive information dissemination approach. Ultimately, the focus on traditional roles will limit collaboration and create an artificial constraint on the depth of learning, metacognitive development of participants, and the prospects for continuous learning. In summary, adding a learner presence construct would undermine the premise of collaboration and severely complicate the CoI framework. If we are to preserve the collaborative constructivist premise of the CoI framework, care must be taken to preserve its integrity and parsimony.

Therefore, in a truly collaborative learning environment, it is contradictory to talk about teacher and learner presence with separate roles and responsibilities. Collaborative inquiry requires learners to develop shared metacognitive awareness through both self- and co-regulatory responsibilities. Self-regulation is a hold-over from conventional higher education and traditional distance education enterprises where the independence of the learner is necessitated by delivery methods or access. The core transactional issue is sustained communication and collaboration regardless of physical separation or time shifting. In this regard, it is assumed "that the collaborative learning model should be the foundation upon which online courses are designed and delivered" and where it has been shown that students report significantly higher perceived learning and satisfaction in communities of inquiry (Arbaugh & Benbunan-Fich, 2006, p. 435). Furthermore, extending discourse and collaboration through an online community of inquiry has shown broader and deeper discussions and more effective outcomes (Warner, 2016).

A Theory?

To begin, it is worthwhile to remind ourselves of the role of theory and its practical value. Theory shapes our view of the world and our behavior. It provides order that helps us make sense of complex situations and in turn creates effective plans to address challenges and solve problems. The goal, however, is that theory not be overly complex and that it conveys the essence of the phenomenon of interest. That is, it provides coherence with parsimony. Good theory has great practical value in that it helps us explain a phenomenon and predict outcomes with the minimum number of con- stituting elements. However, reaching the standard of robust theory is not only demanding to achieve but is constantly open to critique and attempts to invalidate. One framework that has had nearly 20 years of critical study is the CoI.

At this point of theoretical development, it is time to raise the question whether the CoI framework meets the requisites of a theory. In this regard, the CoI framework currently represents a coherent set of articulated elements and models describing the dynamics of a higher educational learning experience. However, to constitute a comprehensive theory, there must be other features present. Dubin (1978) suggests that in addition to units or elements there must be defined relationships (laws of interaction), boundaries that limit its relevance, and system states (how elements act differently in their relations). Once these basic features are in place, then propositions, empirical indicators and hypotheses can be derived. A theory is essential for interpreting the findings of empirical research and the possible refinement of the theory. Based on these criteria, we argue that these basic features of a theory are in place in the CoI framework. Moreover, it has been shown that the CoI framework has the ability to generate hypotheses and provide the theoretical context to interpret results from rigorous research. Therefore, it is argued that the CoI framework meets the test, at a minimum, of a nascent educational theory.

When the CoI framework was first proposed, what was lacking to be considered a complete theory was the detail and completeness of explanation to understand the nature of the relationships among the presences and the development of the system as a whole to rigorously define the relationships and describe system states. In interpreting the data from the research over this last decade (to be discussed in subsequent chapters) it is clear that it has provided a parsimonious structure and the means to understand the complex and dynamic phenomenon of an educational experience. The number of research studies using the CoI framework has clearly indicated its usefulness to make propositions (predictions), generate hypotheses, make observations, empirically test these hypotheses, and provide explanations when interpreting the findings. A decade of research has provided empirical findings to describe the nature of the interactions among the presences as well as the dynamic balance of the CoI system over time. To this point, as we shall see in subsequent chapters, there is considerable evidence that the CoI framework does account for the complexity of an educational e-learning experience.

One final feature that needs further discussion is its boundary or area of application. The reason for mentioning this is that the CoI framework was first proposed to provide order to the complexities of studying and understanding computer conferencing and online learning. It has since been used to study blended learning (Garrison & Vaughan, 2008) and with this its implicit boundary has been expanded to include face-to-face learning environments. This should not be surprising since it was noted at its inception that it was a generic model generated from the general literature and experiences of the authors in traditional higher education (Garrison et al., 2000). The point is that the CoI framework could well be applied to face-to-face educational contexts (Archer, 2010) as well as K-12 (Borup, Graham & Drysdale, 2014; Stenbom, 2015). One other point with regard to boundaries is the perception of factors such as subject matter, student characteristics and technology that were considered exogenous variables in the original description. While these are worthy of study in terms of their relationship to the elements and dynamics of the CoI framework, they continue to be considered indirect variables for reasons of parsimony.

Considering the previous discussion and the theoretical state of the CoI framework, we propose it has evolved rapidly into a comprehensive educational theory. Its adequacy as a theory will be based on its coherence and explanatory power (i.e. logic) (Dubin, 1978). Considering the previous discussion, it would appear that the CoI framework possesses the features of a theory and has sufficient coherence and explanatory power to be considered a theory. However, its validity and usefulness as a theory will be judged by its adoption and the evidence generated to support it. Furthermore, in terms of its citation, the evidence would suggest it constitutes a theory. As a theory, the CoI provides the means to study and understand thinking and learning collaboratively in a community of inquiry. Therefore, we conclude that the CoI framework meets the criteria of what constitutes a theory (Dubin, 1978).

To be clear, much work remains to explore the explanatory power and completeness of the CoI theoretical framework. However, it would seem that it is closer to a comprehensive theory than it is to a framework. For this reason, we shift from the terminology of the CoI framework to the CoI theoretical framework. At the same time, it is clear that judgments of what constitutes a theory are based on complex arguments; so consistent with all scientific endeavors, in the final analysis it will be left to others to judge whether the CoI has reached, or how it might reach, the threshold of a theory.

Conclusion

This chapter has outlined the concepts and elements needed to provide order and insight into understanding the complexities and potential of an e-learning experience. The CoI theoretical framework and its constituent elements have guided the theoretical and empirical investigation described in this book. The evidence suggests that it is the most prevalent and coherent theory in guiding the research and practice of online and blended learning and that it has enormous potential to design, implement, and assess e-learning approaches, strategies and techniques.

Chapter 4

Social Presence

The early adopters of e-learning immediately recognized its potential to support a collaborative learning experience. The obvious and immediate challenge, however, was to create a welcoming learning environment that would serve educational needs. This precipitated considerable discussion with regard to the misplaced goal of replicating a classroom experience. What was not fully appreciated was that creating a community of learners through an asynchronous text-based means of communication represented a qualitative shift from that of a real-time, verbal, face-to-face mode of communication. As such, the challenge of creating a community of learners in a medium that provides no interpersonal visual cues and is limited to words or images on a screen presented a unique challenge for educators.

Re-thinking Social Presence

Community is integral to all aspects of life. Community represents a weaving of individual and group interests; the psychological and sociological; the reflective and the collaborative. This is no less so in terms of creating and sustaining a community of learners. The implicit denial of community has been the greatest shortcoming of traditional distance education with its focus on prescriptive course packages to be assimilated by the student in isolation. This was based upon the misconception that learning is largely an individual cognitive process. However, education is a collaborative experience, which includes a sense of belonging and acceptance in a group with common interests. As such, we must reflect upon what social presence means in an online learning community that is distinguished by the written word as the predominant mode of communication.

Asynchronous text-based communication would appear to present a special challenge in creating a social environment to support a purposeful community of inquiry. Communication theorists have drawn considerable attention to the lack of non-verbal communication cues that are considered to be crucial in forming collaborative relationships. Some time ago, Short, Williams, and Christie (1976) concluded a review of media studies by stating that the "absence of the visual channel reduces the possibilities for expression of social-emotional material and decreases the information available about the other's self-image, attitudes, moods, and reactions" (p. 59). The authors focused on the medium of communication to argue that this presented a loss of intimacy. They used the term social presence to argue that mediated communication is a serious limiting factor to shared social presence. The question was whether this would be fatal to forming and sustaining a community of learners online? Does text-based communication provide the means to communicate social-emotional content necessary for building a social community, of feeling connected, and preventing a feeling of anomie? Or can teachers and students acquire and use compensating communication skills for quality collaborative learning experiences?

Doubts were raised about the hypothesized intimate connection of social presence to the characteristics of the medium. Gunawardena (1995) was instrumental in redefining social presence in terms of whether participants are perceived as "being real" (Gunawardena & Zittle, 1997, p. 8; Kim, 2011). This represented a shift from the technology to the communication characteristics in determining whether individuals are able to connect with each other socially and emotionally. The question was whether the nature of written language can compensate for the lack of visual cues such as body language and verbal intonation which has a profound effect on how a message is interpreted in a face-to-face environment. Or, alternatively, might this medium exhibit other characteristics or properties that provide an advantage to the less extraverted student and, overall, offer the potential for greater equality and participation?

In short, it has been shown that students can and do overcome the lack of non-verbal communication by establishing familiarity through the use of greetings, encouragement, paralinguistic emphasis (e.g. capitals, punctuation, emoticons) and personal vignettes (i.e. self-disclosure) (Garrison & Arbaugh, 2007; Rourke & Anderson, 2002). The fact that text-based communication is a relatively lean medium has been shown not be a serious limitation. While the characteristics of a text-based medium may well have inherent social-emotional limitations, it does have compensatory advantages (reflective, explicit and permanent) in focusing and elevating the academic level of the exchange. That is, written communication may well be more effective for facilitating critical thinking and discourse.

The conclusion is that the apparent limitations of text-based online learning have the potential to offer advantages not possible in a face-to-face educational context. The leanness or richness of the medium will be defined by the task at hand and by the compensating opportunities the medium affords. With regard to the affordance of the medium, research conducted on text-based online learning has consistently demonstrated a capacity for a high level of interpersonal communication resulting in perceived satisfaction and learning (Garrison & Arbaugh, 2007; Kim, 2011). The exact nature of the interpersonal communication will be shaped by the implicit understanding of the specific purpose of the community of inquiry.

It is argued that social presence is an important antecedent to collaboration and critical discourse. Establishing interpersonal relationships and a sense of belonging are important to an academic endeavor. Social presence does not mean supporting engagement for purely social purposes. In a community of inquiry students are expected to be skeptical or critical of ideas and expression must not be restricted for fear that they might damage a relationship. Social presence in an academic context means creating a climate that supports and encourages probing questions, skepticism and the contribution of explanatory ideas. Sustaining critical thinking and discourse requires a sense of purpose and social presence that must develop over time.

> What sustains a dialogue over time is not only lively inter-change about the topic at hand, but a certain commitment to one's partner; a commitment that might not precede the dialogue, but arises only gradually in the spirit of the engagement.
>
> (Burbules, 1993, p. 15)

A community of inquiry must be both inclusive and critical. It is through balancing these seemingly contradictory but complementary social and academic elements that a quality learning environment is created. This is where e-learning can be a very effective medium for supporting an intellectually challenging, yet respectful, community of inquiry.

Creating a purposeful learning community in a virtual, non-verbal environment that would support higher learning requires a new appreciation of social presence. Notwithstanding the importance of social presence for a functional community of inquiry, a key insight (not obvious at the outset) was that creating a cohesive community of learners could not be created based only on establishing social relationships. A cohesive and sustainable educational community was first established through common purpose and academic identity. However, this would not be functional or sustainable without a supportive collaborative environment that did not consider the social-emotional issues of the participants. A sense of belonging, open communication and cohesion are essential conditions for a community of learners.

The original Community of Inquiry (CoI) working definition of social presence was "the ability of participants in a community of inquiry to project themselves socially and emotionally, as 'real' people (i.e. their full personality), through the medium of communication being used" (Garrison et al., 2000, p. 94). The premise was that it is inconceivable to think that one could create community without some degree of social presence. The challenge, however, was to understand the nature of social presence in a purposeful community focused on academic inquiry that involved sustained critical discourse and cognitive presence. The point is that it is the explicit purpose of social presence to support inquiry in the form of reflection and discourse. So the question is what does social presence look like in an academic collaborative online learning environment?

These insights were the beginning of important research into social presence and the catalyst for the development of the CoI framework. The CoI framework with its focus on purposeful academic goals expanded the definition of social presence to go beyond the affective dimension (Garrison, Anderson & Archer, 2000). To reflect a collaborative educational experience, the dimensions of open communication and group cohesion (identity) were included to the early preoccupation with social-emotional concerns. Additional nuances were also incorporated into the definition of social presence to better reflect identity with purposeful academic goals (Garrison, 2009b). This latter development is described in the next section.

In summary, social presence is largely responsible for setting the academic climate and is defined by three overlapping components—interpersonal/ affective communication, open communication, and sustained group cohesion. All are directed to creating a climate for deep and meaningful approaches to learning through practical inquiry (cognitive presence). Therefore, setting climate is a process of creating the conditions for participants to feel sufficiently at ease to engage in meaningful discourse. In essence, it is creating a social-emotional climate for rich open communication (regardless of the medium of communication) that can build group cohesion for sustained collaborative inquiry. A recent study has highlighted the importance of social presence with regard to the richness and flexibility of communication that "co-occur with the cognitive and teaching aspects" of a community of inquiry (Gutiérrez-Santiuste & Gallego-Arrufat, in press). Social presence is concerned with connecting people through both personal and academic communication (open communication) that will build group cohesion and a commitment to purposeful inquiry.

Evidence and Insights

While social presence concerns have attracted great interest from the beginning of computer conferencing and online learning, it is still open to further research. Much of the work on social presence was on the social-emotional component in isolation from the formal academic context. While emotion is clearly associated with intellectual activity, thinking and learning in a collaborative environment presents a complexity that requires consideration of other social-emotional dimensions. It was not until the development of social presence within the CoI framework that social presence moved from a largely affective construct to a more complex and dynamic element that included issues such as communication and cohesion. This was in recognition of the social context—that being a purposeful academic community of inquiry.

What precipitated the latest examination of the social presence construct was the research by Rogers and Lea (2005). They found that when there is shared social identity with the group, group cohesion is enhanced and the group will become more productive. More specifically, social presence is enhanced when individuals identify with the group *and its purpose* as opposed to connecting with specific individual members. Put another way:

> Social presence was enabled through the emphasis on the shared social identity at the level of the collaborating group rather than the creation of interpersonal bonds between individual group members.
>
> (Rogers & Lea, 2005, p. 156)

If this is the case, early in a course of studies emphasis should be placed on the dimensions of open communication and cohesion that are developed in the context of shared purpose and group identity. Climate and interpersonal relationships need to be given time to develop and not distract from the academic purpose of the course of studies.

Such a view of social presence is consistent with a formal educational environment where there is a purposeful community of inquiry and identifying with the goals is an important social-emotional factor that will shape attitudes and behavior. Social presence underpins collaborative inquiry and mediates cognitive and teaching presence. The primary reason students are there is to learn about a specific subject. The sense of group identity is then consistent with the dimensions of social presence—social-emotional commitment, open communication and group cohesion. Identification with the purpose of the group in an educational context has a strong influence on academic behavior. Interpersonal relationships will develop and should be encouraged to the degree that they do not conflict with group identity and the purpose of the community of inquiry.

This insight raises questions with regard to the effect of the social presence dimensions, in particular the affective dimension. Setting climate is more about a feeling of belonging to the group and less about connecting with others on a personal basis. The question is how much emphasis should be placed on affect (interpersonal identity) at the beginning of the course. Perhaps we need to re-examine the affective dimension from the perspective of group identity. Parenthetically, affective concerns were raised by Shea, Hayes, Vickers, Gozza-Cohen, Uzner, Mehta, Valachova and Rangan (2010) when they noted the difficulty of identifying indicators of affect and concluded that social presence is in need of additional specification.

The need to balance the personal and group (academic) identifications in the social presence construct has been supported in recent research. Kovanović, Joksimović, Gašević and Hatala (2014) concluded that "students' social presence develops mostly through interactions focused on learning" (conclusion). The authors argue that engaging students in an exchange of ideas enhanced social presence and a sense of community while affective expressions did not directly contribute to discourse. Similarly, it has been demonstrated that social interactions are directed primarily for learning purposes (Kozan & Richardson, 2014). Another example supporting the importance of focusing on academic purpose is a study by Nippard and Murphy (2007) who found that expressions of social presence were of a digressive nature and often drew attention away from the delivery of the content. This last study supports other research in suggesting that if social presence exceeds a social-emotional threshold, it may well inhibit critical discourse (Caspi & Blau, 2008; Janssen, Erkens & Kirschner, 2012; Lee, 2014). Therefore, the evidence seems to support the position that participants identify first and foremost with the academic purpose of the group and personal relationships should evolve from these interactions.

Notwithstanding the importance of academic identification, the effect of emotions on regulating cognition and decision making is clear (Huntsinger & Ray, 2015; Van Kleef, De Dreu & Manstead, 2010, p. 46). What is less clear is what creates positive emotion and how emotion influences collaborative approaches to thinking and learning. The conclusion of Van Kleef et al., (2010) is that "the structure of the social situation serves as a fundamental moderator of the interpersonal effects of emotions" (p. 81). That is, the larger social context needs to be considered to assess best optimum emotional levels. Emotions play an important role in collaborative learning and the limited access to emotional cues in online environments identifies the need for further study. Development of emotional theory and awareness in online environments would lead to better understanding of emotion and more effective learning in online communities of inquiry (Daniels & Stupnisky, 2012).

Moreover, research on emotion suggests that emotions are associated with motivation and learning strategies which in turn affect academic achievement (Daniels & Stupnisky, 2012). In a summary of several studies on emotion in online learning environments, it was concluded that "there are few differences in emotions experienced in online learning environments relative to face-to-face classrooms" (Daniels & Stupnisky, 2012, p. 222). This may seem somewhat surprising considering the apparent lack of emotional cues and having to deal with the technology. However, greater responsibility appeared to be balanced with the positive sense of control. Regardless, as noted previously, understanding emotion calls for more theoretically based research that includes a clear definition of emotion. In this regard, we shift our focus to the dimensionality of social presence and the place of emotion.

Cleveland-Innes and Campbell (2012) studied emotion specific to online learning environments and concluded "that emotion and cognition are innately intertwined" (p. 271) but have been largely neglected. The authors state that one exception has been the CoI framework but argue for "an expanded role for emotional presence" (p. 272). Their approach was to expand the CoI questionnaire by adding emotional presence measures. Using the results from a survey of 217 students from 19 courses, an exploratory factor analysis was conducted. Their preferred factor analytic solution, shaped by the additional emotional presence items and the hypothesized emotional presence construct, suggested a unique emotional presence factor.

The suggestion of a unique emotional presence element creates significant challenges and raises the question whether this is justified empirically and theoretically. It is argued here that the methodology and factor analytic interpretation is not sufficiently strong to make the argument for a fourth presence. While the emotional component of social presence needs to be explored, the Cleveland-Innes and Campbell (2012) factor analytic interpretation does not warrant challenging the confirmed structure of the CoI framework. What is evident is the need to better understand the pervasive role of emotion in an online and collaborative thinking and learning environment.

Emotion is an affective state that fluctuates with the social conditions and, therefore, is within the purview of social presence. With regard to Cleveland-Innes and Campbell's (2012) argument that a distinct emotional presence would ensure it is experienced "beyond the expression of social presence" (p. 282), it must be pointed out that the existing CoI framework already ensures the interdependence of the presences and that the emotional dimension of social presence influences cognitive and teaching presence. Social presence intersects with the other presences and, therefore, emotion is inherently pervasive as conceptualized in the existing social presence construct. The framework is consistent with emotion playing a key role in guiding judgement, cognition, and decision making. However, creating a distinct emotional presence element based on its pervasive influence is unnecessary and risks fragmenting the social presence construct and complicating the framework.

Emphasizing emotional influence is justifiable considering that, theoretically and empirically, social presence with its affective dimension has been shown to be a mediating influence on cognitive and teaching presence (Garrison, Cleveland-Innes & Fung, 2010; Shea & Bidjerano, 2009a). However, we must be cautious placing undue emphasis on emotion that would not be consistent with a purposeful academic environment (see Jahng, Nielsen & Chan, 2010). That said, there is no question as to the intimate connection emotion has to all aspects of a community of inquiry. It could be argued that emotion is the gravity of a community of inquiry in that it is pervasive, holds things together, plays an essential role in decision making, and is often the prime mover (volition). Clearly emotion and how it fits in the CoI framework needs to be explored and understood. The question is whether it is helpful to see emotion as emanating from social presence or as a distinct generalized environmental influence along with other exogenous factors such as student and contextual characteristics. Regardless, the social presence construct is open to refinement.

The social presence construct has been redefined as the ability of participants to identify with the group or course of study, communicate purposefully in a trusting environment, and develop personal and affective relationships progressively by way of projecting their individual personalities (Garrison, 2009b). Although this is more of a refinement, the significant advantage is that this description better conveys the dynamic nature of the social presence construct in a purposeful and developing community of inquiry. That is, it places a priority on academic goals and communication within the community which leads to increased group cohesion. Through engagement in collaborative academic activities an academic climate develops and personal relationships grow naturally over time. In this way, personal relationships enhance and do not inhibit academic discourse and group identity (i.e. cohesion). Furthermore, the pattern of open communication (purposeful discourse) is set and personal sensitivities (i.e. a reluctance to criticize resulting from close relationships) are less likely to occur. As noted by Lea, Rogers and Postmes (2002, cited in Rogers & Lea, 2005), "environments rich in interpersonal information may, in fact, undermine group identity and result in process losses for the collaborating group" (p. 153).

This discussion of the natural progression of interpersonal relationships raises the important issue of the dynamic of social presence. Theoretically, it was predicted that open communication indicators will be high at the beginning of a community of inquiry and will diminish slightly over time with experience and feedback as to the rules of engagement. A such, it is hypothesized that both group cohesion and interpersonal indicators will likely increase and plateau. In support of this, it has been shown that open communication does decrease over time while cohesion increases (Akyol & Garrison, 2008). As well, interpersonal communication creates camaraderie after a period of intense association (Brown, 2001). This speaks to the development of constructive emotional responses that further open communication and an environment for participants to assume cognitive and teaching presence roles and responsibilities according to their abilities.

Notwithstanding the considerable research into social presence, there is much to understand with regard to the construct itself and its relationship to the other presences. An important area of research that has helped us understand social presence is the empirical testing of the causal relationships among the three presences in a community of inquiry. Only a few years ago it was pointed out that few studies have examined the presences simultaneously (Garrison & Arbaugh, 2007). As noted previously, early research explored this issue and found that social presence plays an important mediating role between teaching and cognitive presence (Garrison et al., 2010; Shea & Bidjerano, 2009a). This mediating role of social presence has been confirmed by a rigorous and comprehensive study and has associated it with higher academic performance (Joksimović, Gašević, Kovanović, Riecke & Hatala, 2015). Furthermore, this study found that teaching presence is essential to establishing social presence. Another recent study also demonstrates the crucial role of social presence in achieving high-level learning objectives (cognitive presence), although it was noted that all three presences need to be considered jointly (Gutiérrez-Santiuste, Sabiote-Rodríguez & Gallego-Arrufat, unpublished).

The relationships among the presences were explored more deeply in a study that looked at their progression over time (Akyol & Garrison, 2008). First, it was shown that each of the social presence categories developed at different rates. For example, it showed that affective expression dropped significantly while group cohesion increased significantly over time. This is consistent with a study by Vaughan and Garrison (2005) who also found a decrease in affective and open communication and an increase in group cohesion. While theoretical predictions of the importance of social presence communication as a whole suggest a decline over time (Garrison & Arbaugh, 2007), fluctuations in social presence have been shown to be affected by teaching presence. Shea et al. (2010) state that "as instructor teaching presence rises or falls, there is a correlating rise or fall in student social presence" (p. 13). One interpretation of this is that this may be the result of the emphasis on social or cognitive presence by the instructor. In other words, a strong focus on the academic tasks may well see a fall in social presence indicators and, conversely, an instructor who models strong social presence will very likely raise the level of social presence in the community as a whole. The key, however, is that this modeling should match and complement the specific academic task.

Another line of research has linked social presence with satisfaction, learning outcomes and retention. An early review of this research found evidence of a relationship between social presence, satisfaction and perceived learning (Garrison & Arbaugh, 2007; Kim, 2011). More recent studies have confirmed these findings linking social presence and satisfaction (Akyol & Garrison, 2008; Akyol & Garrison, 2010b). Zhan and Mei (2013) looked at online and face-to-face learning environments and concluded that the "effect of social presence on student learning achievement and satisfaction were stronger in online environment than in FTF [face-to-face] environment" (p. 131) and added that there is a greater need of social presence in online learning. Consistent with our previous discussion of the importance of identifying with the academic purpose of the group, Leong (2011) found that social presence is associated with satisfaction but is mediated through cognitive engagement. It seems that we cannot disassociate social and cognitive presence with regard to satisfaction. However, there is also a study that has shown a significant relationship between collaborative learning and satisfaction but not between social presence and overall satisfaction (So & Brush, 2008). The explanation is that social presence is a complex concept that is associated with both social and academic factors (reinforcing the interdependency of the presences). The evidence suggests that participants in a community of inquiry distinguish between social interaction and meaningful academic discourse.

Recent studies have also confirmed previous studies that show social presence to be associated with perceived learning (Caspi & Blau, 2008) and final grades (Akyol & Garrison, 2011a; Kang & Kim, 2006; Liu, Gomez & Yen, 2009; Zhan & Mei, 2013). In this regard we have argued that social presence that promotes group identity and cohesion can create a greater sense of perceived and actual learning. Looking at social presence and retention there is one large scale study that provides an interesting insight into re-enrollment in fully online programs (Boston, Diaz, Gibson, Ice, Richardson & Swan, 2009). This study has shown a significant relationship between social presence and retention that is consistent with previous research into social integration in higher education. The authors conclude, "social interaction remains a crucial factor for student retention" (Boston et al., 2009, p. 77). While many exogenous factors influence retention, a sense of belonging to a community can influence motivation to persist.

Finally, this brings us to the need to explore the connection of social presence to motivation as this has been shown to be crucial in sustaining engagement in a learning community. There is a reciprocal relationship between community and motivation. In support of this it has been suggested that task motivation is stronger in groups compared to individual work (O'Donnell & Kelly, 1994). The social nature of humans contributes enormously to motivation which is why a sense of belonging to a group can sustain motivation. Motivation is a social-emotional response that is part of initiating interest, directing effort and maintaining focus. Motivation is associated with social presence but is particularly associated with the commitment and persistence to metacognitively monitor and manage the inquiry process (Malmberg, Järvelä, Järvenoja & Panadero, 2015). Moreover, motivation is essential for active participation in a collaborative learning environment (Kim, Glassman & Williams, 2015). Motivation is an important artifact of the social-emotional dimension of social presence and a community of inquiry. Thinking and learning collaboratively provides an emotional reward and motivational advantage.

The conclusion is that social presence is a multidimensional construct essential to the effective functioning of a community of inquiry. At a minimum, the previous studies point to the complexity of the social presence construct and understanding the social and emotional dynamic of a purposeful community of inquiry. Further study is required to better understand social presence including patterns of development, connection to the other presences, and its influence on dependent variables such as learning outcomes and retention. The first step to achieving these goals is to recognize its influence and continue to refine the multidimensional nature of social presence.

Categories of Social Presence

The original classification scheme for social presence was constructed through a theoretical analysis of the literature as well as the analysis and coding of computer conferencing transcripts (Rourke, Anderson, Archer &

Garrison, 1999). This resulted in three broad categories of social presence indicators consisting of affective communication, open communication, and cohesive communicative responses. However, sharing social-emotional feelings in a purposeful community of inquiry is not the purpose of a community of inquiry. The purpose is to support the achievement of intended academic goals. The view here is that academic goals will be achieved when a climate of open communication is developed. Notwithstanding social presence's importance as a mediating variable between cognitive and teaching presence, the social-emotional dimension needs to be carefully considered and its role articulated within the social presence construct.

Affective Communication

After nearly two decades of research into the CoI framework, attention is being directed to the role of the affective or emotional climate. While the importance of social-emotional environment in regulating cognition is clear, the evidence also suggests that group identity takes precedence over personal identity in purposeful academic environments. Therefore, it is argued here that in establishing a community of inquiry it is crucial to set the academic climate for open and purposeful communication. Open communication and group cohesion extends beyond simply attending to affective communication. Open communication is an essential facilitating condition for engagement in meaningful discourse and developing a sense of purposeful connection to the group. Students join educational environments for academic purposes and not for social reasons. That said, a respectful and supportive climate is important to establish the emotional and intellectual conditions necessary for critical reflection and discourse. It is clear that understanding the pervasive influence of emotion must be a focus of further study.

There are three major indicators of affect communication. First, in online environments when visual cues and vocal intonations are not present, expression of respect and welcome can be communicated through other means such as emoticons and capitalization. Second, beyond the increasingly accepted means of expressing feelings through emoticons, language itself through the content of messages is a very powerful communicator. Perhaps the easiest to appreciate but most difficult to identify is related to humor. Humor and personal references convey goodwill and suggest that there are no serious personal challenges. Third, another very human way of establishing a personal connection is through self-disclosure. Basically, the more we know about other members of the community, the more trustful and responsive we become in terms of academic discourse.

Open Communication

Collaborative inquiry has as a foundation open communication that is reciprocal and respectful. Open communication requires a climate of trust and acceptance that allows questioning while protecting self-esteem and acceptance in the community. Open communication is built through a process of recognizing, complimenting and responding to the questions and contributions of others, thereby, encouraging reflective participation and discourse. Expressing agreement, as well as questioning the substance of messages, reveals engagement in the process of reflection and discourse. Reflective and critical discourse in a community is built upon open communication.

Cohesive Responses

Interpersonal and open communication contributes directly to the third category of social presence—group cohesion. Group cohesion is the dynamic state that is initially the function of establishing social presence. Cohesive communication begins with social presence and simple behavior such as addressing others by name. Group cohesion and association is taken to the next level by using inclusive pronouns such as "we" and "our." It is cohesion that helps sustain the commitment and focus of a community of inquiry, particularly in an online learning group. More specifically, constructing meaning, confirming understanding and completing collaborative activities, will only be successfully in a cohesive community. When students identify with the group and perceive themselves as part of a community of inquiry, the discourse, the sharing of meaning and the quality of learning outcomes will be optimized. Conversely, success in the cognitive domain also has a reciprocal and reinforcing effect on group cohesion.

Group cohesion creates an increased capacity to collaborate. In a community of inquiry, Amemado (2013) has argued that group cohesion needs to be given greater consideration. The importance of group cohesion is supported by research (Baker, 2003; Conrad, 2005). It is recognized that group cohesion is predicated upon a delicate balance of personal and purposeful academic identity. However, it is suggested that purposeful group identity be prioritized recognizing that it serves to strengthen the community at the outset. Thus, social presence develops by attending to each of the categories concurrently but the emphasis should first be on purposeful group identity (addressing why participants are there) while allowing the growth of personal affiliations through social-emotional communication techniques.

Practical Implications

The challenging question is how does one establish social presence in online and blended learning environments that will support thinking and learning collaboratively in a community of inquiry? First, we must appreciate that we are always challenged to find the optimal balance of social presence as tasks and needs change. In general, too little social presence may not sustain open communication and commitment (group cohesion). On the other hand, too much social presence may inhibit meaningful discourse by avoiding critical questioning and constructive disagreement. The primary goal and identity of the group must be deep and meaningful learning experiences and not simply social interactions.

This issue of social presence supporting the larger academic purpose was brought to our attention by Liam Rourke, our research assistant during our early research before online learning became the popular term. Liam noted this important insight with regard to the students' attitudes when coding transcripts:

> Despite theoretical rumors to the contrary, students do not complain that computer conferencing is asocial, terse, hostile, etc. On the contrary, if students complain, it is that the conference is too social, too polite, not critical or challenging, and thus not a productive learning experience.
>
> (Rourke, personal communication, 2000)

The criticism from students was that students were not being challenged when there was too much emphasis on the social and not enough on the inquiry process. Students identified first with the academic goals of the group and secondarily with fellow participants. A student summed up this phenomenon of "pathological politeness" (a phrase coined by our colleague Walter Archer) in the following manner:

> In the context of the [group], it was important to differentiate trust—a willingness to make oneself vulnerable to colleagues—from congeniality. The first is genuinely the basis for posing challenging questions; the latter can actually stand in the way of "straight talk."

Distinguishing between trust and excessive politeness is a crucial distinction for creating and sustaining a community of inquiry. It is not easy for students to engage in critical discourse and this can adversely affect collaboration (Lambert & Fisher, 2013). While collaboration is dependent upon social presence (So & Brush, 2008; Zhao, Sullivan & Mellenius, 2014), there is a risk that this could also inhibit open communication. Establishing social presence must be concerned as much with the academic purpose (cognitive and teaching presence) as with the social-emotional environment.

The possibility that social-emotional issues might undermine cognitive presence was demonstrated in a study by Jahng et al. (2010). They found that increased social communications reduced cognitive communications. They conclude that "there may be an appropriate level of social communication that supports collaborative activity more generally directed at a learning goal [cognitive presence]" (Jahng et al., 2010, p. 54). The bottom line is that excessive emphasis on developing interpersonal relationships may have deleterious effects on the academic functioning of the group if the interpersonal bonds are stronger than the identity to the group and its goals. Therefore, by way of example, excessive time on introductions at the beginning of a course of study may well be counterproductive. The implication from a practical perspective is that while individuals should make personal contact through such means as personal bios, this must not distract from the academic activities of the group. In general, this suggests that members of the community should develop relationships naturally and progressively through the purposeful and collaborative inquiry process. In this way, positive affective responses can be created that support the inquiry process.

This need for a balance of the purposeful and personal is also evident in specific social presence indicators. For example, humor must be used carefully or it can isolate individuals. Due to the risk involved in using humor effectively in a lean, text-based medium, examples of humor are not commonly found in e-learning communities. Certainly, if it is to be used, it is perhaps best to wait until social presence is firmly established and the personalities of the individuals have been revealed sufficiently.

Modeling of appropriate messages and responses can also be crucial in giving the participants a sense of belonging. These messages and responses should set the tone and draw reluctant participants into the discussion. For this reason, teaching presence must be particularly sensitive and responsive at the start of a learning experience while being clear the purpose of establishing a socially secure environment is to facilitate critical thinking and discourse. That is, we must be careful not to emphasize personal identity (interrelationships) at the expense of group identity (academic purpose). Ice breaking activities should not be focused only on introductions but designed around discussing course expectations and establishing group identity by asking students to collaboratively explore and negotiate expectations.

Finally, consideration needs to be given to an initial face-to-face or synchronous online meeting of the group. This can have an accelerating effect on establishing social presence and can shift the group dynamics much more rapidly toward academically productive activities. Learning activities that may be more effectively or efficiently conducted in a face-to-face setting could also be scheduled at this time. Such blended approaches have strong advantages that go beyond social presence. If possible, the loss of freedom with regard to time and location for a face-to-face meeting may well be a worthwhile trade-off.

Conclusion

While strong social presence does provide the basis for respectful questioning and critique, by itself it does not guarantee an optimally functioning community of inquiry. It has been shown that social presence is a mediating variable with regard to cognitive and teaching presence. The optimal level of social presence is dynamic and dependent on the specifics of cognitive and teaching presence. To further understand creating and sustaining an educational community of inquiry, we shift our focus to the academic dynamic as embodied in the cognitive presence construct.

Chapter 5

Cognitive Presence

The Community of Inquiry (CoI) theoretical framework is intended to focus on the challenge of engaging in purposeful collaborative inquiry. From the inception of the Practical Inquiry construct (cognitive presence), the question is whether higher-order thinking and discourse could be realized in an asynchronous, largely text-based educational environment. More specifically, can cognitive presence be created in an online environment and can students successfully move through the phases of practical inquiry that defines cognitive presence? The goal in this chapter is to describe the cognitive presence construct and Practical Inquiry (PI) model and provide an explanation of the nature and quality of inquiry conducted in an online learning environment.

It is to the collaborative thinking and learning experience and the required cognitive presence that we focus our attention. We use the cognitive presence construct to describe the academic process that supports sustained critical thinking and discourse and higher-order knowledge acquisition and application. More specifically, in the context of this discussion, cognitive presence means facilitating the analysis, construction and confirmation of meaning and understanding within a community of learners through sustained reflection and discourse. In an online learning context this includes being supported primarily through text-based communication.

We begin our discussion by turning our attention to the genesis of the cognitive presence construct.

Critical Thinking

Cognitive presence is closely associated with critical thinking. The concept of critical thinking that we build on here is derived from Dewey's (1933) reflective thinking model. For Dewey, reflective or critical thinking has practical value in that it deepens the meaning of our experiences. Making sense of our experiences was Dewey's core educational aim. The adjective "critical" is associated with "reasoning, evaluation and judgment, and these in turn have to do with the improvement of thinking" (Lipman, 2003, p. 3).

Consistent with Dewey's reflective thinking model, Lipman also notes that critical thinking is sensitive to context in terms of exceptional circumstances and generalizability.

Critical thinking both authenticates existing knowledge and generates new knowledge which makes an intimate connection with education. The other dimension that must be noted is the interplay between our private and public worlds. The objective of the reflective paradigm is intellectual autonomy but, in reality, is "thoroughly social and communal" (Lipman, 2003, p. 25). Lipman (2003) argues the importance of interaction in an educational context is supported by the fact that "the reflective paradigm assumes education to be inquiry" (p. 19); therefore, the "only fully appropriate pedagogy [is] the community of inquiry approach" (p. 5). Inquiry is a self-correcting process where members of the community challenge beliefs, suggest alternative perspectives for exploration, and negotiate understanding.

To be a critical thinker is to exhibit considerable independence of thought while not being immune to external challenge. To be clear, it is the individual that thinks and learns, not some amorphous group often associated with group think. However, it is difficult in an educational context to manage this curious balance between the curiosity of the individual and the constructive influence of the group. While the individual's rationality must be challenged, it is also crucial that the group does not suppress curiosity and open inquiry. An educational community is not a singularity where the social group led by the teacher is supreme and intended only to perpetuate the current state of knowledge. Thinking and learning collaboratively must protect and encourage the integrity of the individual from simply mimicking others in the community. Understanding this dynamic such that it will have a beneficial influence on thinking and learning is the function of a community of inquiry.

We are social beings and have an inherent predisposition to get into the minds of others; however, we must learn how to critically and objectively assess our own thoughts. Our conscious thoughts are generated and formed through social interaction. The educational goal should not be simply to transfer information to the individual but increase the awareness of the individual about their thinking process and how to assess the validity of various ideas whether they be socially transmitted or generated by the individual. We must avoid the singularity to think and learn in relative isolation. Personal reflection by itself is not sufficient to increase critical awareness and, therefore, to think deeply about complex issues. Critical thinking extends beyond personal thoughts and experiences. Critical thinking is more effective within purposeful communities of inquiry. The true goal of thinking and learning collaboratively is to increase personal awareness by challenging misconceptions. This is virtually impossible without external input through sustained discourse.

Critical thinking and inquiry provide the means to share and explore personal beliefs and perspectives. The propensity to not see beyond our personal experiences and beliefs and unconsciously ignore contrary evidence is termed confirmation bias (Nickerson, 1998). Addressing confirmation bias is best addressed through thinking and learning collaboratively where learners develop a healthy skepticism and understand the dangers of certainty. Perhaps the great contribution of collaborative inquiry is to challenge inherent confirmation bias and the dangers of ideological certainty. The ability and willingness to step back and critically examine our assumptions and ideas helps us develop a metacognitive awareness essential to worthwhile and continued learning. Moreover, this is inevitably a shared metacognitive awareness.

Critical or reflective thinking is integral to inquiry. However, what exactly we mean by critical thinking is not self-evident. The reason, among others, for selecting Dewey's concept of reflective thinking is that it is comprehensive and coherent. Most forms of thinking (e.g. creative, critical, intuitive) can be interpreted within this framework. Critical thinking is viewed here as an inclusive process of higher-order reflection and discourse. In an attempt to integrate various overlapping concepts associated with reflective and critical thinking, we build on a generic model of critical thinking that has its genesis in Dewey's phases of reflective thought and that considers imagination, deliberation and action (Garrison & Archer, 2000) (see Figure 5.1).

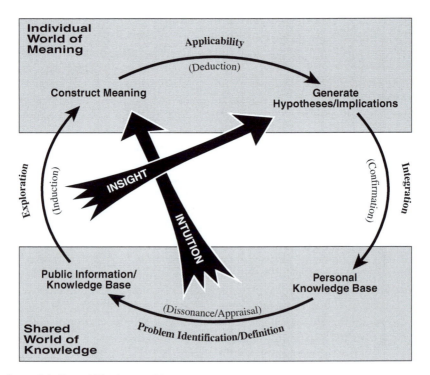

Figure 5.1 Critical Thinking and Intuition

Perhaps the key element of this critical thinking model is the overlay of the concept of the public and private worlds on the phases of reflective inquiry. This is particularly relevant in an online learning experience considering it is largely an asynchronous and text-based environment. The reason is a text-based environment has the potential to provide a remarkable balance between reflection and discourse. This is contrary to verbal discourse which favors a spontaneous and less reflective process. This recognition of two realities is an advantage in appreciating that while all phases of inquiry have elements of reflection and discourse (unity principle), one phase may emphasize discourse over reflection and vice versa. Because reflection and discourse cannot be separated in practice, this distinction makes sense only in the abstract and is intended for purposes of analysis and understanding of cognitive presence.

To this point we have focused on the conscious awareness of our thinking and learning. However, there is much latent cognitive activity at the subconscious level to which we have little awareness. In this regard, the critical thinking model is useful in making sense of related concepts such as creative thinking, problem solving, intuition and insight (Garrison & Archer, 2000). First, creative thinking is clearly a divergent process focused on the early stages of critical thinking. On the other hand, problem solving shifts focus to convergent thinking that emphasizes the latter phase of the critical thinking process. That is, the goal is a solution to a specific problem. The differences between creative thinking and problem solving are a question of emphasis and purpose as both processes include elements of the other and are aspects of critical thinking and inquiry phases. Inquiry includes a blend of both creative (intuitive and insightful) and critical (reasoned) thinking. The key issue is that intuition and insight are legitimate aspects of a rational and collaborative process of thinking and learning. Collaborative constructive dynamics emphasize that learners rationally examine assumptions, ideas and evidence when we engage in discourse to negotiate and confirm understanding. Knowledge is not transmitted in whole from the teacher to the student.

Second, concepts and processes related to intuition and insight cannot be ignored. These are important aspects of rational thought that can be explained and are not simply mystical processes to be rejected as scientifically unworthy of consideration. We have all experienced intuition that guides our conscious thinking. Many have also experienced insights or perhaps epiphanies when dealing with a dilemma or problem that seem to appear when we least expect it. For these reasons, any discussion of inquiry should consider the role of the subconscious mind. Innovation and creativity are neither easily visible nor predictable. The conscious mind is all we can come close to observing, but we must not underestimate the subconscious mind. Beneath our conscious awareness are the creative connections that we struggle to bring to the surface. Yet as unpredictable as the creative process is, evidence suggests that the best way this is done is through the fusion of reflection and discourse—through collaborative inquiry.

Intuition and insight are important creative and subconscious inductive processes that are, according to Dewey, a "product of practical deliberation" (Garrison, J., 1997, p. 33). Intuition is not an "out of the blue" experience but is preceded by purpose and considerable reflective thinking. Moreover, like insight, it inevitably results from a deep and integrated understanding of a phenomenon. Generally, it is seen as a vague, inexact awareness of the key to a problem that provides useful direction to clearly explicate the solution. This differs from insight in that insight is the classic "eureka" experience where clear solutions or coherent conceptualizations occur. While intuition arises more directly from experience, insight arises as a result of considerable reflection (being immersed in a well-defined problem) and the generation of tentative conceptual representations (Garrison & Archer, 2000). Intuition and insight must lead to the union of perception and reason (Dewey, 1967) and are essential to coherent systematic thinking.

However, when individuals are left on their own, thought processes can be suspect and need to be exposed to critical analysis. It has been noted that we "often employ intuitive processes when we make assessments and choices in uncertain situations" (Mlodinow, 2008, p. 4). This is an unproductive process if it is embedded in unreflective ideological perspectives. Too often we confuse wishful thinking with intuitive thought processes grounded in purposeful inquiry. Intuition is a legitimate cognitive process when informed by sound information and argument. In areas of uncertainty, intuition can be more than useful in bringing together disparate ideas that provide direction for further exploration. The key element, of course, is the critical discourse that provides a check on irrational or ideological thought processes. Inquiry embedded in purposeful collaboration can ensure the creativity of intuition is balanced with the test of critical thinking; that is, the integration of perception and reason. In this way, inquiry is an invaluable process to develop all of our thinking and learning abilities.

Educators seek to understand these cognitive processes in order to allow them to design more natural and less contrived educational experiences, that is, educational experiences that recognize how individuals reconstruct experience and construct meaning, thereby not condemning learners to assimilating inert knowledge or moving to predetermined conclusions. This is important in any learning environment where there is intellectual freedom and personal responsibility. The collaborative yet reflective process of inquiry has great potential for facilitating critical thinking that is core to a worthwhile educational experience. The challenge is to use this to build the critical spirit along with discipline-specific, critical-thinking abilities developed through the process of constructing meaning and confirming understanding. We define critical thinking in terms of cognitive presence operationalized through the practical inquiry (PI) model.

Practical Inquiry

Practical inquiry is a generalized form of the scientific method that is grounded in experience (Dewey, 1933). The integration of the public and private worlds of the learner is a core concept in developing cognitive presence for educational purposes. The cyclical two-dimensional PI model is presented in Figure 5.2. The continuum between action and deliberation is reflected in the vertical dimension of the model. This is consistent with the sociological (shared) and psychological (private) aspects of reflective thinking proposed by Dewey. As Dewey (1938) noted, "Any account of scientific method must be capable of offering a coherent doctrine of the nature of induction and deduction and of their relations to one another" (p. 419). This dimension of practical inquiry is the rigorous process of integrating the dynamics of inductive (arrival of generalizations) and deductive (deployment of generalizations) reasoning.

The transition point between the concrete and abstract worlds is reflected in the perception and conception dimension of the PI model. This horizontal dimension of the model reflects the point of fusion of the shared and private worlds. At one extreme is the divergent process of perception and analysis of facts or events. At the other extreme is the convergent process of insight and understanding associated with ideas and concepts. Therefore, the vertical and horizontal dimensions of the PI model reflect inductive/deductive and divergent/convergent processes of critical thinking core to the ideals of higher education.

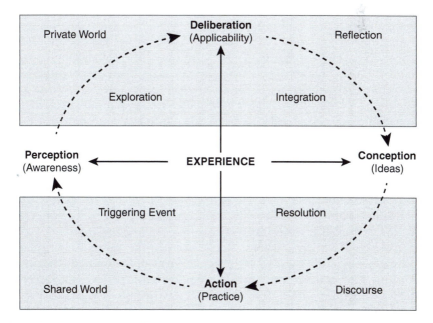

Figure 5.2 Practical Inquiry Model

Beyond the two basic dimensions of the model, practical inquiry includes four phases (trigger, exploration, integration and resolution) that describe cognitive presence in a community of inquiry. To start, we must emphasize that these phases are not immutable. They are generalized guidelines that, in practice, may be telescoped or reversed as insight and understanding are either achieved or blocked. However, a metacognitive understanding of all phases can be of enormous value to both educator and learner in assessing the task at hand, progress achieved and future directions.

The first phase of practical inquiry is the initiation or triggering event. Educationally, this needs to be a well-thought-out activity to ensure full engagement and buy-in from the group. It should also speak to a core organizing concept or issue of the knowledge domain being studied. Preferably, this would be a dilemma or problem that students could relate to, based on their experience or previous studies. While the responsibility of the educator is to initiate this phase of task analysis, this can be structured in a more open and exploratory manner by framing the issue and eliciting questions or problems that students see or have experienced. This has several positive attributes in terms of involving students, assessing the state of knowledge, and generating unintended but constructive ideas.

The second phase of practical inquiry is exploration. The first task here is to understand the nature of the problem and then to search for relevant information and possible explanations. This may be done through group activities and brainstorming and/or through more private activities such as literature searches. The primary dynamic at this phase is the experience of iterating between the reflective and shared worlds as ideas are explored collaboratively and individuals try to make sense of what initially may be complexity and confusion. This recursive process is the essence of thinking and learning collaboratively. The educational challenge is to manage and monitor this phase of divergent thinking in such a way that it begins to become more focused in order to move to the integration phase.

The third phase, integration, moves into a more focused and structured phase of constructing meaning. Decisions are made about integrating ideas and how order and structure can be created. While this is a highly reflective phase, students are also intimately engaged in critical discourse that will shape understanding. It may be during this phase of the inquiry that the characteristics of asynchronous communication come to the fore. The reflective and explicit nature of text-based communication may well facilitate meaningful learning outcomes. For these reasons, this is a particularly challenging phase of cognitive presence. In terms of assessing the depth or quality of learning outcomes, the educator must probe for understanding and misconceptions as well as model the inquiry process. The tendency is to become entrenched in the exploration phase and not move to more advanced phases of inquiry. Developing cognitive presence necessitates engaging students in all the phases of practical inquiry, including a shared metacognitive awareness and appreciation of the inquiry process.

The fourth phase is the resolution of the dilemma or problem, whether reducing complexity by constructing order or discovering a contextually specific solution to a defined problem. This confirmation or testing phase may be accomplished by direct or vicarious action. Direct confirmation is more difficult and often impractical in an educational context. However, in an e-learning environment, with students operating out of work or family contexts, direct applications and testing may be more realistic. In any case, vicarious or mental modeling of solutions is a viable and worthwhile educational activity. In educational environments, as in real life, resolution is seldom fully achieved. Inevitably, results of the resolution phase raise further questions and issues, triggering new cycles of inquiry and, thereby, encouraging continuous learning.

Evidence and Insights

An apparent challenge to the cognitive presence construct emerged early in CoI research. The evidence seemed to suggest that the discourse was not moving discussion to the integration and resolution phases of inquiry. In response to the early findings that inquiry seemed to stall, Garrison and Arbaugh (2007) argued that this was most likely a function of teaching presence such as the design of the task (clear outcome expectation), the need to be more directive in providing crucial information, and moving the discussion forward in a timely manner. This view has been supported in the literature where students were expected to reach resolution and direction was provided (Richardson, Arbaugh, Cleveland-Innes, Ice, Swan & Garrison, 2012). Similarly, Rourke and Kanuka (2007) noted the importance of the teacher and the design in higher-order discourse and concluded that they observed "denser concentrations of postings in the higher phases of critical discourse models when students are presented with structured discussion activities with clearly defined roles for teachers and students" (p. 121). This supports another observation with regard to cognitive presence that inquiry becomes more demanding as it moves to resolution (Garrison & Arbaugh, 2007).

The importance of teaching presence in achieving resolution has been supported in subsequent studies. Studies are specific in pointing to the design and nature of the task as the greatest factor in reaching resolution (Alavi & Taghizadeh, 2013; Bai, 2009; Staley & Ice, 2009). With regard to the importance of design, Richardson and Ice (2010) found higher levels of practical inquiry "with 81% of students at the integration or resolution levels for the case-based strategy" (p. 57). The conclusion from these studies is that tasks designed to achieve resolution will see greater activity at the integration and resolution phases (Stein, Wanstreet, Glazer, Engle, Harris, Johnston, Simons & Trinko, 2007). Beyond design, Bangert (2008) has shown that teaching and social presence, in particular facilitation and direction, were associated with more messages at the highest levels (integration and resolution) of cognitive presence. Similarly, it was found that higher-order critical thinking (i.e. integration and solutions) could be produced in student discussions by specific instructional techniques (Pisutova-Gerber & Malovicova, 2009).

An important insight associated with the phases of practical inquiry note that integration and resolution phases will naturally reflect fewer responses or contributions as participants are challenged and become more reflective when they converge on possible solutions (Akyol, Arbaugh, Cleveland-Innes, Garrison, Ice, Richardson & Swan, 2009). It should also be kept in mind that online discussions seldom provide sufficient time to reach resolution (Richardson & Ice, 2010). In this regard, one study successfully increased activity at the integration and resolution phases by designating a specific and sufficient amount of time for discussion at each of the phases (de Leng, Dolmans, Jobsis, Muijtjens & van der Vleuten, 2009). Another important insight with regard to activity associated with inquiry is that major projects generally reach resolution offline and, therefore, evidence of this activity in transcripts will be largely absent (Akyol & Garrison, 2008; Archer, 2010; Shea, Hayes, Vickers, Gozza-Cohen, Uzner, Mehta, Valchova & Rangan, 2010). In this regard Akyol and Garrison (2010a) noted that with major projects, students believed they reached integration and resolution phases but "most of them thought that resolution is achieved individually through their final projects" (p.10).

Cognitive presence in terms of inquiry has also been found to be associated with the nature of the course and the type of assignments. Evidence of cognitive presence was significant for humanities and social sciences but not for professional courses requiring specific knowledge and skills (Garrison, Cleveland-Innes & Fung, 2010). Similar results were reported by Arbaugh, Bangert and Cleveland-Innes (2010) when they "found significant disciplinary differences, particularly regarding cognitive presence, in soft, applied disciplines relative to other disciplines" (p. 37). More specifically, it was found that courses focusing on acquiring specific knowledge and skills, and the teacher informing the student, do not lend themselves to exploration and integration and, therefore, showed lower scores in cognitive presence (Arbaugh et al., 2010). Consistent with this Gorsky, Caspi, Antonovsky, Blau and Mansur (2010) found that students in science courses with a large number of problem solving assignments were more active and levels of all presences were higher. From a teaching presence perspective, humanities' instructors posted three times more triggering messages while "science instructors posted four times as many messages associated with the category 'exploration'" (Gorsky et al., 2010, p. 64). Not only does this reflect possible differences in disciplines but also supports the importance of appropriate instructional design and the nature of the task in cognitively engaging learners in particular disciplines.

The value of collaboration and discourse is reflected in learning sciences research. With regard to the learning sciences, Sawyer (2008) has stated that "the best learning takes place when learners articulate their unformed and still developing understanding, and continue to articulate it throughout the process of learning" (p. 53). The crucial role of interaction in critical thinking has been confirmed (Saade, Morin & Thomas, 2012) but interaction is not enough. The interaction must display specific characteristics such as purposeful open discussion and be driven by curiosity, skepticism and reason—what we refer to as discourse. However, as we noted, the nature of the interaction and quality of discourse is dependent upon the nature of the task. In this regard, it has been shown that problem solving can engage students and increase cognitive presence (Gorsky et al., 2010). This adds to the evidence that quality learning experiences are associated with collaborative inquiry generally and specifically with critical discourse.

Another area of cognitive presence research has focused on learning outcomes—both perceived and actual. Notwithstanding that cognitive presence is a process model, there has been interest associated with its association to learning outcomes. The question is whether the PI model can be used to predict learning outcomes (Akyol et al., 2009; Rourke & Kanuka, 2009). In this regard, it should be noted that the PI model has been compared to other models such as Bloom's taxonomy and found that practical inquiry predicts learning outcomes with favorable results (Buraphadeja & Dawson, 2008; Cotton & Yorke, 2006; Meyer, 2004; Schrire, 2004, 2006). In fact, in comparing the PI model with Bloom's and the SOLO (structure of observed learning outcomes) taxonomies, Schrire (2004) found the PI model "to be the most relevant to the analysis of the cognitive dimension and represents a clear picture of the knowledge-building processes occurring in online discussion" (p. 491). Buraphadeja and Dawson (2008) also note that the PI model has been widely cited as suitable for assessing critical thinking. Moreover, more recent studies have provided evidence that a community of inquiry can play a significant role in supporting critical thinking and discourse that leads to improved learning outcomes (Rockinson-Szapkiw, Wendt, Wighting & Nisbet, 2016; Warner, 2016; Yang, Quadir, Chen & Miao, 2016).

Perceived learning has been used as a proxy measure for learning outcomes due to the enormous challenge of measuring the quality of learning outcomes. Considering the latent nature of learning, perhaps individuals may be a worthy source for assessing learning. Adding to this dilemma, grades are considered a measure of learning outcomes but too often they simply reflect easily measured surface learning (i.e. recall). However, there is evidence that cognitive presence, as defined by the PI model, is associated with both perceived and actual learning outcomes (Akyol & Garrison, 2010b; Benbunan-Fich & Arbaugh, 2006; Lim, Morris & Kupritz, 2007; Roblyer, Freeman, Donaldson & Maddox, 2007). The point is that perceived learning should not be discounted as a useful measure of learning, especially in the early stages of constructing meaning. Notwithstanding the importance of assessing outcomes, the inquiry process is crucial to inform and assist in the development of the educational process. As Akyol et al. (2009) state: "The point is that understanding the educational transaction and processes of learning not only is the focus of the CoI framework but may well be of much greater value in understanding, shaping and improving the educational experience" (p. 9).

As was noted previously, the CoI theoretical framework is a process model and each of the presences are dynamic and progressive. In particular, cognitive presence provides a model of how to approach learning through inquiry and whose primary focus is collaboratively constructing and confirming meaningful and worthwhile knowledge. Understanding the dynamics of this process is the strength of cognitive presence and the CoI framework. This perspective assumes that participants think and learn collaboratively and, therefore, benefit from the critical insights of others. This is why it is troublesome to hear suggestions that the CoI framework include a fourth presence to accommodate self-regulation behaviors (Shea, Hayes, Smith, Vickers, Bidjerano & Picket, 2012). The reality is that the self-regulation construct on its own fails to explain thinking and learning in a community of inquiry. We must move beyond the self into a shared and distributed learning environment that offers the possibility to collaboratively monitor and manage the learning transaction.

Shared Metacognition

From the perspective of the CoI framework, the intent is to provide a coherent consideration of the shared roles and responsibilities for self and others. This requires an awareness and ability to individually and collaboratively assume responsibility to regulate the thinking and learning process. This executive cognitive process has been referred to as metacognition. In its essence, metacognition reflects the awareness and strategies to assess the learning process (Schraw, 2001, p. 6). The use of the term metacognition has been with us since the late 1970s (Flavell, 1979) but there still remains no general agreement as to its definition. For this reason, there is recognition of the conceptual "fuzziness" surrounding metacognition (Tarricone, 2011). This creates opportunities to explore derivative constructs, especially those associated with collaborative approaches to thinking and learning. Historically, metacognition has been strongly associated with self-regulation as it is central to the control of cognition. However, the challenge is that the focus on "self" creates difficulties when attempting to include socially shared or collaborative thinking and learning activities.

Notwithstanding, the study of metacognition has recognized the importance of social sharing and collaboration in understanding and supporting metacognition (Brown, 1987; Larkin, 2009; Schraw, 2001; Wade & Fauske, 2004; White, Frederiksen & Collins, 2009); subsuming collaborative aspects of regulation within the self-regulation construct created conceptual inconsistencies. To emphasize the process of thinking and learning collaboratively, there has been a recent movement in metacognition theory away from the self and individualistic models to an acknowledgement of metacognition as socially situated and socially constructed (Larkin, 2009). For this reason, metacognition is seen as arising from the interaction among individuals and their environment rather than largely an individual process (Iiskala, Vauras, Lehtinen & Salonen, 2011). Therefore, cognitive sharing and collaboration is an important activity in the development of metacognitive awareness (Brown, 1987; Larkin, 2009; Schraw, 2001; Wade & Fauske, 2004; White, Frederiksen & Collins, 2009).

The perspective here is that the development of metacognitive awareness is dependent upon cognitively and motivationally engaged learners that include individual and shared cognition. In this regard, metacognition is required to explain and justify one's thinking to self as well as to others (Flavell, 1987). The "key mechanism ... is the ability to observe and listen to other perspectives" (Lajoie & Lu, 2012, p. 46) and is best realized through discourse (Brown, 1987; Johansson & Gardenfors, 2005; Larkin, 2009). However, the challenge with social models of self-regulated learning is that "there is great diversity in where social is positioned in the [self-regulated learning] model" (Hadwin & Oshige, 2011, p. 242). Significant questions remain with regard to the constructs and dynamics that need to be included in a definition of socially shared metacognition.

The approach to developing a viable metacognition construct for collaborative learning environments is to subsume self- and shared regulatory functions within a metacognition construct (Tarricone, 2011). Developing metacognitive awareness and ability is core to becoming an effective inquirer since it is essential that regulation of the learning process address monitoring and managing how well the inquiry process is transpiring (White et al., 2009). Viewing regulatory functions within the metacognitive construct has the potential to accommodate both self and shared regulatory processes. Furthermore, metacognition has been generally accepted as consisting of two components—awareness and implementation strategies. Awareness allows the learner to monitor the learning process and then to actively manage the inquiry process. In short, metacognition awareness and implementation ability provides the knowledge and strategies to monitor and manage effective inquiry.

In an educational context, academic achievement has been associated with metacognitive awareness and implementation ability (Stewart, Cooper & Moulding, 2007; Young & Fry, 2008). In online discussions, the evidence is growing that metacognition helps students assess the legitimacy of information (Weigel, Straughn & Gardner, 2010) and the progress they are making in terms of intended learning outcomes. It is essential during the inquiry process that assessments be made about how the individual and group facilitate cognitive awareness and development. This is a central issue in thinking and learning collaboratively and raises the crucial issues about the nature of a community of inquiry that can support and sustain metacognitive awareness and development. We argue that the inquiry process embedded in the CoI theoretical framework provides the context to conceptually and operationally define and operationalize metacognition in a socially shared environment.

Thinking and learning in a community of inquiry is predicated upon participants taking responsibility to personally construct meaning and collaboratively confirm knowledge. Executive cognitive processes are essential in an inquiry approach to thinking and learning. As Lipman (2003) notes, "All inquiry is self-critical practice" (p. 83). Inquiry necessitates the awareness and ability to critically monitor and manage the learning process. That is, there must be a metacognitive awareness of the inquiry process to understand what is required at each phase; then to exhibit the adjustment and flexibility to ensure progression to resolution. This represents iterating between monitoring tasks and managing strategies as inquiry progresses to ensure achievement of intended learning outcomes.

To this point, we have argued that a metacognition construct must accommodate thinking and learning in a collaborative environment; that is, a coherent metacognition construct that is consistent with the assumptions of a collaborative constructivist community of inquiry. The challenge is that the self-regulated learning construct has an individual orientation that does not explicitly address the collaborative nature of regulation in a community of inquiry. As such, new research on regulation has focused on self- and socially shared regulation (Hadwin & Oshige, 2011; Winne, 2015). This also precipitated the development of a shared metacognition construct that proposed two bidirectional dimensions—self- (individual) and co-regulation (distributed cognition) specific to thinking and learning collaboratively in a community of inquiry (Garrison & Akyol, 2013, 2015a, 2015b). As with reflection and discourse, self- and co-regulation are not only iterative/recursive but indistinguishable in practice.

The shared metacognition construct hypothesized that the dynamic self- and co-regulation dimensions each exhibited a monitoring (awareness) and a managing (strategic action) function (Akyol & Garrison, 2011b). This is consistent with the metacognition literature that defined it in terms of monitoring and controlling cognition (Flavell, 1979). The monitoring function is associated with the awareness of cognition and is a process of reflection on thinking and learning in a community of inquiry. More specifically this is a reflection on expectations, meaningfulness of factual content, procedural effectiveness (inquiry process) and conditional knowledge (strategies) and effort required. On the other hand, the management function represents reflection in action. This is the strategic enactment and control of the inquiry process that includes setting goals, exploring and questioning ideas, considering alternate hypotheses, and ensuring timely progress. Consistent with the shared metacognition construct, monitoring and management functions reflect the integration of the private and shared worlds of thinking and learning and the fusion of self- and co-regulation (see Figure 5.3).

The CoI theoretical framework provided the context to rigorously test the shared metacognition construct for its structural and transactional integrity. Research has developed and verified the shared metacognition construct consisting of the self- and co-regulation dimensions each of which include monitoring and management functions (Garrison & Akyol, 2015a, 2015b). This work was facilitated by a quantitative instrument that reflected the shared metacognition construct (see Appendix B). While further validation of the shared metacognition instrument is required, the construct and questionnaire offer a promising means to better understand the structure and dynamics of metacognition in collaborative learning environments. Beyond further confirmation of the shared metacognition construct, research needs to be directed to the dynamic between self- and co-regulation. For example, a recent study found students were more engaged in co-regulation (team regulation) than self-regulation in a collaborative learning environment (Saab, van Joolingen & van Hout-Wolters, 2012). This raises a core consideration about how participants in a collaborative learning environment iterate between self- and co-regulation.

The importance of studying metacognition in communities of inquiry was raised in a recent study. Gašević, Adesope, Joksimović and Kovanović (2015) demonstrated the positive effects of externally-facilitated (shared) regulation on cognitive presence. They integrated shared regulation into the design component of teaching presence which provided opportunities for students to co-regulate their learning. These students used metacognitive awareness of cognitive presence in the context of a community of inquiry. Clearly, shared metacognition holds much promise to understand and

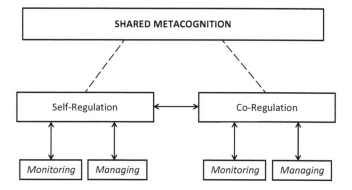

Figure 5.3 Shared Metacognition Construct

support thinking and learning collaboratively. Research has demonstrated that students who provided and received group feedback outperformed students who only used self-explanation strategy (i.e. did not get any metacognitive support) (Kramarski & Dudai, 2009). These self- and co-regulatory dynamics need to be studied both qualitatively and quantitatively to understand how and when shared metacognition functions are most effective. In turn, this research holds the possibility of refining the CoI framework and the development of specific strategies that will effectively guide mutually supported metacognition.

From a theoretical perspective, it is important to understand the place of shared metacognition within the CoI framework. It has been hypothesized as primarily functioning at the intersection of cognitive and teaching presence. The CoI framework provides a broader contextual means to understand the two core functions of shared metacognition. From the cognitive presence perspective, the focus is on awareness and monitoring of thinking and learning; while teaching presence emphasizes the regulation and management responsibilities. This seems to be a natural and logical fit for shared metacognition but considerable research is warranted to fully understand the theoretical and practical implications of the shared metacognition construct. This research will also play an important role in refining and deepening our theoretical understanding of the CoI framework. The next challenge is to demonstrate a positive impact of shared metacognition on learning processes and outcomes in communities of inquiry.

Understanding the impact of shared metacognition on thinking and learning collaboratively is of particular relevance in online and blended learning environments. While metacognition and regulation have been shown to be positively associated with academic achievement, little has been done to understand its role in asynchronous online learning environments (Editorial, 2015). As we have seen in informal online interactions, there is no guarantee of thoughtful collaboration. Simple connectivity does not create productive collaborative thinking and learning experiences. Mediated communication often lacks the social presence that can have a profound effect on commitment and engagement in the learning transaction. With regard to virtual online environments, Volet, Vauras and Salonen (2009) note that "little is known about the extent to which metacognitive regulation is facilitated, maintained, or alternatively inhibited in such contexts" (p. 223). The potential to support and sustain communities of inquiry online have drawn attention to the need to expand our study and understanding of shared metacognition in collaborative learning environments.

Finally, an area of research that has traditionally been associated with metacognition is that of motivation. The reason is that metacognition is predicated upon a willingness to take responsibility to monitor and manage the learning process. As we discussed in the previous chapter, motivation is largely a social-emotional response (social presence), but it is essential in precipitating interest and directing effort (volition). Conversely, motivation grows as a result of being a contributing and valued member of a learning community. Motivation, however, is not simply an emotional response associated with social presence. Shared motivation is associated with engaging and sharing knowledge in an online learning community which can have a significant influence on thinking and learning collaboratively (Kim, Glassman & Williams, 2015; Malmberg, Järvelä, Järvenoja & Panadero, 2015). Motivation emerges at the point of convergence of each of the three presences (i.e. co-determinative) and must be metacognitively managed to maintain a trusting and constructive environment where participants are willing to remain engaged. Motivation is enhanced when social presence is addressed through trust, open communication and a sense of belonging (cohesion). It is also enhanced when teaching presence addresses expectations, interests and support; and when cognitive presence successfully achieves intended learning goals.

Cognitive Presence Descriptors

Practical inquiry is the model within which we operationalize and assess cognitive presence. The goal is to provide a practical means to judge the nature and quality of critical reflection and discourse in a community of inquiry. The descriptors and indicators of cognitive presence generated in our research have considerable potential to assess the inquiry process. The goal is to facilitate discourse to achieve the greater purpose of achieving higher-order learning outcomes and use these indicators to assess critical thinking and discourse with regard to the developmental phases of practical inquiry. In this regard, attention to process in terms of ensuring progression through the phases of inquiry is essential.

Table 5.1 provides the descriptors (adjectives characterizing process) and indicators (manifest examples) that correspond to each phase of the practical inquiry process. These were first based on the socio-cognitive processes that characterized each of the phases of practical inquiry. They were then enhanced and confirmed empirically (Garrison, Anderson & Archer, 2001).

The first phase, the triggering event, is associated with conceptualizing a problem or issue. For this reason, we consider this evocative and inductive by nature. The educational processes would include presenting information that generates curiosity and questions. The triggering event will further discussion in a way that builds into subsequent phases of inquiry. An example might be a statement and question such as: "It has been argued that the only way to deliver effective e-learning is through a Community of Inquiry model or approach. Why do you think that is?"

The second phase, exploration, is a search for relevant information and ideas. For this reason, this is an inquisitive and divergent process. The

Table 5.1 Practical Inquiry Descriptors and Indicators

Phase	Descriptor	Indicator
Triggering event	Evocative (inductive)	Recognize problem Puzzlement
Exploration	Inquisitive (divergent)	Divergence Info exchange Suggestions Brainstorming Intuitive leaps
Integration	Tentative (convergent)	Convergence Synthesis Solutions
Resolution	Committed (deductive)	Apply Test Defend

educational process would include: brainstorming ideas; offering supportive or contradictory ideas and concepts; soliciting narratives of relevant perspectives or experiences; and eliciting comments or responses as to the value of the information or ideas. Following the previous theme, a typical statement corresponding to the exploration phase might be: "One reason I think learning communities are seldom used is that it is too complicated to engage participants collaboratively. Another may be the mindset of those in charge to change practices."

The third phase, integration, is the process of constructing a meaningful solution or explanation. Therefore, this is considered to be a tentative connection of ideas capable of meeting defined criteria, providing meaning and offering potential solutions. The educational transaction would include: integrating information; offering messages of agreement; building on other ideas; providing a rationale or justification; and explicitly offering a solution.

An example would be: "We also had trouble getting cooperation. Often the use of new tools requires new organizational structures. We addressed these issues when we implemented a systems approach, and I think that's why we were successful."

The fourth phase, resolution, critically assesses the viability of the proposed solution through direct or vicarious application. Resolution requires a commitment to test the solution deductively, perhaps through vicarious implementation or thought experiment. This would require a rigorous analysis of the hypothetical test, which could take the form of a presentation and defense with other participants critiquing the suggested application. On the other hand, the test could take the form of a direct application or action research project—either an individual or group project. An example of an exchange consistent with this phase of practical inquiry might be: "A good test would be to ensure that participants understand the expectations, and that collaboration is properly rewarded. Once implemented, this could be assessed by considering project grades as well as the impressions of the participants."

The challenge for educators is to move the discussion and individual cognitive development through each of the phases of practical inquiry. That is, to build the discussion from problem recognition (triggering event) through to exploration, integration and resolution. The tendency is to do the first two phases very well, the third phase less well, and the last phase hardly at all. As discussed previously, this is very likely due to a variety of reasons including the nature of the task, limited time, or a lack of a teaching presence to move the process forward. There must be an appreciation and commitment to the value of thinking progressively through a problem and dilemma such that some worthwhile and lasting benefit ensues. This, of course, is the essential purpose of an educational experience.

Conclusion

Cognitive presence operationalized through the practical inquiry model provides insight into the cognitive aspects of a collaborative learning experience grounded in personal reflection and shared discourse. Cognitive presence operationalized through the PI model is a shared process. Therefore, if educators do not start with a clear outcome, the collaborative dynamics of the thinking and learning process will be severely limited or undermined. While work remains to refine the inquiry process, the PI model with its indicators has been shown to be an invaluable heuristic to guide the development of cognitive presence.

Cognitive presence represents the means to support and sustain a purposeful learning community. The practical challenges, however, are the latent nature of learning and a collaborative approach to thinking and learning. This may partially explain why cognitive presence has been focused upon the least (compared to social and teaching presence) in terms of research using cognitive presence as a treatment variable (Befus, 2016). On the other hand, the Befus study reported a comparable amount of cognitive presence research (compared to social and teaching presence) was focused on using the construct as a measurement device or protocol as well as validating or extending the construct. The interpretation here is that there is a need and opportunity to explore the predictive value of cognitive presence in terms of things such as learning outcomes. A similar opportunity exists to use shared metacognition as a treatment variable to study the quality of the inquiry process and learning outcomes. In general, there needs to be more research associated with learning. In this regard, the constructs of cognitive presence and shared metacognition in the context of a community of inquiry could be very interesting and productive areas for new lines of research.

Notwithstanding the need for more research associated with learning, leadership has been shown to be a crucial responsibility for the success of a worthwhile learning experience. It is to the challenge of providing teaching presence and its role in providing leadership in a community of academic inquiry that we turn to next.

Chapter 6

Teaching Presence

The online and blended learning environment increases access and extends interaction. To be constrained by the closed traditional classroom is to ignore the capabilities and potential of e-learning. While it is clear that the communication technologies associated with online and blended learning provide enormous opportunities and choice for connection and reflection, it also presents significant challenges associated with designing and delivering a meaningful and worthwhile educational experience. The educational opportunities of the Internet and communication technologies present choices that require informed leadership if learning is to be purposeful and developmental. Implicit in this is the need to rethink the purpose, approach and nature of the educational transaction.

The expanded connectivity of e-learning has seen a shift toward collaborative constructivist approaches associated with critical thinking and discourse. This is a learnING-centered approach rather than a learnER-centered approach. From an educational perspective, this distinction is more than a subtlety or nuance. Education is a collaborative process where educators and students have important shared responsibilities. The focus is on learning but not just whatever interests the learner (a risk of the Internet). An educational experience is intended to focus on learning experiences that have societal value as well as the ability for the individual to grow and continue learning. To focus excessively on learner interests (learner-centered approach) risks marginalizing the important educational responsibilities of a knowledgeable teacher. In an educational experience, both the learner and educator are integral participants in the learning process. The role and responsibility of teaching presence is to monitor and manage the transactional balance, and by engaging the learners, collaboratively guide the process of achieving worthwhile and intended learning outcomes in a timely manner.

Dewey (1938) addressed the need for purpose, structure and leadership. The educator must establish aims and activities while not being straight-jacketed by them. In this regard, the educational leader must be focused but flexible as inquiry unfolds and new questions arise. The educational leader must be knowledgeable from both a content and pedagogical perspective while being comfortable with uncertainty. Accepting of uncertainty as a natural dynamic of a worthwhile educational experience allows the educator to adjust to the needs of the learners while considering the purposeful nature of the learning experience. In this regard, Dewey (1933) stated, "thought needs careful and attentive educational direction" (p. 22). Dewey (1938) also recognized that this required developing appropriate social relationships and the social environment of the learning community. As such, teaching presence is an enormously important but complex responsibility that requires sustained adjustment.

Learning-centered approaches are more than simply re-assigning responsibility and control to the learner. This is a violation of the intent and integrity of an educational experience and the responsibility to design, facilitate and direct a constructive learning process. Teaching presence performs an essential role in identifying relevant societal knowledge, creating learning experiences that facilitate reflection and discourse, and diagnosing learning outcomes. In an online learning environment this is both easier and more difficult. It is easier in the sense that the e-learning medium supports sustained and reflective dialogue. However, it is more difficult in that online learning has distinctive communication characteristics that require new approaches and adjustments. In particular, it demands a collaborative approach that recognizes and encourages the assumption and development of teaching presence in all the participants.

To establish appropriate teaching presence, it is necessary to go beyond a list of best practices or techniques for e-learning. More effort and creativity must go into understanding and appreciating the integrating element of teaching presence to facilitate critical thinking and higher-order learning outcomes within a collaborative e-learning context.

Roles and Functions

The core principles and responsibilities of an educational transaction are translatable to online learning environments. While effective teaching can take different forms, principles such as clear expectations, critical discourse, and diagnosis of misconceptions are common to face-to-face and online learning environments. The responsibilities of teaching in any context are complex and multi-faceted. They include being a subject matter expert, an educational designer, a facilitator and a teacher. However, as has been noted, the liberating frame of e-learning significantly alters how the multi-faceted teaching presence responsibilities are realized in supporting collaborative thinking and learning. As a result of the complexities associated with online and blended learning environments, teaching presence provides the essential unifying element to achieve intended learning outcomes in virtual and collaborative settings.

There is consistency in the literature as to what constitutes teaching responsibilities in higher education (see Table 6.1). Although there is some

Table 6.1 Teaching Roles in E-Learning

Anderson et al.	*Berge*	*Paulsen*	*Mason*
Instructional design and organization	Managerial	Organizational	Organizational
Facilitation	Social	Social	Social
Direct instruction	Pedagogical	Intellectual	Intellectual
	Technical		

shifting of roles across the categories, there is a close mapping of the classification schemes associated with teaching in higher education and the categories of teaching presence hypothesized in the CoI framework. While the responsibilities are reasonably intuitive, they also have empirical support (Anderson, Rourke, Garrison & Archer, 2001; Arbaugh, Cleveland-Innes, Diaz, Garrison, Ice, Richardson, Shea & Swan, 2008; Arbaugh & Hwang, 2006). The intuitiveness and consistency of these responsibilities provide confidence and understanding upon which to further explore and explicate teaching presence in online and blended learning environments.

As noted in Table 6.1, the educator's roles fall into three primary categories: design and organization, facilitation and direct instruction. Consistent with this, teaching presence has been defined as "the design, facilitation, and direction of cognitive and social processes for the purpose of realizing personally meaningful and educationally worthwhile learning outcomes" (Anderson et al., 2001, p. 5). Considering the central function of teaching presence, there should be no doubt of the essential role teaching presence plays in integrating the various elements of an educational experience made ever more challenging in a collaborative e-learning environment. Before describing each of the categories of teaching presence, it should be emphasized that teaching presence is what participants do to create a community of inquiry that includes both cognitive and social presence. Therefore, the focus is on the roles of an educator or the actual functions that a teacher must perform to create and maintain a dynamic collaborative learning environment. These functions are integrative in the sense that teaching presence must bring together the cognitive and social in purposeful and synergistic ways. It should be recognized that there is appropriately a cognitive bias in terms of educational purpose but social presence is an ever present and necessary mediating element to collaboratively achieve the intended goals.

Identifying more precisely indicators and corresponding examples for each of the teaching presence categories can provide useful guidelines, especially for those less familiar with online and blended learning approaches. Detailed descriptions of each of the three categories of teaching presence follow.

Design and Organization

Design and organization has to do with macro-level structure and process. Perhaps not surprisingly, the design and organization of an online or blended learning course is, at least initially, more demanding than the design and organization of a similar face-to-face classroom environment. This is due, first, to the technology and the need for educators to design approaches to teaching and learning that maximize the potential of online and blended learning (i.e. sustained collaboration). Second, the entire course architecture and content must be determined well before the launch of the course. This requires considerably more investment of time and expertise on the front end of a course of study. It is no longer possible to determine what to present just before the class is scheduled. Finally, the design may be a considerable undertaking for those who have only had experience delivering a course via lecturing. For these individuals, they first need to understand the design possibilities and adjustments required for an online community of inquiry. This will likely be further compounded by the fact that students may not have experienced an online or blended learning course and new expectations and behaviors will be required.

Building the curriculum is made more complex by having to deal with the apparent contradiction of having to both increase and decrease content. That is, content is increased in the sense of providing links to other sites that may include important learning objects or supplementary material; and decreased in the sense that it must be sufficiently focused to stimulate and support meaningful reflection and discourse. In conjunction with this simultaneous broadening and channeling of course content is the crucial task of selecting collaborative activities and assignments. It is here that an understanding of the possibilities of online learning intersects with the actual teaching and learning transaction. The design work at the front end of a course of studies will pay considerable dividends during the course of study. It will not, however, preclude having to make important design decisions throughout the inquiry process. Table 6.2 provides the design indicators along with exemplars.

The Community of Inquiry (CoI) framework provides the structure in terms of design and organization for a worthwhile educational experience. The difference is that design emphasizes the structural decisions made before the process begins while organization refers to similar decisions that are made to adjust to changes during the educational transaction (in situ design). Organizational comments reflect the flexible and non-prescriptive nature of an educational experience. The structural template is created with the expectation that specific issues and needs will inevitably arise that will necessitate organizational changes in the course of action.

The exploratory nature of a community of inquiry places an increased reliance on organizational issues. The indeterminate nature of the development of

Table 6.2 Instructional Design and Organization Indicators

Indicators	Examples
Setting curriculum	"This week we will be discussing ..."
Designing methods	"I am going to divide you into groups, and you will debate ..."
Establishing time parameters	"Please post a message by Friday..."
Utilizing medium effectively	"Try to address issues that others have raised when you post."
Establishing netiquette	"Keep your messages short."
Making macro-level comments about course content	"This discussion is intended to give you a broad set of tools/skills which you will be able to use in deciding when and how to use different research techniques."

knowledge introduces a degree of uncertainty into the design process and, therefore, a need for flexibility. If online and blended learning is to be a collaborative constructivist process, then students must have influence in what is studied and how it is approached. Therefore, design should not be separated from delivery. It continues in the guise of organizational responsibilities and, as such, there is a need to ensuring continuity from the design to the organization phase. This is best accomplished when both design and organization allows for effective responsiveness to developing needs and appropriate learning activities.

Facilitating Discourse

The second element of teaching presence, facilitating reflection and discourse for the purpose of building understanding, goes to the heart of the learning experience. Facilitating discourse recognizes the purpose of a community of inquiry as enabling and encouraging the construction of personal meaning as well as collaboratively shaping and confirming mutual understanding. This element represents the fusion of purpose, process and product. That is, it is where interest, engagement and learning converge.

Teaching presence plays an essential role in facilitating discourse in a learning experience. Managing and monitoring discourse in an online learning environment is no less important than in facilitating face-to-face discussions. The reflective and rigorous nature of text-based communication demands serious commitment but presents additional opportunities for reflection and engagement. To sustain this commitment and encourage quality contributions requires that the discourse be focused and constructive. Inherent to the open nature of inquiry the paradoxical role of the facilitator must also be noted in that facilitation "aims both at changing and preserving the system, attempts both to exert and not exert control, and teaches by not teaching" (Kennedy & Kennedy, 2010, p. 12). Facilitation is an enormously important and challenging responsibility.

Teaching presence responsibilities require sustained attention to a broad range of issues. The overriding concern is to establish and sustain the learning community to ensure progression toward educational goals. This demands attention to both cognitive and social presence concerns. Postings must be monitored and the nature and timing of responses must be considered. In addition, the community must be somewhat self-sustaining and self-correcting; in particular, too little or too much teaching presence may adversely affect the discourse and the process of building under-standing. It has been shown that high levels of teaching presence can reduce participation and knowledge construction (Zhao & Sullivan, 2016). While maintaining a balance of teaching presence, teacher postings must model critical discourse while shaping the discussion to achieve purposeful goals. Guidance is also required to engage less responsive students as well as curtail the exuberance of those who will inevitably try to dominate the discussion. These skills are not so different from facilitating a face-to-face discussion.

Engagement is not to simply encourage or reward prolific responses. Teaching presence must encourage appropriate and relevant responses by bringing attention to well-reasoned responses and making linkages to previous responses. Participants must feel the discussion is moving in a purposeful direction and in a timely manner. At some point, the threads of the discussion need to be brought together and shared understanding explicitly articulated. All of this requires more than a "guide on the side" but less than a "sage on the stage." That is, the teacher must negotiate something more substantial than a rambling conversation yet not simply provide a prescriptive summary of the topics discussed. When students take responsibility to collaboratively construct and confirm understanding, teaching presence has found the appropriate balance of control. Indicators and examples of facilitating discourse are shown in Table 6.3.

Facilitating discourse for purposes of building understanding involves pedagogical understanding, disciplinary expertise, interpersonal guidance, and organizational direction. Teaching presence must be as concerned with cognitive development as with a positive learning environment, and it must see content, cognition and context as integral parts of the whole. However, opportunity should be provided for interaction that is primarily social and generally off-limits to the teacher. This can effectively be supported in a chat room. Mainstream purposeful discourse is more complex and embeds both cognitive and social elements. This is where the full responsibility of facilitation comes to bear.

Table 6.3 Facilitating Discourse Indicators

Indicators	Examples
Identifying areas of agreement/ disagreement	"Joe, Mary has provided a compelling counter-example to your hypothesis. Would you care to respond?"
Seeking to reach consensus/understanding	"I think Joe and Mary are saying essentially the same thing."
Encouraging, acknowledging or reinforcing student contributions	"Thank you for your insightful comments."
Setting climate for learning	"Don't feel self-conscious about 'thinking out loud' on the forum. This is a place to try out ideas after all."
Drawing in participants, prompting discussion	"Any thoughts on this issue?" "Anyone care to comment?"
Assess the efficacy of the process	"I think we're getting a little off track here."

Direct Instruction

Direct instruction is associated with specific content issues such as diagnosing misconceptions. Academic leadership manifests itself in this situation and is often quite specific in nature. Although direct instruction is a legitimate and important authoritative influence, this essential teaching responsibility is often lacking in informal online learning environments. Notwithstanding its inherent leadership limitations, it has been demonstrated that informal online learning environments can demonstrate teaching presence when well designed (Sun, Franklin & Gao, 2015). Distributed teaching presence including efficient shaping of the learning experience are essential aspects of a sustained and worthwhile educational experience. The challenge is not to lose the educational and intellectual climate when direct instruction may be limited. Participants must take on responsibility for moderation to ensure a productive direction.

The need for direct instruction challenges the "guide on the side" concept. While the concept of a guide or facilitator is integral to teaching presence, in and of itself, it is limited as an educational role. It suggests an artificial separation of facilitator and content expert and speaks to the potential distortion of an educational experience if it becomes pathologically focused on student-centeredness to the exclusion of the influence of a pedagogical and content expert. It has been shown that without strong teaching presence students tend to be overly polite but "without sufficiently deep engagement and … knowledge construction gains" (Joksimović, Gašević, Kovanović, Riecke & Hatala, 2015, p. 650). Such a misguided approach that neglects the need for leadership in purposeful learning environments misinterprets a collaborative constructivist approach to learning and the importance of systematically building learning experiences (i.e. scaffolding) to achieve intended, higher-order learning experiences.

Teaching presence is not possible without the expertise of a pedagogically experienced and knowledgeable teacher who can identify worthwhile content, organize learning activities, guide the discourse, offer additional sources of information, diagnose misconceptions, and provide conceptual order when required. These are direct and proactive interventions that support an effective and efficient learning experience. Indicators and examples of direct instruction are shown in Table 6.4.

Evidence and Insights

The evidence attesting to the importance of teaching presence has grown considerably. In this regard, there is strong evidence of the crucial role teaching presence plays in online and blended learning (Akyol & Garrison, 2008; Arbaugh, 2005; Gallego-Arrufat, Gutiérrez-Santiuste & Campaña-Jiménez, 2015; Garrison & Arbaugh, 2007; Garrison & Cleveland-Innes, 2005; Garrison, Cleveland-Innes & Fung, 2010; Gaševic, Adesope, Joksimović & Kovanović, 2015; Meyer, 2003; Pawan, Paulus, Yalcin & Chang, 2003; Richardson, Besser, Koehler, Lim & Strait, 2016; Schrire, 2004; Shea & Bidjerano, 2009a; Shea, Li & Pickett, 2006; Swan & Shih, 2005; Vaughn & Garrison, 2006; Wu & Hiltz, 2004). Research has also consistently reported

Table 6.4 Direct Instruction Indicators

Indicators	*Examples*
Present content/questions	"Bates says..." "What do you think?"
Focus the discussion on specific issues	"I think that's a dead end. I would ask you to consider..."
Summarize the discussion	"The original question was ... Joe said... Mary said... We concluded that...We still haven't addressed..."
Confirm understanding through assessment and explanatory feedback	"You're close, but you didn't account for..." "...this is important because..."
Diagnose misconceptions	"Remember, Bates is speaking from an administrative perspective, so be careful when you say..."
Inject knowledge from diverse sources, e.g. textbook, articles, internet, personal experiences (includes pointers to resources)	"I was at a conference with Bates once, and he said..." "You can find the proceedings from the conference at http://www..."
Responding to technical concerns	"If you want to include a hyperlink in your message, you have to ..."

the importance of teaching presence for perceived learning and satisfaction (Akyol & Garrison, 2010b; Akyol, Garrison & Ozden, 2009; Joo, Lim & Kim, 2011; Richardson & Swan, 2003; Swan & Shih, 2005; Yang, Quadir, Chen & Miao, 2016) and for academic performance (Paechter, Maier & Macher, 2010; Joksimović et al., 2015; Yang, Quadir, Chen & Miao, 2016). Furthermore, there is evidence that the attainment of intended learning outcomes rely heavily on teaching presence (Szeto, 2015) and instructor preparation and guidance has been shown to significantly increase the completion of learning tasks (Ma, Han, Yang & Cheng, 2015).

Interaction and discourse play an essential role in a community of inquiry and it has been shown that teaching presence is crucial to ensure participation and quality of responses (An, Shin & Lim, 2009; Bliss & Lawrence, 2009; Gorsky, Caspi, Antonovsky, Blau & Mansur, 2010). Instructors who support and moderate communication were also found to support community development (Brook & Oliver, 2007). In this regard, Shea et al. (2006) concluded that strong teaching presence "is related both to students' sense of connectedness and learning" (p. 85). Similarly, teaching presence is associated with a sense of community (Ice, Curtis, Phillips & Wells, 2007; Perry & Edwards, 2005; Shea et al., 2006). Design and a shared understanding of the goals have been associated with variables such as engagement and cohesion (Tsiotakis & Jimoyiannis, 2016; Unwin, 2015). Gasevic et al. (2015) demonstrated that design along with expert role facilitation resulted in significantly high levels of cognitive presence. Design was also shown to be important for academic performance (Joksimović et al., 2015). As the evidence pointing to the critical importance of teaching presence continues to grow, it seems increasingly clear that teaching presence is central to purposeful deep and meaningful learning experiences in collaborative learning environments.

The importance of teaching presence for higher levels of cognitive presence has been associated with timely feedback that included the "facilitation of learning and development by providing encouragement and direction [coaching]" (Stein, Wanstreet, Slagle, Trinko & Lutz, 2013, p. 79). Randomly selected treatment and control groups showed that learner-led discussions can promote critical thinking and responsibility for learning if "continuously coached and provided with feedback in teaching presence and social presence … compared to members of an un-coached group" (Stein et al., 2013, p. 83). This study also concluded that this is congruent with predictions of the CoI framework. Similarly, it has been shown that the teaching presence role to scaffold discussion strategies can facilitate cognitive presence and critical thinking (Darabi, Arrastia, Nelson, Cornille & Liang, 2011). Scaffolding teacher presence in the form of shared regulation in student-led discussions has also shown a higher effect on cognitive presence (Gaševic et al., 2015).

Notwithstanding the central importance of teaching presence, the interdependence of all the presences must be recognized and addressed. A recent study looked at the importance of teaching presence by comparing under-graduate and graduate students (Sheridan, Kelly & Bentz, 2013). They found all the teaching presence dimensions were important and there was no differ-ence between undergraduate and graduate students in terms of importance. What was most interesting, however, was the importance of instructor dis-position (social-emotional). The insight was to have an instructor that is understanding, flexible and helpful and who can project themselves into the learning environment. A similar insight was also reported in terms of the importance of encouragement and affirmation in addition to practices associated with design and facilitation (Wisneski, Ozogul & Bichelmeyer, 2015). This explains the finding that teaching presence is largely responsible for both social and cognitive presence (Joksimović et al., 2015; Savvidou, 2013; Rubin & Fernandes, 2013) and reinforces the core assumption of a community of inquiry that teaching presence must consider both cognitive and social presence.

The importance of concurrently considering all three presences was revealed in a study by Clarke and Bartholomew (2014) who took an in-depth look at teaching presence. It was found that students favored instructors who balanced their comments across all three presences. However, the important message here is that for discourse to move through the inquiry process, teaching presence must exhibit a balance between facilitation and more directive input. The conclusion of Clarke and Bartholomew (2014) was that instructor participation in online discussions is a balancing act that requires careful thought and action. In this regard, we must keep the academic goals clear through facilitation and direction while maintaining social presence through encouragement. Therefore, if asynchronous online discussions are to be more than chat rooms, then the nature of instructional leadership is crucial—interaction is not enough (Garrison & Cleveland-Innes, 2005). Teaching presence, which includes strong leadership, is crucial to achieve intended academic goals. The study of deep and meaningful learning suggests "that neither social presence alone nor the surface exchange of information can create the environment and climate for deep approaches to learning and meaningful educational exchanges" (Garrison & Cleveland-Innes, 2005, p. 144).

An aspect of teaching presence that has only recently been addressed is in understanding the changes in emphasis of its dimensions over the duration of a course of studies. Insight into this phenomenon was initially reported by Vaughan and Garrison (2006) when they found that design and facilitation comments decreased over time while direct instruction comments increased considerably. This pattern was confirmed when it was found that direct instruction increased significantly over time (Akyol & Garrison, 2008). The caveat is that direct instruction must not limit student participation and assuming increased responsibility. The dynamic nature of teaching presence must not be lost as the complexity of balancing facilitation and direct instruc-tion over time presents a special challenge (Rienties, Giesbers, Tempelaar &

Lygo-Baker, 2013). As with social and cognitive presence, more research is required into the dynamics of all the presences as a course develops over time. This dynamic variation of the presences is complicated by a range of contextual factors that include student characteristics, disciplinary challenges and communication technologies.

The teaching presence construct has been confirmed through both qualitative and quantitative studies (Anderson et al., 2001; Garrison & Arbaugh, 2007; Arbaugh et al., 2008; Ke, 2010). However, a question has been raised as to the dimensional structure of teaching presence. Shea et al. (2006) conducted a factor analysis of over 2,000 college students and concluded a two-factor solution was most interpretable. The students apparently were able to only distinguish between facilitation and direct instruction. On the other hand, another study suggested that students may view design and direct instruction similarly (Arbaugh et al., 2008). While these studies raise questions about the original definition of teaching presence, they provide an important insight. The results can be explained from two perspectives. First, teaching presence dimensions are interdependent variables and, therefore, there are situations where the overlap may cloud the distinction. Second, and perhaps more importantly, the characteristics of this sample of students may be that they were not able to fully appreciate the distinction among the responsibilities associated with teaching presence. That is, considering their educational development, they may not have the pedagogical understanding to distinguish the dimensions of teaching presence. Considering these explanations, it may not be surprising that there were difficulties in identifying the dimensions.

One of the most important areas of research and application of the CoI framework has to do with using it as a template to design courses and programs. Befus (2016) conducted a thematic synthesis of the CoI framework and stated that "Researchers, instructional designers, learning strategists, and practitioners have found the CoI framework to be a pragmatic and valid tool upon which to structure rich online and blended courses and empirical studies" (p. 23). Added to this, it has been shown that students value clear course requirements (Saritas, 2008; Sheridan & Kelly, 2010) and this is associated with students' perceived likelihood of success (Kupczynski, Ice, Wiesenmeyer & McCluskey, 2010). Similarly, the importance of design to ensure an active role for the participants has been revealed in terms of the construction of knowledge (Lai, 2015).

There are a growing number of examples of the use of the CoI framework to design and assess course development initiatives (Ice, Gibson, Boston & Becher, 2011; Kumar, Dawson, Black, Cavanaugh & Sessums, 2011; Moore & Shelton, 2013; Rubin & Fernandes, 2013). At the heart of the use of the CoI framework to design and assess a course is the intention to build and sustain collaborative presence. In this regard, Swan, Day, Bogle and Matthews (2014) have used the CoI survey instrument to assess course implementation and have found "significant increases in student learning outcomes" (p. 79).

A study by Yang, Quadir, Chen and Miao (2016) has noted the importance of cognitive presence design for predicting both subjective and objective learning outcomes. The use of the CoI framework for design has also been used to develop courses at the secondary school level (Jackson, Jackson & Chambers, 2013).

Another promising use of the CoI framework for design purposes is in professional development. The first professional development initiative that was designed around the CoI framework was provided by Vaughan and Garrison (2006). The goal was to have faculty learn how to design a community of inquiry by experiencing a professional development community of inquiry. This proved to be successful as faculty learned to think collaboratively and share ideas in a trusting environment. This worked particularly well in a multi-disciplinary setting that allowed the participants to consider a wider range of possibilities and with peer support they believed they could be successful.

Finally, considering the importance of teaching presence, it is a bit surprising that it has been reported that this is the least studied presence (Befus, 2016). There is much still to understand from both a theoretical and practical perspective regarding teaching presence and its interaction with the social and cognitive presences in a dynamic community of inquiry (Richardson et al., 2016). Research approaches must also use both qualitative and quantitative analyses if we are to fully understand the full range of teaching presence behaviors and their relationship to social and cognitive presence mapped over time. Using the CoI framework to guide the design of online and blended courses and programs (not to mention face-to-face learning experiences) may well be the lasting pragmatic legacy of this research.

Conclusion

The dimensions of teaching presence provide a template that can be of considerable value to designing, facilitating and directing a collaborative learning experience. Notwithstanding the essential role of the educator, it needs to be emphasized that in the CoI framework, all participants have the opportunity to contribute to teaching presence. Teaching presence "is a distributed responsibility in that all participants are required to actively engage in shaping the thinking and learning experience congruent with their ability" (Garrison, 2016, p. 77). Moreover, if the ultimate goal is to continue to learn, students must be supported to develop metacognitive awareness and regulative abilities as they take responsibility to manage and monitor their learning. As participants develop cognitively and socially, the more distributed teaching presence becomes.

To this point, we have provided the framework and elements of a deep and meaningful learning experience. We have not attempted to identify principles or suggest specific guidelines with regard to the practice of e-learning. This means recognizing the possibilities for creating communities of inquiry where thinking and learning collaboratively can be sustained over time. The full potential of an e-learning community of inquiry requires a full understanding of new and emerging information and communication technologies. It is these technologies that have reshaped society and are transforming educational approaches to learning.

Part II

Applying the CoI Framework

The goal of this section is to explore issues of practice. Here the principles associated with the application of e-learning are described. These principles provide the foundation of informed and adaptable practice that is applicable to a broad range of purposes and contexts. The section begins with a discussion of e-learning communication technologies and its practical implications in rethinking and redesigning higher educational learning experiences. Evidence and insights are explored throughout.

Chapter 7

Learning Technologies

Learning technologies continue to play an important enabling role in the transformation of teaching and learning in higher education. These technologies have become a catalyst to rethink the teaching and learning transaction. Educators are realizing that new and emerging communications technologies are radically changing the educational landscape in terms of connectivity and collaboration. They provide the means to create cohesive communities of learners independent of time and space. These technological innovations are not exotic or expensive; they are technologies that have permeated most segments of our increasingly connected society. The opportunity to connect instructors and students in a sustained manner has changed the expectations and approaches to teaching and learning.

Information and communication technologies have created the opportunities for shared cognition previously not possible. These technologies have made thinking and learning more accessible and effective through an alteration of the time and space dimensions. The result is that we are able to access information and connect with others at any time and in any location. The distributive and collaborative possibilities are transforming how we think about and approach learning. The theory and practice explored here is circumscribed by the ability of learning technologies to create and sustain discourse and precipitate reflection in purposeful communities of learners. In particular, it has been a catalyst in exploring and adopting collaborative approaches to thinking and learning—approaches that speak to the essence of critical and creative thinking and learning.

Historical Perspective

The word technology drives from the Greek *tekhnologiā*, meaning a systematic treatment of an art or craft (American Heritage Dictionary, 2000). This original emphasis on systematic treatment and an implied adherence to the tenants of science has inspired the field of instructional technology to embrace a scientific view of its activities. It can be confusing, however, when we label all systematic designs, thoughts, expressions and plans as technologies. The more common understanding of technology is that it is a tool as opposed to a systematic process or technique. Therefore, for our purposes, we distinguish the technology as a tool from scientific or academic procedures.

Notwithstanding this distinction, it is limiting to analyze a technological tool outside of the context in which that tool is applied. In an educational context, instructional technology implies a discussion of the way in which a tool is used as well as the characteristics, limitations and applications of that tool. That is, instructional technology must be seen from the perspective of its intended purpose as a means to access information and support discourse within a community of learners. This focus on the technological tools, therefore, cannot be separated from the mindful application of these tools. Therefore, e-learning represents the practical application of information and communication technologies to create more effective approaches to learning generally and the educational transaction specifically.

Learning technology emerged as a field of study in the 1960s. With this came a series of technological innovations but with little influence on instructional practice. Looking back over the last half century, technological development focused on audio-visual presentation devices. With the development of personal computing in the 1970s, computer assisted learning emerged but was seen to be largely prescriptive drill and practice activities. However, the 1990s represented a sea change with the emergence of the Internet and the widespread adoption of communication technologies. There was a transformation of how we viewed and used technology in society generally. Educators slowly began to appreciate that information and communication technologies were transforming society and this would soon include educational institutions. Beyond access to information, communication technologies demonstrated capabilities that could enhance the quality of the learning experience from the perspective of sustained communication and collaboration. Developments in information and communication technologies set the stage for the rapid development of e-learning at the turn of the 21st century. The digital age was upon us.

Personal computing combined with advances in mediated communication created a great interest in computer conferencing and its possible application for educational purposes. Computer conferencing represents the origin of online learning. Early in the development of computer conferencing, it became apparent that it did not replicate a face-to-face classroom experience. It was quickly realized that because of the asynchronous and text-based nature of this communication, computer conferencing for educational purposes represented a qualitatively different approach to learning (Kaye, 1987; Harasim, 1987). An important historical and theoretical point is that e-learning did not evolve from traditional distance education (Cleveland-Innes & Garrison, 2010). Historically, distance education was purposed to bridge geographical distances and was embedded in the industrial model with institutions focusing on cost-effective access. The ability of online learning to support a collaborative learning experience very much challenged the dominant world-view of distance education as being a largely independent, self-instructional approach to learning. This perspective is supported by Guri-Rosenblit (2009) who states that "most e-learning in American higher education is not used for distance teaching purposes" (p. 94). Therefore, while there is overlap with distance education, e-learning must be considered a distinct branch of the educational evolutionary tree.

E-learning caused significant disruption in the field of distance education. Traditionally, the values and practice of distance education were to cope with the challenge of access to education. Independent study made possible through self-directed learning packages was the standard approach to reach out to learners at a distance. This reality was solidified through Peters' (2007) industrial model of distance education characterized by division of labor, mass production and economies of scale. The great success of this approach was the efficiencies gained through adopting industrialized economies of scale. The downside was the isolated educational experience that required students "to become autonomous and self-regulated with regard to goals, methods, and media" (Peters, 2007, p. 61). There was little opportunity for meaningful feedback which contributed to an extremely high dropout rate (Garrison, 1987).

This inherent limitation on feedback and meaningful discourse was also embedded in traditional face-to-face or campus-based education dominated by a process of talking to students who passively tried to record the thoughts of the teacher. The goal in higher education too often was to transfer information verbally in contrast to the written word employed by distance education. However, in both approaches, learners were left to make sense of the material primarily on their own. This is why research consistently reported "no significant difference" when distance education methods were compared to campus-based learning experiences. The explanation is that in both situations they were assessing information recall. This may be acceptable in courses that only require information recall (Cho & Tobias, 2016). However, in higher level courses whose goals are to develop critical thinking and inquiry abilities, technologies that support discourse become extremely relevant and advantageous. What is required is a new conceptualization and approach to thinking and learning; a more collaborative approach to thinking and learning that would take advantage of new and emerging communication technologies.

E-learning has significantly altered the practices of both distance and campus-based educational institutions. This change in practice with regard to collaborative approaches to learning began to emerge in significant ways at the turn of this century. The principles and practices of distance education as a self-paced and independent form of learning began to be seriously questioned (Garrison, 2000). The flexible and collaborative potential of e-learning is in stark contrast to the traditional practices of distance education. Similarly, passive lecture approaches were seriously being questioned. Attention began to be directed to blending online and face-to-face approaches. Moreover, with the convergence of face-to-face and online learning, we have seen the further marginalization of passive, independent approaches to learning. E-learning has become a tool of transformation and as higher education addressed passive information delivery methods, a new pedagogy began to emerge—a pedagogy that is based on a changing sense of thinking and learning collaboratively guided by inquiry-based approaches. As a result, e-learning has blurred the distinction between online and campus-based learning and collaborative approaches to thinking and learning are moving into the mainstream of higher education.

E-Learning Approaches

The task of scholars is to create conceptual models that allow us to better understand the world we inhabit and create. A core concept in the quest for educational models is the realization that the essence of education is communication. In this regard, technology should be used to create environments that support academic communication. The assumption here is that thinking and learning is greatly influenced by "characteristics of the medium, designs that take advantage of these characteristics, and the characteristics of learners and tasks" (Kozma, 1991, p. 180). In e-learning environments, learning management technologies are important in creating and sustaining successful communities of inquiry (Rubin, Fernandes & Avgerinou, 2013); however, it has been stated that there is gap between current learning management systems and the changing needs of higher education. The argument is that new approaches need new learning management systems that meet the "next generation digital learning environment" (Brown, Dehoney & Millichap, 2015, p. 2). A major criterion is that "support for collaboration must be a lead design goal" (Brown et al., 2015, p. 7) for the next generation digital learning environment.

However, the interactive potential of the technology is not enough. While technologies can have an enormous influence on the type of communication, the potential will be determined by the vision and design of the thinking and learning experience. A recent meta-analytic study of technology-supported student interaction revealed "that collaborative qualities purposefully added to technology-supported student-student interaction substantially add to learning" (Borokhovski, Bernard, Tamim, Schmid & Sokolovskaya, 2016, p.15–28). Therefore, it is important to move beyond simple interaction and technology that may support such interaction. Teaching presence in the form of collaborative design is required. In this regard, Borokhovski et al. conclude that special attention needs to be paid to "designing tasks and activities that would elevate interaction to the stature of collaboration" (p. 23).

We must be much more specific about the purpose and nature of the transaction that is most appropriate for the desired learning experience. This perspective is central to understanding the technological contributions to e-learning. Meaningful collaboration online is more than social interaction. In addition, accessing information online does not constitute collaboration. Collaboration is dependent upon a sense of purpose and commitment to explore and question. To this end:

> Collaboration implies more than just passing data back and forth in an attempt to develop what is often a non-descript deliverable that can be as forgettable as the interactions themselves. Genuine collaboration is achieved through ongoing meaningful exchanges between people who share a passion and respect for one another. Trading ideas and taking risks on behalf of others and the organization is key. Ultimately, new innovations and critical problem solving are realized through relationships.
> (Sobel-Lojeski, 2015, 4th paragraph)

While the previous quote was written from a business perspective, it really speaks to purposeful inquiry and meaningful discourse central to a worthwhile educational experience. The message here is that we must avoid the "connectivity paradox" where people are increasingly connected but feel more isolated (Sobel-Lojeski, 2015). Connectivity is not enough. The challenge is to use technology to create shared environments where participants can engage in purposeful inquiry.

By necessity, the technology of distance education in the past focused on access and economies of scale that had the unfortunate effect of shifting attention from two-way communication and critical discourse that is considered to be the essence of an educational experience. Somewhat ironically, the focus on technology-based e-learning has moved us back to considering the possibilities of sustaining meaningful connections. However, this is understandable since the antecedents of e-learning are associated with computer conferencing and before that, it had its roots in computer assisted learning, educational psychology and instructional technologies. In addition, e-learning has as its theoretical foundation collaborative constructivist approaches to learning. E-learning has carried forward the educational imperative to engage students in collaborative forms of inquiry.

Therefore, e-learning is less about issues of technology and bridging distances as it is about creating communities of learners engaged in collaborative inquiry (Garrison, 2009a). In much of higher education, this represents a significant shift in core assumptions, goals and practices. The result has been to demonstrate that with advances in e-learning technologies, interaction and independence were not mutually exclusive. With the advent of the Internet and a wide range of ancillary communication technologies, distance education was no longer a zero sum game with regard to interaction and independence. Educators could design collaborative learning experiences while maintaining independence. Despite the great fanfare and enthusiasm for various technological innovations over the years, instructional technologies are only beginning to have a significant practical impact on mainstream education as a result of the emergence of online and blended design approaches to learning.

To reiterate, e-learning is more than just a form of distance education. The acceptance of e-learning has been associated with its ability to create communities of inquiry either at a distance or in a blended manner where learners can sustain purposeful and meaningful discourse. In this way, online and blended learning has transcended the notion that it was just an efficient means to deliver course materials or a lecture. E-learning has shifted the thinking of distance and campus-based educators in significant ways. A few of the key information and communication technologies that have been the catalyst for this rethinking are described next.

Web 2.0

The first decade of this century saw the emergence of what has been termed Web 2.0 technologies that gave greater flexibility to the user to communicate and control information. This refers to the use of World Wide Web technology that can make accessible information and enhance collaboration. Web 2.0 represented a shift from accessing information (read-only Web 1.0) to a means of accessing others and participating in a collaborative form of thinking and learning. This included a range of tools that included discussion boards, blogs, wikis, social networking and mobile learning. While Web 2.0 has become well established, it has not diminished in importance. New Web-based applications and information sites have exploded. The challenge is to understand its potential as an educational platform. That is, how do we capitalize on its technological possibilities for thinking and learning collaboratively—where individuals can contribute to a larger purpose and source of new insights?

At the same time, the administrative backbone of e-learning has been the course management system (CMS) that provides the platform to support e-learning. More specifically, the CMS provides a means to organize and deliver content as well as support assignments, discussion boards and assessment. Course management software is the backbone of online learning and is becoming an important tool for campus-based classrooms. Some of the indispensable features are control of class registrations, management of documents, communication among students, and a means for assessment. Not surprisingly, course management systems are the most used learning technology in higher education, but there remains some resistance among faculty as it has been reported that just over half of students have used it in most of their courses (Dahlstrom & Bichsel, 2014, p. 10).

Notwithstanding the enormous potential of Web 2.0 technologies for collaboration, we need to take a close look at these tools as they apply to approaches to thinking and learning. It is essential to keep in mind that the key to adopting technologies for e-learning is to recognize their potential to support collaborative constructivist approaches to teaching and learning. To assess these technologies for educational purposes, it is extremely helpful to have a coherent framework to make sense of and assess their impact socially, cognitively and pedagogically. For these reasons, there is much work to be done about how to effectively use these tools for a worthwhile educational experience.

Social Media

We use the term social media to apply to specific applications that support social networking and relationship building (e.g. Facebook) through the creation of personal profiles, the ability to add and interact with friends, and share information. Social media are a means to share activities, photos and ideas with others. Another application is a form of blogging that allows subscribers to send short messages on a particular topic (e.g. Twitter, Instagram, Snapchat). The focus here is more on sharing news and images than on social networking. The risk is superficiality and less sustained thinking. Regardless, these applications have gained worldwide popularity. The challenge for educators is to understand the possible value that social media might add to an educational experience.

Based on the widespread popularity of social media, social networking has entered the mythical phase. This is the phase where the power and impact of the technology are hyped to a point that there will be inevitable disenchantment and problems with privacy. With regard to social media, however, this necessitates a critical examination of their place in the world of higher education. As such, we need to take a serious look at social media and understand how these applications may well benefit an educational experience. On the surface, examples of social networking such as Twitter or Instagram with their requirement for short messages certainly suggest a high degree of spontaneity and superficiality. On the other hand, education is the antithesis of superficiality and it begs the question whether higher education risks a surface approach to learning with the uncritical adoption of social media and networking?

A recent study of social media and reflective thought reinforces our concern about the superficiality of frequent exchanges of short messages. It was concluded that "participants who frequently texted or used social media were less likely to engage in reflective thought" (Annisette & Lafreniere, in press). The implication of these findings is disturbing considering the prevalence of social media and the obsessive use among young people most highly engaged in formal education. Annisette and Lafreniere (in press) point out that this age group "is often in the midst of their academic careers with perhaps the greatest reliance on reflective thought is a cause for concern" (4.2 Implications). This is magnified with the realization that "reflective thinking is related to academic performance" (Phan, 2009).

The reality is that social media have not translated well to supporting effective collaborative learning experiences. Lim and Richardson (2016) reported in a study of online learners that no significant relationship was found between students' perceived social presence and the intensity of social networking. It would seem that there is not an easy transfer of social networking to formal educational settings. Social learning is part of a community of inquiry but it is not synonymous with collaborative constructivist approaches to deep and meaningful learning processes and outcomes. While students may be open to the use of social media in the classroom, there is a "significant difference between the perceived role of this tool [Facebook] as social, rather than educational" (Roblyer, McDaniel, Webb, Herman & Witty, 2010, p. 138). As such, it is unclear at this point whether social media have a significant role to play in mainstream education. An educational experience is about the context and process of worthwhile learning. The reality is that there is little evidence as to the benefit and learning effectiveness of social networking. As Sanger (2010) states, "There is no reason to think that repurposing social media for education will magically make students more inspired and engaged" (p. 18).

Sanger goes on to say that what engages people about social media is the passion for their personal interests and to stay in touch with friends. And to the heart of the matter, Sanger (2010) asks, "is fostering a deeply networked online social life among the proper tasks of education" (p. 22)? This should cause serious educators and researchers to take pause about the role of social media in higher education. At what point does condensing a message result in dumbing down discourse? In support of common logic, it has been reported that participants are reluctant to speak out on social media (Hampton, Rainie, Lu, Dwyer, Shin & Purcell, 2014). Social connections outside a purposeful learning community seriously restrict expressing disagreement. The reality is that most of us seek the approval of others; therefore, we are exposed to like-minded people and the reinforcement of existing biases and perceptions. There is an inherent avoidance of contrary perspectives which reduces the incentive to challenge ideas and think creatively. Dron and Anderson (in press) make this point when they state that large-scale social media "are not designed with learning in mind and tend to use and magnify implicit or explicit preferences/actions rather than target learning needs" (section "The Stupidity of Mobs", 5th paragraph).

Social media may well be the best example of connectivity paradox in that being connected does not necessarily reduce isolation. The lack of a shared purpose and collaborative environment does not encourage constructive questioning and meaningful exploration. The risk is that social media only attracts like-minded individuals and encourages confirmation bias. There is an absence of a sense of a learning community based on shared purpose, trust and responsibility. Participants connect on a superficial level but are isolated on a deeper more meaningful level. Social media without cognitive leadership do not create the focus, commitment and trust to critically explore, challenge ideas, and seek innovative perspectives and solutions.

Notwithstanding the pervasive presence and experience with social media, it remains unclear how the popularity of social media will impact educational environments. However, at a purely social level, there may well be value for social media in creating and sustaining learning communities. For example, there is evidence that students who are satisfied with the campus climate also persist (Schreiner, 2009). The argument is that if students feel connected and part of the larger community, they will be happier and persist. Not only might social networking contribute to social presence in the classroom, but it could become an important ingredient in campus life for those commuter institutions where students spend so little time on campus. If social media help students persist and be successful, then this technology could find a useful role in higher education.

Mobile Learning

Social media are very much linked to mobile technologies. These include a wide range of devices from laptops to cell phones. They go hand in hand with social networking and the ability to send email, access the Web, and record audio and video from any location. While the most common use of mobile devices is to support social networking, they also can be used for a range of educational purposes. While students are increasingly reliant on mobile communication devices, it is not entirely clear what advantages it may offer e-learning. In this regard, Brown and Mbati (2015) address the misconceptions of mobile learning and begin with the recognition that it is not simply learning while in motion or the use of mobile technologies. Mobile learning represents a range of potentialities that can offer "seamless access to learning support" (Brown & Mbati, 2015, p. 116).

The need for a cautious approach to technologies such as mobile communication devices is expressed well in an ELI (2010) resource. It is stated that "applications used in mobile learning generally focus on brief interactions … [and] enable the quick review of information rather than prolonged deep learning" (2nd paragraph). While there are legitimate uses of mobile devices, the reality is that most of these situations do not lend themselves to sustained educational discourse and reflection. Participating in a reflective discussion using a cell phone in a public setting may not be a strong argument for mobile learning. In this regard, Brown and Diaz (2010) make the point that smart phone use by undergraduates is for short term applications (it is hard to imagine typing a lengthy message or document using the keyboard of a smart phone). At this point, the best argument for mobile devices would appear to be rapid access to, or recording of, information in a field situation.

An interesting study compared the perceived usefulness of a variety of mobile devices in accessing course materials and activities (Koole, McQuilkin & Ally, 2010). Notwithstanding the arguments for more freedom and increased connectedness, the study concluded that "respondents may not consider mobile access as important as basic desktop computer access to their LMS [Learning Management System]" (Koole et al., 2010, p. 73). This was supported by a more recent study of mobile technology where they found that tablets were found to influence learning but only "very minor ones were found to support leaning on a smart phone" (Reychav, Dunaway & Kobayashi, 2015, p. 148). More telling in the Koole et al. study, students felt that mobile access did not increase their sense of connectedness and rated studying through a mobile system extremely low. In assessing the reality of mobile devices, the question is what value does it add to current desktop LMS access? Speculation here is that mobile devices may add significant value in specific contexts where immediate access to information and guidance in real world environments such as the health professions or those who study in the field.

The question is what effective role is there for mobile technologies in an educational environment as these technologies proliferate. The reality is that few studies have explored this question (Shin & Kang, 2015). To address this central issue, a recent study explored student intentions to adopt mobile learning, student satisfaction and student achievement. Notwithstanding the perceived indispensability of mobile technologies as a social tool, the acceptance of mobile learning systems compared to pre-existing e-learning systems appears to be dependent upon "support for optimized functions, information, and follow-up services" (Shin & Kang, 2015, p. 123). Shin and Kang (2015) found that acceptance of mobile learning management systems influence learner satisfaction and subsequently learner achievement. While mobile technology would appear to have the potential to contribute to learner satisfaction and achievement, this is dependent upon ensuring "that students are afforded a comfortable mobile learning environment while continuously receiving information of relative advantage to mobile learning" (Shin & Kang, 2015, p. 124). As encouraging as these results appear, the generalizability of these findings are limited considering sampling and methodological factors. As a result, we are still left questioning the productive role of mobile technologies in educational contexts.

Some have argued that portable communication devices could provide an opportunity for communication within the classroom. Here mobile devices can be used for a number of useful purposes but this requires a shift in how teaching and learning is designed. Mobile devices have been shown to be problematic during a lecture as students' are often distracted with social networking. While the natural reaction is to ban mobile devices, this is not the long-term solution. This situation reinforces the position that higher education must significantly rethink the design of the face-to-face classroom. For these devices to add value and be used to enhance the quality of learning, the classroom must become a more engaging learning experience. Consideration needs to be given to distinguish between those educational activities that are best done in face-to-face or online environments.

The use of mobile technologies for educational purposes raises questions about potential limitations. It is crucial that we understand the benefits of mobile devices for specific educational purposes. Conversely, care must be taken not to replicate technological mistakes of the past and design learning environments simply to incorporate mobile devices. The risk here would be that the technology would be driving the educational transaction which has never proven to be sustainable. The ultimate advantage of online learning is that it connects individuals over time and space. The question is the educational purpose and quality of this experience when one is limited to mobile devices? The point is that mobile communication may be great for personal communication, but it may not be best for serious academic discourse. This is also reflected in student and faculty concerns. As alluded to previously, "students are not necessarily ready to fully move into the mobile space for their coursework" (Brown & Diaz, 2010, p. 5) and faculty are not keen on learning to use yet another technology and having to adapt their curriculum accordingly. In a recent study, nearly two-thirds of faculty indicated they were concerned mobile learning is more of a distraction than a learning enhancement (Brooks, Dahlstrom, Grajek & Reeves, 2015). If we expect faculty to adopt mobile technologies, the benefit must be transparent.

While mobile learning may be a subset of e-learning, it is not equivalent to or a replacement for a range of technologies and learning support represented by e-learning. The fundamental question is whether mobile learning is appropriate for complex tasks that require concentrated attention and extended discourse. As with social networking, the question is the educational value-add for the use of mobile communication. While there may be educational value in connecting individuals socially, the question is how can mobile communication technology be usefully adapted for purposeful academic communication? While understanding the possibilities and limitations of mobile learning to meaningfully support an educational experience, e-learning is in its early stages, the Community of Inquiry (CoI) framework provides a comprehensive perspective to explore its use.

MOOCs

Another educational approach reliant upon learning technologies that has drawn considerable attention in recent years is Massive Open Online Courses (MOOCs). MOOCs are essentially online courses that provide opportunities for participants to access information and connect with others. These large enrollment courses are "facilitated" by an instructor and participants had the option to "engage" with other participants. The reality is that optional participation in discussion forums does not encourage or explicitly support meaningful discourse. In this regard, serious questions are raised with regard to the quality of the learning experience (Toven-Lindsey, Rhoads & Lozano, 2015).

The question, therefore, is why have MOOCs drawn so much interest. The primary reason for the interest in MOOCs is clearly access cost. The contention has been that MOOCs will transform higher education. However, the Achilles heel is the nature of the learning experience. The reality is that MOOCs cannot be defended from a quality perspective. MOOCs do not offer qualitative improvements as evidenced by the high dropout rates. Massive online courses simply do not offer quality teaching presence engagement. MOOCs are essentially large-scale distance education that has been with us since the advent of the open universities that provided access with limited opportunities for meaningful discourse. Access and connection by itself does not create a cohesive learning community that engages students in critical discourse. Dron and Anderson (2014) have noted the difficulty to provide structured courses such as MOOCs "where it is all too easy to become lost in social space" (Dron & Anderson, 2014, p. 12). Recent results have shown that "Completion rates (defined as the percentage of enrolled students who completed the course) vary from 0.7% to 52.1%, with a median value of 12.6%" (Jordan, 2015, p. 341). Since participants in MOOCs have trouble connecting with and sustaining meaningful discourse, we speculate that this may be the primary contributing factor for low completion rates.

It has been observed that few MOOCs have been recommended for credit; many MOOCs are poorly designed; they have insufficient quality control; and are not well managed at the point of delivery (see Are Massive Open Online Courses (MOOCs) Enabling A New Pedagogy? 2015). On the upside, however, MOOCs have drawn attention to online learning and, in particular, to blended learning. Israel (2015) reviewed various approaches to blending MOOCs with conventional classroom courses and the preliminary finding was, "Students in blended MOOCs in traditional classrooms performed almost equal or slightly better than students in only face-to-face class environment" (p. 115). However, Israel (2015) also concluded that there were "lower levels of student satisfaction, and limited participation in discussion forums provided by MOOCs" (p. 115). The findings of Israel (2015) led to the conclusion that "MOOCs, in general, have the potential to offer excellent resource materials in the form of video lectures, quizzes, and assignments, though there are challenges in synchronizing them with in-class traditional courses and repurposing MOOCs with on-campus LMS and policies" (p. 115).

Notwithstanding that MOOCs have raised awareness to online learning, the reality is that "MOOCs will be seen as a limited-purpose tool that conveys limited benefits in a limited set of contexts" (Wasson, 2013, p. 194). The contexts where MOOCs have had an impact are addressing the demand for informal learning experiences. From a formal educational perspective, the most promising application of MOOCs may be to support face-to-face courses but this undermines the ethos and economic argument for MOOCs.

Learning and Technology

E-learning is an important element of a connected knowledge society. For this reason, we must understand this relationship between technology and learning, especially the nature of learning in a connected society. In this context, learning is intimately connected to the technology that connects society. It is imperative that those involved in the educational enterprise come to grips with the reality that technology is an increasingly important element of the educational experience and represents opportunities and constraints for interaction that can significantly influence the quality of this experience. With the emerging presence of e-learning with its associated communication technologies, it becomes crucial that we explore and consider how this is impacting learning. The medium of communication does send an implicit message and that message can enhance or diminish the intended educational message. Participants in an e-learning experience must perceive the benefit of the technology and technology must serve worthwhile purposes or genuine participation will be compromised. In this regard, it is important to demonstrate "the importance of technology in facilitating all three presences of the CoI framework" (Rubin et al., 2013, p. 54).

Researchers have questioned statements such as that of Clark (1983) who declared, "media are mere vehicles that deliver instruction, but do not influence student achievement any more than the truck that delivers our groceries causes changes in our nutrition" (p. 445). His argument was that it is the instructional design, mediated through learning activities that affect learning outcomes (Clark, 1983; 1994). While the paramount importance of instructional design cannot be denied, the issue is whether this generalization holds across various intended learning outcomes or, to express it another way, whether characteristics of the technology of communication (specifically e-learning) can, in fact, have a significant influence on higher-order learning (Kozma, 1994). The null hypothesis that the means of communication has no effect on facilitating critical thinking and discourse and the achievement of higher-order learning outcomes has become less acceptable.

The research into media use in educational contexts has consistently demonstrated no significant differences in learning outcomes when different delivery media were compared. However, it is important to note that much of this research did not control for the nature and quality of learning outcomes. In fact, most often the intended learning outcomes measured in these studies were the outcomes expected from low-level, information-assimilation educational experiences; that is, the memorization and re-statement of static information. But does the "no significant difference" generalization hold with higher-order learning outcomes?

At least one pioneer in the use of written communication for educational purposes suggests that the null hypothesis does not hold. Feenberg (1999) states that writing is "not a poor substitute for physical presence and speech, but another fundamental medium of expression with its own properties and powers" (p. 345). The differences in the nature of spoken and written communication are, in fact, a key to understanding the effective use of online and blended learning. This echoes comments made by media researchers such as Olson (1994) who asserts that the written language is not just a pale shadow of the spoken language but rather an independent entity with distinctive characteristics worthy of study in themselves. As Stein (1992) notes, a new, interdisciplinary "science of the text" is emerging. Add to this research that indicates the superiority of blended learning with its integration of verbal and text-based communication over both face-to-face and online learning alone (Means, Toyama, Murphy, Bakia & Jones, 2009). As important as instructional design is, the medium of communication can significantly affect specific learning activities.

The critical point is that contextual variables (including specific technologies) can influence the nature and quality of learning outcomes. Contextual contingencies and learning activities must be congruent with intended and desired outcomes. What is learned is inseparable from how it is learned (Marton, 1988). What is learned can also overcome contextual constraints through well-designed and facilitated learning experiences. This, of course, is a crucial realization when utilizing a technology that has unique communication characteristics. The method of transmission or communication is an important contextual influence that can be strengthened with good design or, on the other hand, limitations mitigated with appropriate teaching presence. Regardless, the characteristics of the technology can influence the educational transaction for better or worse and educators must be cognizant of the learning environment they are creating from both a pedagogic and technology perspective.

Conclusion

Notwithstanding that the Internet and communication technologies have been the catalysts for the proliferation of e-learning, ultimately e-learning is not about technology but about connectivity and community. The challenge to the educational community is to design collaborative constructivist learning experiences that can incorporate the advances in information and communication technologies. These technologies have the enormous capability to bring people together to share and create knowledge. Brown and Adler (2008) properly shift the focus of these learning technologies when they state, "communities are harbingers of the emergence of a new form of technology-enhanced learning—learning 2.0—which goes beyond providing free access to traditional course materials and educational tools and creates a participatory architecture for supporting communities of learners" (p. 28).

Notwithstanding the important role played by communications technology, sound pedagogical ideas must be merged with the ubiquitous and powerful capabilities of the new and emerging communication technologies. These tools must be used to approach educational ideals and meet the demands of a rapidly changing knowledge society. We must not be seduced by the trivial applications of technology masquerading as an educational experience. It is important that we not make the mistakes of the past by becoming overly enamored by the technology but instead ask what the technology can do to enhance a worthwhile educational experience. Higher education must critically evaluate what "role these innovations should play in effective teaching and learning" (Roblyer et al., 2010, p. 134). It must also not overestimate student use of technology. Perhaps, surprisingly, technology only "has a moderate influence on students' active involvement in classes" (Brooks et al., 2015, p. 4). In this regard a very large international study concluded:

> Although technology is omnipresent in the lives of students, leveraging technology as a tool to engage students in meaningful ways and to enhance learning is still something of a promise rather than a practice.
>
> (Brooks et al., 2015, p. 34)

Unfortunately, the finding of the previously noted study is consistent with other studies that have noted that technology is not consistently being employed to address and improve educational experiences. Educational institutions need to use technology to actively engage students in thinking and learning collaboratively. It is through collaborative inquiry that technology can best serve the educational experience. With regard to technology adoption, institutions have a responsibility to provide the leadership "to make significant and sustained progress and to facilitate buy-in" (Brooks et al., 2015, p. 34).

The lesson to be drawn here is that "institutions should not think in terms of a single technological paradigm shift, but rather adopting a culture of continual change" (Ice, 2010, p. 158). Technology is in a constant state of flux and the needs and challenges of higher education are also changing. The one thing that higher education has not been very good at is change. E-learning has been a catalyst for change as it has offered solutions to the challenges of educational effectiveness and efficiency. When technological innovation is understood within the paradigm of e-learning, the focus is directed to using advances in information and communications technology to improving the educational process, most notably through the creation of collaborative thinking and learning experiences. E-learning is a promising means to explore and understand how technology can transform the educational enterprise through the adoption of collaborative approaches to thinking and learning.

Chapter 8

Blended Learning

The focal point of the adoption of learning technologies in education has become the blending of online and face-to-face learning experiences. Nearly a decade ago, it was reported that approximately 80 percent of higher education institutions in the USA offered blended learning courses (Allen, Seaman & Garrett, 2007). More recently, a study of North American undergraduate students reported that nearly four out of five had taken a blended course (Dahlstrom, Walker & Dzuiban, 2013). This shift to blended learning has also been noted by a panel of experts who have stated that "blended learning is on the rise at universities and colleges" (Johnson, Adams Becker, Estrada & Freeman, 2015, p. 16) and has been termed the "new normal" (Porter, Graham, Bodily & Sandberg, 2016). What is evidentially clear is that blended learning is at the center of contemporary educational approaches to thinking and learning.

As blended learning becomes embedded in educational institutions concomitantly, we are witnessing a transformation focused on engaged learning experiences. Our increasingly connected world with its knowledge economy makes the provision of sustained collaborative thinking and learning not only a rational but essential response. Blended approaches to learning that maintain connectivity over time and distance have demonstrated the ability to create and sustain communities of learners focused on the advantages of thinking and learning collaboratively. That said, the theoretical concepts and principles outlined in previous chapters apply particularly well to providing blended learning experiences.

Blended Learning Described

The obvious distinguishing feature of blended learning is the integration of face-to-face and online activities. From this perspective, blended learning was defined as "the organic integration of thoughtfully selected and complementary face-to-face and online approaches and technologies" (Garrison & Vaughan, 2008, p. 148). However, it was noted that simply adding optional or supplemental online activities to essentially a face-to-face learning experience did not meet the threshold of a blended learning design. The underlining distinction was integration of face-to-face oral and online written and visual communication such that the individual strengths were fused in a way where the results were greater than the best of the single constituting elements. The defining characteristic of the early descriptions was largely the technological structure of the design.

Early exploration of blended learning saw discussions regarding the threshold of what constitutes a blended learning experience. From the beginning, some of us were not comfortable setting narrow and rigid boundaries. The exact percentage of time spent in face-to-face or online communication did not seem to be a distinguishing feature of what should constitute a proper blended learning experience. The main concern was that this would not encourage innovation associated with the integration of online and face-to-face learning experiences. This position was the right one as it became clear that the true defining characteristic of blended learning was the opportunity to meaningfully engage learners in ways simply not possible with either face-to-face or online. The central proposition of blended learning became a fundamental rethinking of educational approaches from the perspective of sustained student engagement.

Rethinking of educational approaches was essential to not find ourselves in a position of simply layering on more activities and responsibilities without a consideration of what is important and reasonable from a time perspective. The goal was to design collaborative learning experiences that would take advantage of the technological possibilities to achieve a more effective learning experience. In its simplest form, this meant replacing passive listening with engaged and reflective learning experiences. In this regard, blended learning is more than blending face-to-face and online learning experiences. The essence is the blending of individual and collaborative learning activities using synchronous and asynchronous verbal and written modes of communication that are congruent with the intended goals. At the macro level, this also includes a range of face-to-face and online courses that constitute a blended program of studies.

While this description of blended learning reflects considerable complexity and some imprecision, it also represents a powerful range of possibilities and opportunities to connect learners congruent with the needs of a connected knowledge society. The great advantage of blended learning is that it represents a convergence of approaches to address the specific needs of a range of learning environments. The possibilities of blending approaches to learning are only limited by educational imagination and academic needs.

Scenarios

Considering the potential breadth of blended learning designs, it is a challenge to provide representative examples. There are, however, several scenarios where blended learning designs have particular value and that reflect its particular strengths. In this regard, the most common challenge that a blended learning design is asked to address is the large enrollment course. Typically, this is a first-year undergraduate large enrollment class delivered by a lecture approach. It was recognized early that these classes could benefit substantially from a blended learning design by providing opportunities for interaction and collaboration. The goal is essentially to replace some or all of the lectures with activities and assignments. This could be accomplished by placing course content online through recorded lectures or readings, and students would then be expected to come to class better prepared to more deeply inquire into the subject matter. Limited face-to-face class time would be used for more productive team projects, labs or individual/small group interaction with the instructor. Sustainable online activities might include tutorials, discussion groups or assessment. If lectures were to be retained, they could be used to introduce core ideas with the opportunity for students to question and interact in small groups. In large classes, personal response systems can be used effectively to engage students by having them report back individually or from a group perspective. For some subjects, more radical examples could be adopted by dropping all formal classes and creating drop-in labs with personal assistance where students could work individually receiving immediate feedback and assessment. This investment in creating labs and software may be more cost-effective for math/science classes with hundreds of students each semester.

A blended learning approach could also be applied to medium-sized classes and be achieved with modest investment of resources. In addition to increased student engagement, the goal may be more effective and efficient use of the instructor's time. With some investment at the front end of the blended design, an important pay-off for the instructor is a much more engaging and enjoyable teaching experience. Similar to large enrollment classes, lectures can be recorded and made available online for students. Again class time could be used for discussion and group tasks. A good example of this approach is in writing courses that shift from passive lectures to devoting greater time to the writing process itself (focus on applying knowledge). Face-to-face class time may be reduced and replaced with online or drop-in labs. A corollary benefit is that this may prove to be beneficial from the perspective of the commuter student who would be afforded the convenience of reduced travel without compromising the quality of the educational experience.

Online Blended Learning

There is another form of blending that combines *asynchronous* (written) and *synchronous* (verbal) online learning. Because this does not include face-to-face interaction, it is not technically blended learning as we have described it. However, it is an important form of e-learning and a form of blending worthy of consideration. Blending asynchronous and synchronous communication in an online environment has a significant advantage. In particular, the immediacy of synchronous verbal communication can enhance the development of a sense of community. Synchronous verbal communication has a sense of immediacy that can be very effective in establishing social presence (trust, open communication and group cohesion) and perceived learning (Baker, 2004; Swan & Richardson, 2003). This may be especially effective at the beginning of a course to create identification with the course, instructor and fellow students. Verbal immediacy can also be a great benefit in an online environment when introducing a new topic by efficiently focusing activities and addressing concerns.

Two leaders in this blending of asynchronous and synchronous communication in an online educational environment are Michael Power and Norman Vaughan (2010). These researchers have begun investigating what they call blended online learning designs (BOLD). They argue that there are important limits to asynchronous online learning.

These quality concerns are associated with learner isolation that have been mitigated with online learning designs but have prevented a breakthrough in mainstream higher education (Power & Vaughan, 2010). What appears to be lacking is spontaneous dialogue and negotiation of meaning to counter the structure of the asynchronous online course package. Tentative early findings suggest that synchronous communication offers more of an opportunity for dialogue and perhaps lower attrition. This latter benefit is congruent with research noted previously associated with a sense of community (cohesion) increasing persistence. Regardless of the design, blended learning is made possible by online learning opportunities and the adoption of thinking and learning collaboratively.

Why Blended Learning?

Understanding why educators would want to include online learning experiences in a campus-based learning environment is best explored from the perspective of a community of inquiry. Halverson, Graham, Spring, Drysdale, and Jeffery (2012) have stated that the Community of Inquiry (CoI) framework is "one of the most utilized theories for blended learning at this time" (p. 24). The primary reason for this is the ability of a blended learning design to engage participants in critical reflection and discourse through inquiry by creating a flexible and sustainable community of learners. As we have noted, blended learning is about actively involving all participants in the educational experience. Its essence is moving away from using scarce face-to-face time for information transmission. To use blended learning to disseminate content is to ignore its inherent advantage to engage learners (face-to-face and online) and sustain these connections over time and space.

Blended learning designs extend time on task beyond the limited frame of the traditional face-to-face classroom. The range of design possibilities becomes apparent when we look at the combinations of face-to-face and online learning experiences and then imagine how they might be integrated for specific educational purposes.

Online learning provides a unique dimension to the face-to-face learning community that builds group cohesion. It encourages greater participation and, thereby, creates a greater sense of belonging to a purposeful group of learners. Asynchronous written communication is not only reflective but it is less intimidating and encourages intellectual risk-taking. This freedom of expression in turn enhances the face-to-face session as more students participate and increasingly feel more comfortable participating. In a counter-intuitive manner, online learning allows participants to reveal themselves in ways they may not be encouraged to do in a face-to-face environment. The reality is that learners are less intimidated by the immediate presence of others. There may also be increased opportunity for formal small group activities, while informal relationships have more time to build as communication is extended beyond the face-to-face classroom.

Notwithstanding the theoretical arguments for the power of blended learning and the significant shift in pedagogical thinking it constitutes, there is growing evidence of its effectiveness. A landmark meta-analytical study and review of e-learning by the U.S. Department of Education has provided powerful results as to its effectiveness (Means, Toyama, Murphy, Bakia & Jones, 2009). The study initially identified 176 experimental or quasi-experimental studies of online learning from 1996 through 2006 (most were from higher education). The main finding was that "Learning outcomes for students who engaged in online learning exceeded those of students receiving face-to-face instruction" (Means et al., 2009, p. xiv). The two significant influences on effectiveness were the use of blended approaches and time on task. There were 99 studies that contrasted online or blended learning with face-to-face. Here it was found that "Instruction combining online and face-to-face elements had a larger advantage relative to purely face-to-face instruction than did purely online instruction" (Means et al., 2009, p. xv).

In other studies, blended approaches have been shown to be effective in small liberal arts colleges that pride themselves on "intimate classroom experiences" (Kolowich, 2012). The expectation is that blended approaches will reinforce intimate classroom experiences. In fact, when blended learning was compared to historical results of the traditional courses, performance was superior. Other examples of blended learning found students "learn the material as well or better than in a normal lecture course—but in half the time" (Kolowich, 2012, 7th last paragraph). These findings strongly suggest a distinct advantage of blended learning over not only face-to-face but online learning as well.

Insight into the reasons for this blended learning advantage can be found in the significant influence associated with time on task. Both online and blended learning provide increased time on task. Moreover, it is argued here that time on task is not only greatly extended in a blended learning design, but the quality of that time is significantly greater when integrating the interactive strengths of verbal and written communication. Finally, the previously noted meta-analytical study concluded that "contrasting blends of online and face-to-face instruction with conventional face-to-face classes, blended instruction has been more effective, providing a rationale for the effort required to design and implement blended approaches" (Means et al., 2009, p. xvii). These findings are powerful statements about online learning in general and blended learning in particular. It must be concluded that online and blended learning (i.e. e-learning) is a viable option in higher education to deliver superior effectiveness and efficiency.

To add to the previous studies supporting blended learning, studies using the Community of Inquiry (CoI) theoretical framework have provided interesting insights into the benefits of blended learning. One study focused on the perceptions of cognitive presence and the actual learning outcomes in an online and blended environment (Akyol & Garrison, 2010a). While the actual grades were identical, it was found that "students in the blended course had higher perceptions of learning, satisfaction, cognitive presence, teaching presence and social presence" (Akyol & Garrison, 2010a). Clearly there were perceived advantages to the blended learning approach beyond grades. Considering there was no significant difference regarding grades, one area that may be worth looking at would be persistence or completion rates. In this regard, it has been found that blended learning completion rates have been reported to be higher than online and many face-to-face courses (Dziuban, Hartman, Moskal, Sorg & Truman, 2004).

Another study using the CoI theoretical framework focused on how blended learning supported the inquiry process. This was in partial response to earlier studies that appeared to show inquiry stalling at the exploration stage. In this study, Vaughan and Garrison (2005) found that the face-to-face environment was preferred for initiating discussions, but the online environment was useful for expanding and sustaining the discussion. The results of this study suggest that online learning required participants to engage in greater integrative thinking (Vaughan & Garrison, 2005). This study also suggested that the resolution phase of inquiry may well be best done in a face-to-face environment.

Along these same lines regarding the progression of inquiry, Akyol and Garrison (2011a) found increased frequency at the integration phase for blended learning compared to online learning. The explanation was an advantage of blended learning to use the face-to-face sessions to trigger the task and begin the exploration. While the nature of the task and teaching presence is still crucial for progression, it was concluded that blended learning may provide enhanced conditions for critical thinking. This is supported by other researchers in suggesting that the speed and energy of a face-to-face discussion at the exploration phase has been reported to benefit from a face-to-face environment (Meyer, 2003). Moreover, considering online discussions tend to be more reflective, focused and thoughtful, this may well favor designing greater online discourse at the integration phase.

However, as has been discussed in previous chapters, all elements of the community of inquiry must be working in concert if inquiry is to be effective in reaching intended learning outcomes. A research priority is to simultaneously examine the three CoI presences. In this regard, one study focused on social, cognitive and teaching presence while exploring the differences between online and blended learning designs (Akyol, Garrison & Ozden, 2009). Differences in the social and cognitive presence dimensions were found between the online and blended design. In terms of social presence, group cohesion messages significantly favored the blended design. This is not surprising from a theoretical perspective as the blended students could make interpersonal and affective connections much more quickly. Online students apparently had to make more of an effort to create an affective presence. In this regard, class size was more of a problem for the online students in developing social presence. In short, developing social presence online took time.

With regard to teaching presence, Akyol, Garrison and Ozden (2009) reported that, because blended learning students could meet with the instructor face-to-face, blended students required less teaching presence online and assumed more responsibility for facilitating and directing the discussions. Face-to-face access to the instructor also explained why students in the blended course had greater cohesion which supports increased collaboration and the ability of the students to assume teaching presence responsibilities. Therefore, the fact that students in a blended learning environment demonstrated increased teaching presence is a considerable advantage in achieving intended goals and enhancing metacognitive awareness and ability (learning to learn).

On another front, it has been recognized that there is a significant role adjustment to online learning (Cleveland-Innes, Garrison & Kinsell, 2007). The ease of adjustment to online learning afforded by blended learning needs to be recognized as higher education transitions to more technologically mediated forms of communication. The first challenge is to ensure that the technology is appropriate for the educational task. The core challenge, however, is creating and sustaining a community of inquiry where the social, cognitive and teaching presences are in dynamic balance. In this regard, Rovai and Jordan (2004) provided evidence that "blended courses produce a stronger sense of community among students than either traditional or fully online courses" (abstract, lines 5–6). This was also supported by Tayebinik and Puteh (2012). It would seem that an effective community of inquiry may well be best realized in a blended environment.

While we focused on the effectiveness of blended learning, there are considerable administrative efficiencies to be gained with its adoption. The efficiency of blended learning approaches is best evidenced in the work by the National Center for Academic Transformation (NCAT). The NCAT database of hundreds of course redesigns demonstrates conclusively that effectiveness and efficiencies are not mutually exclusive. The results of the initial course redesign projects, confirmed by numerous subsequent projects, found that institutions significantly reduced costs while increasing completion rates, student satisfaction, and improving or maintaining learning outcomes (Twigg, 2003). The ability to both improve effectiveness and efficiency should be seen as some kind of miracle for resource challenged educational institutions. This may be why the vast majority of courses in higher education incorporate some form of blending online with face-to-face learning experiences. For very good reasons, blended learning approaches have become the norm in higher education.

Finally, considering the increasing adoption of online learning in all educational spheres, some thought needs to be given to the continuing value of the term blended learning. It is argued here that this term served a useful purpose to identify the strengths and weaknesses of face-to-face and online learning. More significantly, however, it drew attention to sustained collaborative approaches to learning and the blending of personal reflection and collaborative thinking and learning. Blended learning has become more identified with innovative engaging approaches to learning than it is simply with the blending of technologies. In the future the blending analogy may prove to be less than useful as the focus shifts to sustained engagement of learners. As the adoption of blended learning designs continue to evolve and more and more courses meet the minimal requirement to be considered blended, the term may well become superfluous. It is suggested that this may not be far off as the effectiveness and efficiency of blended learning is being demonstrated and adopted.

Conclusion

Research has shown that blended learning has had a significant impact on the transformation of teaching and learning with its focus on sustained interaction and collaboration. Dzuiban, Hartman, and Mehaffy (2014) state "findings make a clear case that blended courses provide a superior environment for students to develop their skills and concept of understanding through multiple reinforcing study opportunities" (p. 326). Moreover, the authors state that the key is attending to student cohorts. That is, creating and sustaining learning communities through both face-to-face and online approaches focused on personal reflection and critical discourse. The distinguishing feature and strength of blended learning approaches is bringing learners together in purposeful communities of inquiry.

It should be emphasized that blended learning represents a significant conceptual and practical breakthrough in enhancing the quality of teaching and learning in higher education. It is inherently transformative and has quietly pervaded higher education. The "impact of blended learning is potentially monumental—permanently changing how students interact with higher education" (Laumakis, Graham & Dziuban, 2009, p. 86). In this regard, blended learning is a powerful strategic approach to teaching and learning. It is a thoughtful approach to the important challenge of engaging learners in purposeful discourse. The great advantage of blended learning is that while it is transformative, it builds upon traditional ideals of communities of learners and familiar face-to-face learning. Notwithstanding the congruence of blended learning with traditional values of higher education and its capabilities to create and sustain communities of inquiry, blended learning initiatives are not always well received. Faculty need to be reminded of the traditional values of higher education associated with critical discourse and be shown successful examples of blended learning designs that effectively and efficiently achieve these ideals. Blended learning may well be the only reasonable means in a context of mass higher education to create a community of inquiry that can support critical and creative thinking and learning.

While the impact of blended learning in education is clear, the pragmatic success does not diminish the need for more studies looking into the range of its applications and pedagogical complexities. To move this research forward effectively, it is essential "that clear theoretical frameworks be articulated that can provide coherency and depth to the research conversations" (Halverson et al., 2012, p. 397). In this regard, it has been noted that blended learning has been significantly impacted by the CoI framework (Dziuban et al., 2014). With the exception of the CoI framework, there is "a lack of attention to coherent theory building" (Burkhardt & Schoenfeld, 2003 cited in Halverson et al., 2012) that risks incoherence. While we must recognize the value of diversity in the field of blended learning research, there is a responsibility to provide coherence that is only possible through greater attention to theory building.

Notwithstanding the need for continued study of blended learning and the development of theoretical frameworks, there is a literature base in both face-to-face and online teaching and learning in higher education that can inform the study and practice of blended learning (Vaughan, Cleveland-Innes & Garrison, 2013). From a pragmatic perspective, there are generic principles of teaching and learning in higher education that have relevance to the design and delivery of blended learning (see next chapter). However, future research needs to place greater emphasis on issues of how to meaningfully engage learners effectively in face-to-face and online contexts as we move to sustained collaborative forms of learning. Institutionally, an immediate area of research is associated with student and faculty support, both in terms of pedagogy and mastering software.

Chapter 9

Guidelines for Practice

There is no shortage of craft "know how" books offering guidance on how to conduct online and blended learning experiences. However, effective teaching requires more than a repertoire of techniques or recipes. These compendia of techniques provide little in the way of a coherent perspective or understanding of the interplay between the collaborative (social) and constructivist (cognitive) dimensions of a teaching and learning transaction. Nor do they provide an appreciation of the elements and unique characteristics of the online or blended learning experience.

As compelling as the research evidence is in support of a community of inquiry approach to achieve deep and meaningful learning experiences, the reality is that no two educational environments are the same. There is no exact reproduction of a community of inquiry across contexts. That is, it is not possible to reproduce the same context in which one particular approach proved successful. The goal is integrity of implementation that "allows for programmatic expression in a manner that remains true to essential empirically-warranted ideas while being responsive to varied conditions and contexts" (LeMahieu, 2011). This requires that we think through and understand the theoretical underpinnings of any new approach. This can be greatly assisted by identifying the principles of the approach and adapting them to the particular needs and demands of the environment. Moreover, this is made considerably more effective through collaborative design, testing and redesign strategies. There is no one-to-one translation with regard to educational innovation.

In the first part of this book, the Community of Inquiry (CoI) theoretical framework described the foundational concepts, principles and organization of an e-learning experience. This chapter provides a pragmatic discussion of an online and blended learning experience. The following discussion is embedded in the CoI framework that provides a coherent context to understand the purposes and functions of collaborative constructivist methods and techniques. The framework also reflects the dynamics of a community of inquiry. Therefore, flexibility in terms of goals and methods must also be part of the transaction as the educational experience develops. Inherent is also the recognition of the need for connection between learning activities and learning outcomes. Learning activities must be congruent with intended outcomes but context dependent in terms of the learners, subject matter and technology. This complex and challenging task of designing, facilitating, and directing worthwhile learning activities is the focus here.

Learning Activities

Simple lists of learning activities or the latest popular technique provide little rationale for designing learning experiences and selecting appropriate activities that address the subject matter and larger intended academic goal. The following classification (see Table 9.1) identifies the four fundamental learning activities: listening, talking, reading and writing. This figure helps us to understand the purposes and strengths of each learning activity. These activities are organized and understood from a cognitive or content perspective as well as from an organizational and transactional perspective.

For example, content has traditionally been assimilated largely through listening and reading. The counterpart to listening, that is, talking or verbal discourse, is severely limited in most face-to-face environments due either to large classes or inappropriate educational approaches. The result is that less emphasis is placed on the collaborative construction of meaning and confirmation of understanding manifested largely through discourse. Similarly, from the individual perspective, we see a bias toward reading but fewer opportunities to rigorously bring ideas together coherently through reflection and written assignments. This is often due to the cost of marking written assignments in large enrollment classes. Educationally, we appear to be emphasizing information acquisition while limiting opportunities for critical discourse and higher-order knowledge construction and confirmation.

From an online learning perspective, the bias shifts as listening and talking are replaced by reading and writing. However, in online and blended learning environments, reading and writing are both an individual and collaborative means of communication. When properly designed from an interactive perspective, reading becomes both a means to acquire information as well as "listen" to the views of the instructor and students. Correspondingly, writing becomes the means to both construct meaning and communicate questions

Table 9.1 Learning Activities

	Exploratory *(information acquisition)*	*Confirmatory* *(knowledge construction)*
Group	Listening	Talking
Individual	Reading	Writing

Source: Adapted from Garrison & Archer, 2000

and ideas with members of the learning community. With online and blended learning, we are able to listen by reading and talk by writing.

What place is there then for the traditional group activities of listening and talking? Are these activities simply abandoned in fully online learning experiences? If so, what do we lose educationally? It has been our experience, supported in the literature, that students very much value real-time verbal interaction. The question is how important are listening and talking activities and what is their function in a community of inquiry. As we have seen, synchronous verbal communication can be blended with asynchronous communication in a fully online environment. In this way the blending of verbal and written communication can move academic discourse to another level in constructing meaning and confirming understanding.

In the previous chapter, it was noted that verbal dialogue may have an advantage in the early, exploratory phases of practical inquiry. However, there is perhaps a stronger connection between verbal discourse and social presence. Experience has shown that online learning students very much seek out other students, either face-to-face or by phone. Real-time, sustained verbal discourse is of considerable advantage in establishing social, cognitive and teaching presence, particularly in the early phase of an educational experience. The challenge is to recognize the various strengths of verbal and written communication and design learning experiences that can maximize the transaction.

Before turning specifically to online and blended learning guidelines, we must emphasize that teaching presence assumes an approach that is neither a "sage on the stage" nor a "guide on the side." We believe that one is as biased as the other in approaching the design and delivery of an educational experience. There is a place for either or both as the demands of a worthwhile educational experience develop. The central point here is that an educational experience is properly composed of teacher and student with a shared purpose but with shifting responsibilities. While considerable emphasis must be placed on teaching presence, this is not the sole responsibility of the educator. The ultimate responsibility of the educator is to distribute this responsibility and help learners increase their self- and co-regulation (shared metacognition). This important role and dynamic will become apparent as we explore the dimensions of teaching presence.

Teaching-Learning Guidelines

Coping with this complexity and the adoption of new technologies necessitates that teachers have a theoretical framework and set of guiding principles. The following principles reflect a transactional perspective and deep approach to learning consistent with a community of inquiry. In essence, these principles are able to guide the creation of a supportive and critical community of inquiry. We define an educational community of inquiry as a group of individuals who collaboratively engage in purposeful reflection and discourse in the construction of personal meaning and confirmation of mutual understanding. In this regard, the CoI theoretical framework represents the process of creating a deep and meaningful (collaborative constructivist) learning experience through the development of three interdependent elements—social, cognitive and teaching presence.

The principles are derived from the CoI framework and are organized around the dimensions of teaching presence (design, facilitation and direction); each of the teaching presence dimensions incorporate issues of social and cognitive presence.

The seven principles are:

1   Plan for the creation of open communication and trust
2   Plan for critical reflection and discourse
3   Establish community and cohesion
4   Establish inquiry dynamics (purposeful inquiry)
5   Sustain respect and responsibility
6   Sustain inquiry that moves to resolution
7   Ensure assessment is congruent with intended processes and outcomes

Within each of the dimensions of teaching presence, we discuss issues of social and cognitive presence that the teaching function addresses. Teaching presence encompasses more than the exchange of messages. In addition to the facilitation of critical discourse, activities may include readings, exercises, Web explorations, blogs or wikis and collaborative projects, to name a few. The first challenge is to consider which activities to include and how they will be integrated into a coherent and meaningful educational experience. Design is the first dimension of teaching presence that must concurrently consider social and cognitive presence issues.

Design and Organization

To begin, we must appreciate that the roles of the educator and student in online and blended learning transactions are both congruent with, and different from, their roles in a traditional face-to-face classroom experience. First, in any educational context there is an essential leadership role that the educator must assume, especially at the outset in terms of providing an initial design or plan. At the same time, in terms of asynchronous text-based communication and the accessibility to resources, online and blended learning represents a significant shift in how the teaching and learning transaction plays out. This is consistent with a collaborative constructivist inquiry approach where all participants must begin to assume teaching presence responsibilities. It is to these transactional issues and their practical implications that we turn our attention.

Adjustment to an e-learning context includes the need to plan for both social and cognitive presence responsibilities. Responsibilities of all participants will require adjustment. This is particularly true for first-time online students who have to adjust to written communication and participation in a virtual community of inquiry. While students will need to adapt to a more collaborative approach, educators will have a greater challenge in learning how to balance facilitation and direction to achieve a deep and meaningful level of interaction. Identifying with and engaging in an online community of learners is unlike most traditional educational classrooms. Design considerations need to recognize adjustment challenges and provide technology support.

The process of planning a quality online or blended learning experience is very likely to be more complex and time-consuming than planning a conventional classroom experience. Thinking through the structure, process and evaluation aspects of an online or blended learning course raises special challenges. The introduction and orientation will greatly influence sustained motivation and must, therefore, be carefully considered. These challenges also present opportunities to educationally enhance the learning experience through more transparent teaching presence and modeling. Teaching presence must be an integral dynamic of a community of inquiry and not be perceived primarily as an authority function. To ensure a true inquiry-based approach, teaching presence responsibilities must be shared by all participants to greater and lesser degrees as the course of study progresses. For this reason, much of the success of the learning experience depends on design and organization.

It is important to appreciate that in a collaborative constructivist approach design is not a rigid template that is imposed on the learning situation from the beginning. The design must be inherently flexible and adaptable to unpredictable and individual learning needs as they arise. Giving form to a course is not a one-time responsibility but will be devolved to greater and lesser degrees to the participants as learning progresses. Design and redesign continues throughout the educational experience as collaboration and shared control introduce a creative element of uncertainty. This constructivist freedom with an educational purpose takes advantage of the great strength of e-learning and outlines a major advantage over conventional lecture style face-to-face approaches or prescriptive, self-instructional course packages characteristic of traditional distance education. Curriculum must be relatively open and all are active participants. Moreover, students must have an appropriate degree of shared control and responsibility over the management and monitoring of their activities and learning. In this way, shared metacognitive awareness develops. Responsibility and control must naturally evolve and grow as the learner progresses socially and cognitively. This developmental theme is reflected in each of the subsequent sections on the design of social and cognitive presence. This helps us understand what kinds of activities and support are needed in progressive phases of learning.

Activities must be considered in depth both before and during the learning experience. During the design phase, instructors must do their best to provide reasonable structure (goals, expectations) and anticipate as best they can the evolving needs of the students. Planning and structuring a course can effectively be accomplished by following the phases of practical inquiry. That is, starting with defining the challenge. Next, consider bringing on board individuals or a team that can bring specific expertise, whether that is design or content experts. A collaborative approach during the exploration and integration phases can encourage creative ideas and an innovative design. Finally, the initial design implementation needs to be considered a prototype that will require an iterative process of testing and revision.

Particular macro components to consider are:

- establishing curriculum;
- identifying resources;
- defining clear expectations and goals (process and content);
- addressing technological concerns;
- structuring activities (collaborative and individual);
- setting time frames;
- devising assessment processes and instruments.

While specific design suggestions will follow, a comment about addressing technological concerns is appropriate here. It is easy to say that technology should be transparent (not consciously aware of the technology), but this is an ideal, predicated on training and support. The transparency issue is compounded by the constant introduction of new media and standards. It may be a special challenge to provide technology training and support for students at a distance. (It should be noted that technology and associated training is crucial but exogenous to the core of the CoI theoretical framework.) While educator in-service in the use of technology can often be done in face-to-face seminars and workshops, consideration must be given to continuing online support. It has been shown that faculty and students "are open to learning how to use technology that can connect and engage students" but need evidence of benefit and support in adopting technology (Brooks, Dahlstrom, Grajek & Reeves, 2015, p. 34). Moreover, technology training will invariably require more time than is initially estimated. For this reason, the greatest success may be achieved when training is offered over time.

Social Presence

In any educational setting, one of the first and most important challenges is to establish social presence. It is crucial that each student feels welcomed and is given the reassurance that they are part of a purposeful community of learners. This sense of belonging and security facilitates open communication and creates group cohesion—elements essential to a collaborative learning experience and establishing cognitive presence. From a social presence perspective, it is helpful to understand the dynamics of group development. Even though groups do vary considerably in their cohesiveness and evolution, some insight into group dynamics can be useful in anticipating social conflicts or reduced motivation. There are several group development theories that essentially confirm that groups evolve in a relatively systematic manner (Pratt, 1981). This fact has been confirmed by Akyol and Garrison (2008).

In the initial phase, students must feel they belong if they are to form a cohesive community of inquiry. In the middle, or productive phase, there will inevitably be conflicts and the need for resolution, although it is difficult to predict when, and to what degree, conflict will manifest itself. One should be aware of this difficulty because the process might not surface in an overt manner but may still have a detrimental effect on open communication and group cohesion. If students are to take responsibility for their learning, then instructors must expect challenges and conflict. The key is to address these conflicts constructively with respect and negotiation. As groups bond, endings become important. Preparation for transition and emotional closure are issues that should be addressed. Consideration of these dynamics provides the social presence essential to establish and build cognitive presence.

As noted, conflict may be inevitable if critical reflection and skepticism are to be encouraged. The goal is to create trust but not discourage respectful dissent or criticism. Here, teachers can model the appropriate behavior by opening themselves to challenges from students. Paralleling the characteristics of reflection and discourse inherent in inquiry, students must be separate but part of the community. That is, they must be allowed and encouraged to maintain cognitive independence to construct personal meaning while contributing to mutual understanding through discourse where perspectives and ideas are respectfully challenged.

Preparation for the first session is important in any educational experience but crucial in an online learning context. In establishing social presence, paradoxically, the vehicle should be educational concerns and issues. Certainly, efforts must be made to allow participants to introduce themselves, but the first session should not be just a social event. It must be remembered that the purpose of establishing social presence is to support and enhance a purposeful community of inquiry. Through the use of chat rooms, collaborative assignments, and discourse associated with subject-related critical inquiry, students will gain trust and develop relationships over time. Once established, social presence will recede to the background as academic challenges take greater precedence.

While student motivation may initially be high, sustaining this motivation throughout the course of studies will be a function of collaboration and cohesion. Consideration must be given to anticipating how to involve reluctant students as well as focus or limit contributions from over-enthusiastic participants. Not all students will feel comfortable in an online or blended learning environment and they will need to know the rules and understand academic etiquette. Here, clear expectations as to the length and frequency of contributions should be provided before the course begins and reinforced throughout the course. Although not all students need to participate at the same frequency as their peers, they should be instructed to show their presence on a regular basis. Accommodation must be made for individual differences and this is why assigning grades based upon participation needs to be made with care.

The great challenge for teachers in establishing social presence is setting the right tone at the right time. The right tone may range from nurturing and emotional support to questioning and providing analysis. The tone of the conversation should correspond with the issues and goals. At times, the educator may be a "guide on the side" (a facilitator), and at times, a "sage on the stage" (provide direct instruction)—or, at other times, something in-between in the role of an active participant. The specific educational tone will require a form of teaching presence congruent with the educational challenge at hand.

The first sub-element of teaching presence, design and organization, should build a social presence that establishes:

- a feeling of trust and being welcomed;
- a sense of belonging to a community of learners;
- a sense of control;
- a willingness to engage in discourse;
- a conversational tone;
- a questioning attitude.

Suggested activities to establish social presence to be considered at the design stage might include:

- introductory email or video from instructor, include short bio;
- student Web pages sharing a short bio and expectations;
- discuss and negotiate expectations in small groups;
- informal coffee shop chat board;
- netiquette and code of conduct.

Cognitive Presence

Ultimately, the purpose of any educational experience is learning but not just fortuitous or indiscriminate learning. The focus here is on purposeful learning that is more than an exchange of opinions. Higher education places value on reflective thinking, critical discourse and higher-order learning outcomes. The critical thinking process required to achieve these results necessitates complex and sustained communication between and among the teacher and learners. Understanding and acceptance of the dialogic writing process in an online learning environment are essential.

To provide insight specific to thinking and learning collaboratively, we have focused on a community of inquiry and the cognitive processes associated with the Practical Inquiry (PI) model. Cognitive presence is created directly through critical reflection and discourse and described by the PI model. The four phases of practical inquiry derived from Dewey (1933) are 1) a triggering event and sense of puzzlement or dissonance; 2) exploring an issue or problem through gathering and exchanging relevant information; 3) integrating or making sense of this information by connecting the ideas in a meaningful way; and 4) resolving the issue by applying and testing the ideas either directly or vicariously.

Progressing through these phases will not likely happen without some guidance and this must be carefully considered when designing and organizing an educational experience. The transformation from the triggering and exploring stages to the integration and resolution stages of inquiry will depend on the nature of the assignment. If the goal is to resolve a dilemma or solve a problem, then teaching presence is essential to ensure movement to the integration and resolution phase. The division of the plenary group into smaller groups for discussion can be very beneficial for establishing cognitive and social presence. While social presence may benefit from smaller groups, there is evidence to suggest that cognitive presence may benefit from increased activity in dyads (Puzzi, Ceregini, Ferlino & Persico, 2016). Another study has shown more thoughtful engagement and achievement scores through the use of broader and small project teams (Warner, 2016). From a social presence perspective, it has been shown that a higher level of social presence can be achieved through small group discussions (Akcaoglu & Lee, 2016).

One of the first important tasks associated with teaching presence is the responsibility to design a variety of appropriate learning activities appropriate for the intended learning outcome. In designing an effective educational experience, particular consideration should be given to the use and development of case-based studies. Case studies focus discussion using a real-world perspective that is relatable. Case-based discussion has "demonstrated both greater and deeper problem space coverage during facilitated discussions" (Ertmer & Koehler, 2015, p. 69). Teachers can utilize small and large group discussions, encourage learners to take responsibility for extracting meaning, and provide opportunities for learners to moderate discussions. Used in these ways, case-based studies can provide a constructive environment to explore an important issue, introduce an organizing concept (big idea), and to reach resolution.

There is a growing interest in using problem-based inquiry learning activities in online and blended learning. Problem-based inquiry learning focuses learning by confronting students with ill-structured problems that mirror, as closely as possible, authentic issues and concerns. The teacher's primary role is to construct authentic problems. These problems are based on the curriculum or domain of knowledge about which students are expected to gain knowledge and competency. The instructor then makes available an appropriate set of resources that students can use to find solutions to the problem. As noted previously, case studies are excellent examples of a problem based activity that reflects authentic issues. They encourage students to be actively involved in their learning as problem solvers as opposed to content receptors found in dissemination-based educational practices.

During the problem-based inquiry learning process, the teacher acts as a coach and a role model. Coaching functions include helping students to attack the problem at the correct level, assisting with structuring and documenting their tentative solutions, and helping students organize their learning activities. Of course, problem-based inquiry learning inevitably includes false starts and trips down paths that are unproductive; however, the educator should not short circuit this important exploratory component of the inquiry process. The educator thus acts as a co-investigator in the problem solution, fading into the background as students' ability to solve problems grows.

Problem-based inquiry learning in an online learning context is not significantly different than that which is orchestrated in a classroom setting. However, since most problem-based inquiry learning activities are structured to allow group investigation, collaborative dynamics such as group synchronization, document management, discussion, and task assignment must be supported. Providing opportunities for synchronous activity through real-time audio or text chat is helpful for students to efficiently plan and undertake group activities. In environments that are based solely on asynchronous interaction, it is often difficult for groups to quickly allocate tasks and plan their problem-solving activities. Time must be allotted accordingly and consideration must be given to synchronous communication on the front-end.

From a cognitive presence design perspective, two issues stand out—content and assessment. First, if higher-order learning outcomes are valued, then learners must not be overloaded with excess content. The great risk in too much content is that it sends the implicit message that the goal is to assimilate information. Students must have time to reflect, make sense of the content, and share understanding with participants in the learning community. Cognitive tasks will change, but the process of iterating between reflection and discourse is a necessity. With virtually unlimited access to information in an e-learning context, considerable thought needs to be given to organizing information so students do not get lost in the details.

Second, cognitive presence will be overwhelmingly influenced by assessment and grading. Simply put, assessment must be consistent with intended learning outcomes. If the educational goals are higher-order learning outcomes, then assignments must be congruent with and tests must assess this level of learning. It is not good enough to emphasize critical discourse when students will be tested and graded only through information recall. In this situation, the quality of discourse and participation will inevitably drop as students will devote their limited time to activities that are rewarded. This incongruence between activity and assessment creates frustration for all and limits deep and meaningful approaches to learning. We do not need the power of a collaborative, constructivist e-learning experience if all we intend to do is transmit information and assess recall.

Asynchronous communication provides for both reflection and discourse. The challenge for the teacher is to balance and integrate them. At the beginning of a learning experience, considerable structure and support is required to establish cognitive presence. Beyond clear content goals, it is extremely advantageous to provide a metacognitive map of the inquiry process (PI model) so students have an awareness of their responsibilities in constructing meaning and understanding the progression of their learning activities and tasks. One technique that should be considered is to have students label their discussion contributions according to the phase of inquiry. This will create both knowledge and management of the inquiry process. Students need to understand that greater cognitive presence (i.e. responsibility) will be expected as the course progresses.

Cognitive presence issues associated with design and organization include:

- expectations of assessment of cognitive development;
- organization and limitation of curriculum;
- selection of appropriate learning activities;
- provision of time for reflection;
- integration of small discussion groups and sessions;
- provision of opportunities to model and reflect upon the inquiry process;
- design of higher-order learning assessment rubrics.

Suggested activities to establish cognitive presence to be considered at the design stage might include:

- plan for question-driven and problem-based learning activities;
- use small breakout groups;
- allow time to engage and complete the assignment;
- have students share a powerful learning experience and discuss why it was eventful;
- have a WebQuest to collaboratively search, analyze and synthesize information from the Internet

Facilitating Discourse

The approach advocated here is not simply that of a "guide on the side." The educator plays a key role throughout the learning experience—even when discourse and activities are largely regulated by the students. The teacher is ever-present and essential in providing oversight to the managing and monitoring process. There is always a need for an educator to structure, shape and assess the learning experience if it is to be more than an informal or fortuitous experience. However, the goal of the educator is to engage learners in discourse and caution must be exercised not to be too present as it may limit participation and gradually assuming teaching presence (Zhao & Sullivan, 2016).

Discourse goes to the core of the e-learning experience. Interaction and discourse is the strength of online and blended learning and is the essence of a community of inquiry experience. Facilitation is a key responsibility in monitoring and managing educationally worthwhile discourse. Facilitating discourse for the purpose of constructing meaning and confirming understanding requires a delicate balance between too little and too much intervention. Facilitating discourse first requires a climate that will precipitate participation and reflective discussion.

Social Presence

Education by definition is socially situated and the need for social presence is derivative of this reality. Moreover, social presence is essential to creating a learning community that is more than transmitting and assimilating content. It should be a process of inquiry associated with reflecting on, questioning, analyzing and testing ideas. These basic activities do not thrive in a group without personal affiliation and where expression is open and risk-free. A sense of isolation or of not being connected will not encourage or support critical and creative thinking, nor will it engender motivation resulting from a shared experience that acknowledges contribution and accomplishment. Without these affective and interpersonal elements, engaging students and realizing cognitive attitudes and skills to sustain learning are less than certain. The intersection of social and teaching presence addresses a number of practical issues (netiquette, to model interactions, facilitate ice-breakers) that establish the appropriate interpersonal relationships that make participants sufficiently comfortable to engage in substantive discourse.

It is difficult to discuss social presence in the absence of cognitive presence. Social presence does not exist simply for itself; social and cognitive presence are mutually beneficial. In an educational context, the purpose of social presence is to support cognitive presence that serves the intended academic goal. For example, providing insight or expressing reasoned agreement to an individual's message adds to both social and cognitive presence. A collaborative constructivist educational experience is predicated on, and sustained by, the social relationships and cohesion of the group. Practical inquiry is an inseparable iteration between personal reflection and public discourse. This inherent fusion of the public and private worlds means that the separation of social and cognitive presence does not exist in practice. Therefore, while we focus first on social presence guidelines and suggestions, cognitive presence issues are ever present.

In addition to having students post short bios (preferably in a chat room), a good start to an online or blended learning course is to form the students into small groups and ask each group to identify questions they may have about content, process and assessment expectations. These issues can then be brought to the class as a whole. This not only creates an opportunity for the instructor to set the right tone for inquiry by clarifying process concerns and negotiating course expectations, but it allows students to become familiar with other students and the technology. Through open communication, teachers can reveal their thought processes, thereby, enhancing shared metacognitive awareness and making themselves personally more accessible to students. Although the teacher must remain professional, revealing aspects of one's academic qualifications and, to some extent, personal interests can contribute to a welcoming and more relaxed environment. It has been shown that in higher education, teacher self-disclosure is more critical in building interpersonal relationships in online classes than in face-to-face classes (Song, Kim & Luo, 2016). This is to compensate for limitations in revealing personality that is more readily available in face-to-face settings and that may challenge establishing teacher-student relationships online.

Students must feel secure while engaging in discourse that is purposeful and cognitively challenging. For this reason, it needs to be made clear that purely social or personal exchanges are welcomed but may be best conducted in a chat room or coffeehouse.

Suggestions to facilitate social presence and establish a community of inquiry are:

- acknowledge participation;
- be encouraging and supportive while directing discussion;
- project your personality as a teacher and allow students to get to know you as a person to the degree appropriate for the context;
- suggest that students log-on at least three times per week;
- encourage students to acknowledge contributions when responding;
- be conversational and not too formal in communications;
- encourage "lurkers" to participate;
- express emotion but avoid flaming;
- be cautious using humor, at least until familiarity is achieved;
- encourage students to inform the teacher by e-mail of tensions or anxiety.

Cognitive Presence

Cognitive presence goes to the heart of an educational experience. That is, creating and sustaining a community of inquiry where students are engaged in a collaborative and reflective process which includes understanding an issue or problem, searching for relevant information, connecting and integrating information, and actively confirming understanding. The focus here is managing the process and monitoring the depth of understanding. This involves facilitating and focusing the discourse, providing appropriate insights and information when needed, and seeking common understanding or insight.

The first challenge from a community of inquiry perspective is getting the attention of the students and engaging them in meaningful discussions. Depending on the learning objective and the subject matter, there are typically two ways to approach this. The first approach is to provide one or two intriguing questions along with some associated readings or a case study. Posing questions has been shown to be effective in generating constructive discourse (Zhao & Sullivan, 2016). The goal is to have the students define the key question or issue, find the relevant information, suggest some meaningful connection or order, and agree on a resolution. Students may be expected to explore the Web for additional relevant information that can be reported on and bookmarked for future reference. Here the instructor is very much a moderator and guide. This approach is inductive, with the emphasis on creating academic order. The second approach is more deductive in nature and is more appropriate with well-ordered or defined subject matter. The goal of this approach is to provide a model or framework (perhaps competing models) with the challenge to the students to gain understanding by testing applications in contexts familiar to them.

The core responsibility in either example is facilitating (initiating, sustaining and summarizing communication) and stimulating meaningful discourse where students actively participate, critically challenge arguments, and take responsibility for making sense of the course content. To lecture online is to negate the power and capability of the technology and, most detrimentally, to turn students into passive receptors of information. Critical inquiry is content specific and needs to be led by an educator with content knowledge as well as context (pedagogical) expertise. That is, they must know their subject but they must also have pedagogical expertise to moderate critical discourse whether it is a synchronous face-to-face or asynchronous text-based learning environment. Facilitating deep understanding necessitates questioning, searching for core concepts, making connections, injecting new ideas or concepts, diagnosing misconceptions, constructing coherent knowledge structures, and reviewing and summarizing. This requires knowing when to give and assume control, when to encourage student input, and when to inform.

Particular care must be exercised when moving the discourse to the latter phases of inquiry. Due to tasks or assignments that do not explicitly require resolution or a facilitation approach that may be too passive, many inquiry learning experiences stall at the exploration phase and students are left to their own devices to resolve the dilemmas and construct meaning. When resolution is the expectation, participants must have it clearly in mind that this is the goal of the educational experience. Resolution may be predictable or it may not, depending on how well defined the subject matter or task. In any case, there must be a relentless shaping of the discourse through the phases of inquiry. That does not mean that it is a simple linear process or that all phases are of equal importance. In practice, there will be iteration between and among phases and more time will be spent on some phases than others. For example, in less well-defined subject areas, the focus may be on exploration and integration. In well-defined subject areas, the focus may be largely on resolution and finding solutions to specific problems.

One constant in this process is the need for discourse to stimulate and guide reflection. This is often best done in smaller groups. These discussions may be done in private to encourage participation, unless the educator is invited in. Each group is expected to assume responsibility for providing teaching presence and be required to report back to the full class. It is here that students are free to share their learning experiences and attempts to construct meaning. They will also learn how to facilitate critical discourse and direct the progress of the group. Small group discussion can be used in all phases of inquiry to foster increased participation and develop responsibility to construct meaning. It has been shown that small group discussions provide opportunities to clarify questions with peers and this has a positive effect on achievement (Sun & Wu, 2016). However, it should be noted that large or whole class discussion sessions have the advantage of more ideas and a diversity of viewpoints (McCarthy, Smith & DeLuca, 2010).

Small groups provide an opportunity to allow the students to moderate discussions. Student moderation can attenuate the authoritative influence of an educator and encourage freer discussion. On the other hand, student moderated discussions may lack needed content expertise and, therefore, may not have the same ability to weave responses, add important information, and encourage critically reflective comments. Student moderation can be a very valuable experience but should have some guidance and oversight (Rourke & Anderson, 2002). It should be kept in mind that students can be resentful if they feel abandoned by the instructor. By encouraging students to collaboratively monitor and manage their learning is the means of increasing shared metacognitive awareness. Considerable attention should be directed to increasing shared metacognitive awareness to give students a better understanding of critical thinking and the inquiry process. This cognitive map of the inquiry process can be a guide for the educator and students in thinking and learning collaboratively. Consideration should be given to introducing the CoI framework and PI model before engaging in discourse. This will increase awareness of inquiry and shared metacognition and strongly shape the nature and quality of contributions.

Research has shown that tagging discussion contributions encourages students to reflect on their thinking and "stimulates more in-depth and focused contributions" (Schellens, Van Keer, De Wever & Valcke, 2009, p. 77). This technique can help to overcome the tendency of students to resist challenging arguments and being overly polite (Rourke & Kanuka, 2007). Similarly, labeling discussion contributions was also found to attain a higher level of cognitive processing which "mirrored a higher degree of metacognitive regulation in relation to planning, achieving clarity and monitoring" (Valcke, De Wever, Zhu & Deed, 2009, p. 165). This technique has value from both a pragmatic and research perspective in understanding and promoting shared metacognition in an e-learning environment. Finally, the essence of most practices to improve metacognitive skills is to engage students in collaborative activities such as peer assessments, collective reflection, and modeling metacognitive processes (Choi, Land & Turgeon, 2005; Kramarski & Dudai, 2009; White, Frederiksen & Collins, 2009). Communities of inquiry have enormous potential to support shared metacognition through critical discourse that includes questioning, feedback and direction.

In a modern connected society, learners must be cognizant of the process of thinking and learning collaboratively. A major part of this is an awareness and understanding of shared metacognition as constituting a fusion of self- and co-regulation responsibilities. Students should be provided opportunities to manage and monitor their learning activities in context if they are to judge the success of these strategies and tactics. That is, students need to be aware of their thinking and that of others to effectively regulate thinking and learning collaboratively. This awareness will go a long way to move discussion beyond the early exploratory phase and move the discourse on to the integration and application of new ideas and concepts. This raises the importance of shared metacognitive awareness (Garrison & Akyol, 2015a). Students must not rely on external (teacher) regulation exclusively. This requires activities that are not overly scripted where shared metacognition is developed through distributed or shared teaching presence.

A great technique to have students increase their metacognitive awareness (knowledge) and management (regulatory) skills in a collaborative environment is to have students think about their online contributions. One effective way is to have them label their responses and keep track of discussion responses from others (Pawan, Paulus, Yalcin & Chang, 2003). Within the context of the CoI framework and the PI model, this would mean labeling responses according to each of the phases of inquiry. This has been shown to produce a higher level of cognitive processing (Valcke et al., 2009). Another practical advantage of shared metacognitive awareness is to have learners progress through the inquiry phases in a timely manner without stalling on one of the phases.

Cognitive presence issues associated with facilitating discourse can be summarized as:

- provide stimulating questions;
- identify puzzling issues arising from responses;
- challenge ideas and precipitate reflection;

- moderate but do not overly direct discussion;
- test ideas through application theoretically or vicariously;
- move on when discussion ebbs or has served its purpose;
- facilitate shared metacognitive awareness by having students label the nature of their comments in terms of the phases of the PI model.

Direct Instruction

Direct instruction is an essential function in a formal learning experience to provide academic and pedagogic leadership. In higher education, the educator is expected to set the intellectual climate, design the curriculum, model the characteristics of an inquisitive scholar, and initiate students into the nuances of the discipline. Inevitable academic challenges will require direct intervention but with openness such that the learner is a respected participant in the transaction. Scaffolding (temporary support to develop higher cognitive skills) is an important component of most socially shared (collaborative constructivist) models of purposeful learning. Thoughtful and sustained support is not accomplished through a laissez-faire or authoritarian approach to learning.

Social Presence

While on the surface it might seem that direct instruction would diminish social presence, it in fact has the opposite effect. First, let us reiterate that cognitive and social presence issues are interdependent. Regardless of the cognitive challenges facing instructors and students, education is a social enterprise. When done with moderation, direct input from the educator can develop a sense of accomplishment and group cohesion. Second, direct instruction can reinforce important social-emotional considerations, such as demonstrating respect and relating to individuals in a non-threatening way. Students very much value teaching presence, but they must also be comfortable questioning or even challenging direct instruction.

Another area justifying direct intervention is when a few students dominate the discussion or intimidate others and create barriers to participation. Here, direct instruction is required to encourage dominant students to listen to others and reflect upon the discourse. Similarly, in a highly interactive learning environment, conflict may arise that needs to be managed. While intervention may be required if conflict interferes with class dynamics, in general, students should be left to their own devices for minor disagreements. Over time, it can be expected that students will become increasingly socially and academically responsible. However, a single student can be disruptive to the point that open communication and discourse is seriously compromised. For the sake of group cohesion, disruptive individuals should be confronted directly through personal communication.

Social presence issues associated with direct instruction must be approached with particular care as the comments are specific and often directed to individuals. Some suggestions are:

- shape discussion but don't dominate;
- provide feedback with respect;
- be constructive with corrective comments;
- be open to negotiation and providing reasons;
- deal with conflict quickly and privately.

Cognitive Presence

The virtual nature of an online learning experience only enhances the need for teaching presence. Students need feedback and direction for academic reasons or managing time constraints to expedite the educational process. As a subject matter expert, answering questions or clarifying misconceptions are not only constructive but essential teaching presence responsibilities. It is strongly suggested that a knowledgeable educator has the responsibility to frame the content and direct attention to specific concepts that form an organizing framework for the specific content. In this way, students have, or can construct, the schema that goes beyond isolated facts and provides the foundation to facilitate continuous knowledge development. Inevitably, this will necessitate appropriate engagement and intervention. Teaching presence goes beyond a neutral weaving of participants' contributions.

There is evidence that educators are not always very good at moving discourse through the stages of inquiry (Clarke & Bartholomew, 2014). The bias often mistakenly has been towards facilitation as opposed to challenging and directing thinking. To be clear, teaching presence responsibilities go beyond facilitation and must provide a balance of facilitation and direct instruction specific to the particular need of the task at hand. Teaching presence in the form of direct instruction is needed to ensure that discourse remains focused and developmental. Teaching presence must be focused on the quality of discourse, ensuring that the intended goals are achieved in a timely manner. Therefore, educators must be prepared to move beyond facilitation and provide suggestions or specific information to move the discourse to integration and resolution phases of inquiry. Teaching presence that included feedback and coaching has been shown to be associated with higher levels of cognitive presence (Stein, Wanstreet, Slagle, Trinko & Lutz, 2013).

Direct instruction should be approached with the intent of taking the learner to higher-levels of academic development than they might have otherwise reached if they were left on their own. This means implementing, monitoring and ending a range of learning activities and tasks when specific learning objectives are achieved. This requires solicitation of formative feedback and direct instruction when required. Deep and meaningful learning depends on diagnosing misconceptions and formative evaluation that the teacher can use to intervene directly in a timely manner. These are important teaching presence responsibilities. On the other hand, lecturing and dictating values and viewpoints represent a lack of understanding of the potential of information and communication technologies and online and blended learning to connect learners and sustain discourse over time and space. Similarly, too much direct instruction will assuredly reduce interaction and limit critical reflection to the detriment of deep and meaningful learning experiences (Zhao & Sullivan, 2016). Students must have the opportunity to develop their ideas through discourse. This requires a delicate balance where the situation may call for learner control, while at other times the discussion may need direction or be brought to a close. Direct instruction often obliges students to look deeper into a topic.

Finally, summarizing discourse segments at the end of a course is also a crucial direct intervention. At these points, it is often appropriate to extract key concepts and direct students to further learning challenges. This is important from both a cognitive and social presence perspective. Cognitively, it can create a sense of accomplishment, offer direction for further study, and provide an assessment of achievements. Socially, it is an opportunity to have some closure and allow participants to bid others farewell.

Cognitive presence issues associated with direct instruction can be summarized as:

- offer alternative ideas and perspectives for analysis and discussion;
- respond directly to and elaborate on inquiries for all to absorb;
- acknowledge uncertainty where it exists;
- make connections among ideas;
- collaboratively construct knowledge structures;
- summarize discussion and move on;
- provide closure and foreshadow further study.

Assessment

Assessment is considered a separate principle because of its crucial role and pervasive influence across all aspects of a community of inquiry. From a design perspective, we must keep in mind that in educational environments how learning is rewarded will overwhelmingly shape approaches to learning. Therefore, it is essential to reinforce and reward thinking and learning activities in ways that are congruent with intended learning outcomes. Assessing learning activities and their formative results is the primary responsibility and challenge in a Community of Inquiry framework that is focused on the inquiry transaction. The goal is to create an environment for thinking and learning collaboratively based on authentic and constructive feedback. This form of feedback will include presenting new ideas, guidance in shaping discourse, reinforcement, and enhancing shared metacognitive awareness. Educational assessment also includes the reality of assigning grades. If not thoughtfully designed, formative assessment that is not congruent with the processes and intended outcomes of a collaborative community of inquiry will fatally undermine constructive efforts in this regard.

Formative and summative assessment is integral to the inquiry process and maintaining a constructive learning environment. Assessment is critical to cognitive presence to assess conceptual understanding and the progression of inquiry. Similarly, with regard to social presence, participants must be able to assess how they project themselves in socially constructive ways that facilitate open communication and commitment to community goals. Therefore, because of the strategic and tactical nature of assessment, it is argued that the generalized and crucial nature of assessment necessitates that it be seen as a larger contextual influence. Speaking to the overarching nature of assessment, we must reiterate that assessment with feedback is the responsibility of all participants, otherwise it risks constraining thinking and learning collaboratively. For this reason, we have identified assessment for special consideration and will be the focus of the next chapter.

Conclusion

The focus of this chapter has been on the practical aspects of teaching presence associated with a community of inquiry. In each of the three teaching presence dimensions (design, facilitation and direct instruction), relevant issues of social and cognitive presence were discussed and broad guidelines provided. While we have explored a set of specific principles associated with each of the elements of a community of inquiry, we must keep in mind that any derivative strategy or technique may have a direct impact on one presence but will inevitably impact other presences as well. An effective community of inquiry must keep intended academic goals front of mind if discourse is to be more than an informal chat room. Clarke and Bartholomew (2014) in their study of teaching presence state that their findings further "the idea that we need all three parts of the COI framework to be effective but how we employ this framework takes a careful and thoughtful balancing act" (discussion, last sentence). This represents a considerable challenge where educators need to be teaching scholars. Implementing e-learning requires extensive time to prepare and manage and this can be a major barrier to adoption (Martins & Nunes, 2016).

Chapter 10

Assessment and Evaluation

The critical role of assessment and evaluation in ensuring a collaborative constructivist educational experience is examined in this chapter. We have reserved a full chapter to this topic due to the pervasive and significant influence that assessment has on learning. While it is seen as a teaching presence responsibility, it is integral to establishing effective social and cognitive presence. Therefore, assessment is an essential process to maintain a dynamic balance among the presences in the complex environment of a purposeful community of inquiry.

Although the terms assessment and evaluation have occasionally been used synonymously, there is an important difference between the terms. Assessment is associated with determining students' learning processes and outcomes. Such assessment is, by necessity, multifaceted and can include acquisition of skills and behavioral competencies; competency in applying cognitive skills, including capacity to apply critical and creative solutions to complex problems; and attitudinal demeanor, including capacity to be positively engaged in a community of inquiry. Generally, assessment occurs throughout the course, thereby, providing formative feedback to students; and at the completion of the course, providing summative information on successes and failures from student and teacher perspectives.

On the other hand, the term evaluation is used to refer to the act of comparing a unit, course, or program against some set of performance or outcome criteria. These criteria are often set by external agents or organizations, but the interests of the teacher and students are also driving forces within evaluation policies. Comprehensive evaluation includes measures of learning, satisfaction, costing and cost-benefits, and other criteria for program success as defined by any or all relevant stakeholders or participants. While this is often externally driven, evaluation should be open to analysis and understanding by the learning community, even if this is nonnegotiable.

Assessing Learning

The importance of assessment in an educational experience cannot be overestimated. As Rowntree (1977) states, "If we wish to discover the truth about an educational system, we must look into its assessment procedures" (p. 1). This is one of the great truths and constants of a formal educational program of study. There is consensus that assessment fundamentally shapes learning, particularly if we hope to approach learning in a deep and meaningful manner (Garrison & Archer, 2000). When it comes to the pedagogical importance and influence of assessment in an educational experience, online and blended learning are not exempt.

The focus of the discussion here is from an educational perspective and, therefore, much of the theory and practice of a quality educational experience that has been developed for campus-based education are directly relevant for the design of assessment in online and blended learning contexts. Assessment in an online learning context is complicated by many factors, including the effects of the communication media; the lack of physical proximity and body language used for feedback in classrooms; the limited instructor supervision over the learning process; the difficulty of authentication and cheating on exams in distributed contexts; and the likely reduction of informal, after-class interaction.

Assessment is directly linked to effective teaching and learning by revealing student understanding and achievement. For assessment to be successful, it must first be congruent with intended learning outcomes. For example, if the goal is to realize deep understanding of concepts and develop critical thinking abilities, the focus of assessment must be understanding and thinking—not the recall of fragmented bits of information. Therefore, assessment should diagnose misconceptions during the learning process and assess the quality of intended learning outcomes. This form of in-depth assessment is not for the faint of heart in any educational experience and it is no less challenging in an e-learning environment. However, the challenges can be mitigated through the effective use of the interactive and collaborative activities made possible by the technology and the use of assessment techniques consistent with the potential of online and blended learning for collaboration.

Functions of Assessment

With online and blended learning, the focus must be on assessing thinking and learning collaboratively. Unfortunately, the tradition of education is that assessment is focused on individual content assimilation and instructor-centered activities. If we are to capitalize on the collaborative potential of e-learning, we need to include techniques that recognize and reward collaborative learning. When collaborative learning is not valued and reflected through assessment processes, authentic participation and deep learning will be compromised. Considering the strengths of e-learning in supporting collaborative constructivist learning, this "requires a radical rethinking of assessment methodologies" (Swan, Shen & Hiltz, 2006, p. 46).

Collaborative thinking and learning is more than a means to an end in terms of content acquisition. It is the means to deep understanding and shared metacognitive awareness of the collaborative inquiry approach that makes possible continuous learning. For this reason, it is important to have formative feedback and assessment of the collaborative process. Students should be asked to comment on what went well and what did not in terms of the educational transaction. At the same time, assessing collaborative learning should not be done at the expense of assessing individual learning. Assessing collaborative and individual learning reflects the shared and private worlds inherent in the process of practical inquiry. A means must be found to provide a grade for both collaborative and individual accomplishments. Consideration must be given to assessing collaborative assignments. One way to do this is for the group to collaboratively design and submit the comprehensive product but have each participant submit their particular contribution to the project. Other means are self-assessment, peer assessment and group presentations.

The Community of Inquiry (CoI) framework speaks to the educational transaction and the need to provide feedback on a continuous basis. Much of this feedback is provided continuously by all the participants in the learning community assuming responsibility for teaching presence. Formative assessment provides feedback on the progress of participants toward attaining educationally intended objectives. Formative assessment provided by the community motivates and guides participants in an efficient manner. In addition, students are more likely to persevere when their learning activities are acknowledged and rewarded. In this way, formative assessment serves the fundamentally important role of providing feedback to students on their complex and challenging collaborative learning efforts.

Assessment also plays a critical function by providing external benchmarks that can be internalized. Since knowledge and understanding are both externally and internally defined, assessment provides an integrating mechanism whereby external measures of learning accomplishments are matched with a personal understanding of the learning process (metacognition). Metacognitive awareness must be developed collaboratively during the discourse to ensure that worthwhile and intended goals are being reached in a timely manner. Shared metacognitive awareness operates at the intersection of teaching and cognitive presence (i.e. regulation and learning) but also is impacted by social presence. Effective instructors use assessment techniques strategically to emotionally engage and motivate learners to persist in productive learning activities. To do this, learners need to understand and have input on the learning activity and collaboratively assess the strategy if we are to build shared metacognitive awareness. Similarly, effort and pace of progress need to be brought into conscious awareness and discussed by the community.

Having articulated the role of assessment in an educational learning experience, we now turn the discussion to the means by which assessment is best used in online and blended learning contexts.

Assessing Participation

Assessment must be linked to, and be congruent with, course objectives and activities if it is to be useful in achieving intended outcomes. Many of us have had the experience of devising enrichment or suggested activities for students, only to realize that most students are too instrumentally focused and too busy with other commitments to undertake uncredited tasks. However, throughout this book we have been arguing for the integration of cognitive, social and teaching presence through participation in communities of inquiry enhanced through sustained communication. Therefore, educational tasks and activities should be consistent with outcome expectations and be assessed openly. Given the necessity to relate effort to reward, we must confront the question of how best to assess and reward student participation in asynchronous and synchronous discourse.

It is clear that students must perceive participation in online discourse as a core component of the program of studies. Thus, assessment activities must be integrated within learning activities in addition to being worthwhile and relevant. However, teachers must also be careful not to overly structure the discourse through excessive assessment and personal intervention. The natural flow of the inquiry process (flexibility to attend to curiosity) must be ensured. The social presence of the learning environment must be welcoming and positive enough that students willingly respond and support each other in the academic process. On the other hand, omnipresent assessment may lead students to conclude that the discussion is a "teacher tool" and not one over which they have any control to modify to meet their individual interests and educational needs. Students must have input into assessment if they are to be encouraged to be responsible learners and develop shared metacognitive awareness that will ensure continuous learning.

Students must perceive that their participation is congruent with the grades assigned for participation. Such reward for participation is unlike most classroom education where it is common not to provide grades for attendance and participation. Jiang and Ting (2000) in their report on college students studying via networked learning found that students' perceived learning was significantly correlated to the percentage of grade weight assigned to participation and their resulting participation in discussion. Thus, it is important for teachers to value students' participation both informally, through frequent interaction among themselves, and formally, through feedback and assessment.

In a community of inquiry, discourse is a critical component of the learning process. Palloff and Pratt (2005) argue that given this emphasis on the learning process, participation must be assessed and appropriately rewarded. Most students are pressed for time and are unlikely to participate in activities that are marginal or viewed as supplemental to the grading assessment. For this reason, it is crucially important that students be provided guidelines for arguing a position and be given grading rubrics that state assessment criteria and percentage of final grade for participation. Research has shown that effective discussion is associated with assessment and, more specifically, there is evidence to suggest that discussions shaped by assessment rubrics show "more posts, more threads, and a greater depth than … discussions in the classes given no discussion criteria" (Swan, Schenker, Arnold & Kuo, 2007, p. 78).

The following rubric (Table 10.1) was designed to assess an online discussion moderated by a student. The goal was to identify the key components or responsibilities for moderating the discussion and then to define the quality characteristics or performance levels associated with each component. This rubric was created by a colleague, Dr. Norm Vaughan, when we

Table 10.1 Discussion Rubric

Component	Beginning	Developing	Accomplished	Score
Participation	1 point Only contributed and participated in one of the online discussion forums	3 points Contributed and participated in three of the online discussion forums	5 points Contributed and participated in each of the five online discussion forums	
Moderation	1 points Posted an initial online discussion forum question	3 points Posted several discussion forum questions	5 points Posted several discussion forum questions and responded to the postings of other students	
Summary	3 points Provided a general summary of the online discussion forum	5 points Summarized the important ideas that emerged from the discussions	7 points Summarized the important ideas that emerged from the discussions, the unresolved and contentious topics, and key concepts that captured the discussion	
Resources	1 point Incomplete list of resources and citations	2 point Core list of resources cited in APA format	3 points Extensive and relevant list of resources cited in APA format	
			Total Score	/20

co-taught a blended course on the topic of blended learning (see also Vaughan, Cleveland-Innes & Garrison, 2013). Another rubric that might be developed would be to assess the quality of participation according to the phases of the Practical Inquiry (PI) model. For example, the vertical column would have three phases of inquiry—exploration, integration and resolution, while the performance levels could be judged by relevance (integral to thread), clarity (succinctness) and argument (references). For more ideas of discussion rubrics see Swan et al. (2006).

Most course management systems provide tracking features that allow teachers to monitor the number of logons and contributions to online forums. Thus, it is possible to quickly compile data about student participation. However, tabulating the number of postings is not an accurate measure of meaningful contributions or student achievement and growth. We are also aware of a tendency in formal education for some students to adopt "instrumental" attitudes towards learning, wherein they strategically focus only on teacher-defined outcomes. Like much quality educational research, quality student assessment is multifaceted and uses a variety of measuring devices. We next examine some of the means to assess participation and contribution.

The computer systems that underlie online learning communications can relatively easily be used for quantitative analysis of student postings. Instructors who measure the number of postings, with few guidelines or feedback mechanisms for shaping quality of the messages, usually succeed in getting participation, but it is unclear if this assessment influences the quality of the discourse and learning outcomes. The growing interest in assessment is being assisted by developments in learning analytics (Johnson, Adams Becker, Estrada & Freeman, 2015). This can support deep and meaningful educational experiences but must provide a grounded educational perspective that engage learners in critical reflection and discourse. At the same time, this should not be at the expense of pedagogically sound assessment of student participation from a qualitative assessment of participation that displays postings in context. When undertaking the task of assessing messages in context, one must be diligent to make the assessment criteria as open as possible and to share these criteria at the beginning of the course.

Ideally, students should be given the opportunity to reflect on their contributions and the inquiry process. Students' own postings can be used as the basis for reflection on learning activities and assessment (Davie, 1989; Paulsen, 1995). This can be shared in the form of an online journal or blog. Another tactic is metacognitively labeling contributions according to the phases of the PI model (i.e. cognitive presence) which could then be a source for assessing the quality of contributions. At the end of the course, students may be asked to illustrate their contributions and evidence of learning by composing a "reflection piece" in which they quote from their own posting to the course. In this regard, students should be given guidance to help them extract quotations that illustrate their contributions. Obviously, students who have not participated will not be able to provide transcript references from their own postings and, thus, will generally receive lower assessment ratings. Alternatively, a student may still be able to show learning by selective extraction of relevant postings, thus providing an opportunity to make-up for vicariously participating (lurking).

Self-assessment of contributions can be further refined by having students undertake moderating functions during specific time frames of the course. They can then be asked to demonstrate their contribution to the class and the discourse by quoting their contributions to teaching presence (such as summaries, welcoming comments, learning instigations, and other contributions). They should also be asked to reflect on their metacognitive knowledge and awareness and how this was enhanced through the transaction. Finally, students could be presented with a summary of social, cognitive and teaching presence indicators and asked to describe which of the categories their postings contribute most significantly.

Assessment Activities

A community of inquiry learning experience contains a balanced set of learning activities that work individually and together to precipitate and support purposeful discourse and reflection. The online and blended learning environment is highly advantageous in supporting a community of inquiry focused on thinking and learning collaboratively. The reason is that information and communication technologies are continuing to develop and are understood to provide combinations of text, voice and multimedia interaction that can occur in both synchronous and asynchronous formats for the purposes of thinking and learning. Examples include performance assessments (wikis), authentic assessments (real-world case studies), portfolio assessments (journal or blog), and online computer generated tests and quizzes (Palloff & Pratt, 2009). A common assignment in higher education is finding, reading and critiquing a relevant published article of particular interest to the student. Guiding students and fairly assessing such work can be greatly facilitated through the use of an assessment rubric. Table 10.2 is a rubric designed to assess a reading assignment developed by Dr. Norm Vaughan.

Consistent with the increased emphasis on active learning and authentic assessment is the increased use of portfolios of learner products or artifacts. Portfolios "evidence understanding of important concepts or mastery of key skills by requiring students to organize, synthesize, and communicate their achievements ..." (Swan et al., 2006, p. 53). The construction of learning artifacts demonstrates knowledge acquisition in a very fundamental and explicit manner. It can include demonstration of individual understanding as well as collaborative contributions. Portfolio assessment also is congruent

Table 10.2 Article Critique Rubric

Component	Beginning	Developing	Accomplished	Score/ Comments
Synthesis/ Summary	1 point Incomplete synthesis— missing components	2 points All components of the synthesis are present but not completely developed including the: Principal question, argument or thesis statement Theoretical framework Methodology Study findings Conclusion and/or recommendations	3 points A complete and fully developed synthesis of the article	
Critique	1 point Incomplete critique— missing components	3 points All components of the critique are present but not completely developed including a discussion of: The validity and reliability of the study findings Why you agree or disagree with conclusion/ recommen-dations	6 points A complete and fully developed critique of the article	

with strategies that allow significant input from students into their own learning goals. Students can then embark on individual and collaborative learning paths and demonstrate their accomplishment through the artifacts as demonstrated in their portfolio. The transcript can be used as a very useful component of the portfolio and teachers can ask students to annotate, summarize or otherwise add reflective metacognitive comments to their archived contributions.

Each of the activities and strategies employed to assess student learning have methodological and epistemological limitations. While using these strategies, we are attempting to measure complex domains of knowledge as they are instantiated in individual and collaborative contexts. It is important for assessment strategies to "ensure both group interdependence and individual accountability" (Swan et al., 2006, p. 53). Interdependent accountability may be as straight forward as documenting the sharing and use of resources. Clearly a successful undertaking of these assessments is an immense challenge. Furthermore, teachers are compelled to undertake these assessments in a transparent, reliable and authentic manner that allows students or college administrators to challenge them. In order to reduce the error inherent in over-reliance on a single assessment activity, a sound educational practice is to use a variety of assessments throughout the course. Variety should occur in the format of assessment:

- quizzes, short answer, longer articulated response, and term paper;
- in the degree of collaboration required from individual to group assignments;
- in the role of assessor from self to peer to teacher assessment;
- from assessing broad theoretical understanding to assessing very practical applications of new knowledge.

Student assessment in problem-based inquiry learning contexts is more challenging than assessing traditional educational outcomes in terms of content acquisition. Problem-based inquiry learning attempts to induce deep levels of learning and to encourage students taking increased responsibility and developing metacognitive awareness. As such, simple measures of knowledge retention are not able to assess student growth in these important areas. Because of this, a variety of assessment activities are often built into problem-based inquiry learning. These can include presentations in which students demonstrate or post their solutions to the problem; self- and peer assessments in which students assess their own contributions and the contributions of other group members; and the development of concept maps that document problem solutions and the processes used to achieve those solutions.

Finally, one of the inherent advantages of collaborative approaches to learning is the capacity to discuss the critical role of assessment with students. The inherent communications capacity of the Internet can be used to allow students to comment upon and negotiate the type of assessment so that students understand the purpose to ensure it adequately reflects and guides their learning objectives. Student input and appropriate control of the learning program is central to effective higher education. If students are expected to assume increasing control of their learning, they must have some input and choice over the content and process. Moreover, control must extend beyond choice of goals to choice of how these goals are assessed.

Course Evaluation

Assessment of student learning is a key component of the evaluation of online and blended learning, but it is only one of the factors in which educators have responsibility. The online and blended learning context is complex and made up of many components. All these components must work together in a seamless fashion if a quality educational experience is to be realized. Palloff and Pratt (2009) list eight elements when evaluating an online course:

- perception of the course experience;
- orientation to the course;
- quality and quantity of content;
- discussion and interaction;
- self-assessment of participation and performance;
- course management system;
- technical support;
- access to resources.

Evaluation begins by determining the strategic intent of the program. In this regard, clearly identifying why the particular course has been developed and delivered is crucial to assessing its effectiveness. Traditionally, distance education courses have been offered in order to increase access to education opportunities by spanning geographic or temporal distance. While access is a component of online learning, added value speaks to issues of quality reflected by collaborative thinking and learning experiences. Institutions also attempt to use online and blended learning as a means to increase revenues, to increase or retain market share of students, and to enhance institutional or national recognition or prestige. The knowledge of the potential of online and blended learning is critical to establishing mechanisms for measuring the achievement of these goals. It should be noted that these goals are often hidden and implicit; therefore, the first role of the educator must be to explicate these hidden agendas.

Another element in proactive evaluation is to look closely at the content of the courses. Sims (2001) points out that content for any course exists along a continuum from the static content that is predetermined by the developer before students are enrolled, to content that is open to the contributions of the students and teacher as the course progresses. However, with regard to content flexibility, the challenge is coherence and congruence with the larger purpose of the course. Moreover, writing style should be consistent and match the reading level and the degree of familiarity with vocabulary appropriate to the average learner enrolled in the course. The content of the course material must be accurate and authors should acknowledge biases they bring to the discussion. While this seems to be a common sense requirement, it is essential in critical discourse as the learners contribute content in collaborative learning environments.

Effective evaluation of course material requires a close examination of the instructional design incorporated in the course. All courses reflect the pedagogical biases and understandings of their creators. There are many examples of online content that is based on instructivist designs masquerading as constructivist designs. Despite differences in design every course should:

- be aligned with the prior experience and knowledge of the learners;
- provide pathways and sequencing that are coherent, clear, and complete;
- provide opportunities for discourse;
- provide means by which students and teachers can assess the learning experience and expected outcomes;
- clearly articulate the ways in which these outcomes are to be achieved.

Specific to the point of this chapter, course evaluation should address evaluating the quality, quantity and thoroughness of the assessment of student learning. As discussed previously, assessment drives learning behavior and in many ways defines the course. A proactive evaluation of the course looks closely at the assessment activities and notes how accurately they measure both the espoused and the hidden course objectives. Most quality courses will have multiple forms of assessment, including assessment of both individual and group work. The means by which the evaluation is authenticated against discipline or community norms is also a challenge.

The degree of student support is another element of course evaluation. Since students are unique, there are an infinite number of issues that may challenge student learning. To address these concerns, a variety of student support services must be available. These resources need to focus on both the content (remedial activities for some and enrichment for other students), technical issues (especially if the technology used for delivery support is novel, sophisticated or complex), and personal issues (various types of counseling support).

The final area of course evaluation relates to assessing the degree to which outcomes have been met. Are the learners satisfied with the courses? Are credentialing or accreditation organizations able to certify those who have successfully completed the courses? Are teachers satisfied with the work conditions and the workloads associated with the course? Are there mechanisms in place so that the course will be continuously improved during subsequent iterations? It may also be relevant to evaluate whether the course is affordable to students and cost effective for the institution and makes a difference to the students?

Course and program evaluation is challenging and often not of immediate concern to the educator responsible for the course or program. However, these macro-level concerns cannot be ignored for the long-term success of the course or program. Senior administrators must be intimately connected to evaluation of online and blended courses if they are to develop progressively and grow the support and confidence of their place in the institution.

Conclusion

As the breadth of the discussion above illustrates, judging the worth of online and blended learning experiences is a broad and complex topic that includes much more than merely assessing student performance and their perceptions of the course. Sustained evaluation is required to address the complexity of the development and delivery of an online and blended community of inquiry. It is only through rigorous and systematic assessment and evaluation that educators and administrators will be able to develop an understanding of the complex issues associated with judging the worth of the educational experience.

Assessment and evaluation raise our awareness of the enormous administrative responsibilities and organizational issues that need to be navigated. For this reason, designing online and blended learning experiences will need institutional leadership (policy), incentives, and instructional development support. These larger organizational traditions and structural realities can constrain the adoption of e-learning approaches and associated possibilities for thinking and learning collaboratively. Therefore, we turn to organizational issues and leadership essential to the adoption and sustainability of online and blended learning.

Chapter 11

Organizational Issues

Institutions of higher education are strategically positioning themselves with regards to adopting online and blended learning approaches. They are shifting from the public relations rhetoric associated with being innovative to moving ahead in drafting vision, policies and goals with regard to collaborative approaches to teaching and learning relevant to a connected world. These forward looking institutions are redefining their conceptions of what constitutes a quality learning experience in the context of ubiquitous, mediated communication environments. The answer as to what distinguishes institutions of higher education is increasingly being seen in terms of the quality of the learning environment, not simply being able to access information. By revisiting their core values and culture, institutions are recognizing a need to move away from passive lectures and are realizing that thinking and learning collaboratively are the means to significantly enhance the scholarly culture and learning environment in a knowledge society.

Expectations are changing and there is little doubt that educational institutions are being transformed as a result of online and blended learning innovations. However, the question is how to lead and manage this transformation. Institutions face the challenge of developing a vision and strategic direction that will position them to move forward in a way that provides the greatest flexibility to continue to adapt to new innovations. Meeting this challenge demands insightful, collaborative organizational leadership. Leaving it to the first adopters will not sustain teaching and learning innovation.

Strategic Innovation

Blended and online approaches to learning are no longer interesting experiments. They have moved into the mainstream of higher education and are recognized as strategic imperatives. The reason is the recognition of the pressing need to address inherent deficiencies in higher education related to overreliance on lectures and information dissemination. The reality is that added value is no longer associated with accessing course content but the transactional quality of the learning experience. In short, the goal is the enhancement of the quality of the learning environment through meaningful engagement. More time and effort, however, must be expended on understanding the e-learning experience and how it can serve core educational values and goals. Too much effort continues to be expended to sustain the status quo and too little time is given to developing approaches that enhance the quality of the learning experience.

Katz (2010) has stated that the digital age will reshape higher education and the "leaders of today's traditional scholarly enterprises must rethink a number of fundamentals behind the higher education institution" (p. 52). The central issue that educational institutions are struggling to adapt to is the reality of a continuously connected society and why students need to be on campus. Traditionally, higher education institutions were defined by place in terms of where the repositories of knowledge physically existed. Clearly, in the Internet age this proposition no longer holds. The real issue is not physical presence but a sense of belonging to a scholarly community. From the perspective of a quality educational experience, place will more and more be addressed by embracing blended approaches to learning that extends the academic community over time and distance.

It is no longer a rational option to reject online and blended approaches to learning. Online and blended learning is transforming educational institutions for the better. Most importantly, they have been shown to have the potential to enhance the traditional values and ethos of higher education by fostering communities of learners and the integration of research methods through inquiry into the curriculum. Traditional higher education teaching and learning practices (the lecture) that limit engagement put institutions at a serious disadvantage pedagogically. The credibility of passive information transmission approaches inherent to most higher education institutions has been eroded. The inevitable challenge for these institutions is to face the disruption of adopting transformative approaches to teaching and learning that fully engage learners.

Online and blended learning are disruptive technologies because they threaten the sustaining technology—the face-to-face lecture. Disruptive technologies are invariably a threat to established organizations (Yamagata-Lynch, Cowan & Luetkehans, 2015) and, in the longer term, if they do not adjust, will inevitably be the source of their demise (Christensen, 1997). According to Christensen, disruptive technologies have caused dominant firms to fail because those firms have refused to adapt. The existential challenge for these organizations is to transform themselves during periods of technological change. Such fundamental change is currently being experienced in higher education. It is becoming ever more evident that e-learning's ability to facilitate an enhanced, yet more convenient and in many cases less expensive, educational approach, is not hyperbole. The viability of many higher education institutions will depend on how they address this transformational challenge.

According to Christensen (1997), the winning strategy is to find relatively low-risk niche areas in which the technology can be understood and incubated and where, if there are failures, they will come early and be less expensive. From a business perspective, Christensen suggests, the "innovator's task is to ensure that this innovation ... is taken seriously ... without putting at risk the needs of present customers" (p. xxiv). However, "Attention to new, disruptive technologies should not preclude sufficient attention being paid to the sustaining technologies that will allow the central core of the institution to maintain its favorable position in the marketplace" (Archer, Garrison & Anderson, 1999, p. 24). When adopting disruptive approaches, the legitimate needs of campus-based learners and the core values of the faculty and the institution must be recognized or the innovation will be greatly resisted— even at the institution's own peril. This has been the case with regard to e-learning innovations until it was recognized that these approaches were not only congruent with but enhanced the values and ethos of higher education. Notwithstanding the congruence with core values, institutional leadership has a very challenging balancing task that must begin with development of sound policy and support of e-learning innovation.

Policy Development

Many educational institutions are making substantial investments in blended and online learning. However, because of the lack of strategic direction and sustained commitment, fundamental change has been slow. Institutional policy must be developed to provide direction and focus sufficient resources to facilitate what will be a difficult process—the transformation of the sustaining technologies and vested interests of large institutions.

Some of the topics that a policy document and strategic plan should include are:

1   Vision

    • understand background
    • define core values
    • describe strategic goals

2   Needs and risk assessment

    • identify issues
    • identify challenges
    • identify best practices

3   Educational principles and outcomes described
4   Implementation initiatives and strategy

- link to institutional priorities
- create a steering committee
- identify communities of practice

5   Infrastructure

- design multi-media classrooms
- describe administrative processes

6   Support services

- provide professional development
- provide learner support

7   Resources, incentives and recognition
8   Benchmarking and research

- establish success criteria
- assess progress
- communicate direction and accomplishments

In addition, there are several issues that must be addressed to ensure that an e-learning vision and strategic plan are effectively created and implemented. First, the vision and strategic plan must have attainable goals and initiatives that have the support of the institution's leaders. Strategies must be seen as flexible actions that will inevitably need to be rethought and reshaped as the realities of implementation arise. Second, there must be collaborative leadership that includes senior leaders throughout the entire process. A more inclusive approach will provide an opportunity to build trust and create a sense of ownership. Third, research and evaluation is necessary to remain current and to stay on track. This is really a corollary of the first point in that implementation of a strategy must be continually informed with new ideas internally and externally. Finally, considerable effort must be given to communication to sustain the collaborative leadership such that successes are shared and support maintained.

Lasting innovation does not occur from the top down nor does it grow from the bottom up. More often than not, effecting change is an iterative process where mid-level leaders (who have the expertise and commitment) with the sustained collaboration of both senior management and the grassroots are in a position to provide strategic input. The vision must have practical value and be seen to be an imperative. For senior leadership to commit to this vision, they must see the potential benefits, address uncertainties, and be assured of success (Yamagata-Lynch et al., 2015). This means that senior leadership must be provided with evaluation data on a sustained basis in which they can be assured of success. Only with this commitment will policy and resources be directed to the systemic development of disruptive innovations such as blended and online learning.

Infrastructure

It should be clear that a vision and strategic plan must be systemic. It is not sufficient to select elements of the strategic plan in a fragmented or ad hoc manner. All the elements of the plan must be integrated in a coherent and timely manner. The technological infrastructure is no exception. The technology of learning management systems can create an enabling environment and provide much of the functionality for online and blended learning. The support and maintenance of technology is essential to sustaining an e-learning initiative (McGill, Klobas & Renzi, 2014). Learning management systems is the needed "middle ware" that links repositories and the educational process. It is the infrastructure that will empower the organizational communities who will ultimately provide the buy-in and sustainability. This infrastructure will support the creation of knowledge as well as managing its preservation and dissemination.

Equally important is the recognition and integration of communities of practice where teachers and students can manage and share information and knowledge with regard to curriculum, course management and pedagogical processes. Knowledge management builds upon the foundation of communities of inquiry that involves both creation and application of knowledge (know-how embedded in the wisdom of practice). As Rosenberg (2001) states, the "importance of community cannot be overstated" and its real power "is that it creates opportunities for people to go beyond interaction with content to contributing information and sharing" (p. 80). That is, knowledge management encourages members of the community to consider new ideas, grow and innovate. Institutional investment in e-learning and associated technology infrastructure will require not only the full support of senior administration but the commitment of leadership across the organization.

Leadership

It has been commonly accepted that higher education stands apart in its determination to resist change and the adoption of technology (Duderstadt, Atkins & Van Houweling, 2002). While there are traditions in higher education that should be protected, there are legitimate calls for change when it comes to increasing recognition for the need to more effectively engage students in the educational experience. In times of change, too often the missing element is leadership. There is a core set of leadership characteristics required for transformational change. The values and personal virtues essential to a leader are integrity and openness. Successful leaders treat people with fairness, honesty, openness and respect. These values and virtues are manifested in terms of vision, commitment, decisiveness and the ability to recognize talent. These leadership qualities instill the confidence in others to engage in effect change.

Leadership must have a vision and be willing to advocate for change. This vision must then be translated into understandable and achievable strategic goals and actions. Leadership must next show commitment to action and a willingness to make difficult decisions. Commitment to action reflects decisiveness. Decisiveness is a corollary to change that requires conviction and mediates vision and action. Moreover, decisiveness represents the courage to move forward with the expectation that adjustments will need to be made. The future can never be fully anticipated; consequently, surprises and failures will inevitably occur along the way. Leadership must expect these setbacks, learn from them and move forward.

While innovation may be relatively commonplace, true transformation occurs only rarely. Adopting e-learning in its full potential is a transformative process that requires strong leadership and sustained commitment to overcome resistance and setbacks. Decisiveness is having the courage to make timely decisions and to seize opportunities, invariably without as much information or consultation as may be desirable, or even prudent. Leadership must listen and reflect very carefully but not be afraid to take action. Innovation and transformation do not emerge from consensus but, rather, consensus results from open communication and collaboration. As in a community of inquiry, open communication and an ability to listen can identify and refine ideas. However, the value of collaboration is to enhance individual creativity, responsibility and action. Perhaps the most important attribute of successful leadership is being able to work collaboratively.

Leading Collaboratively

While educational institutions are facing the winds of change, their traditional hierarchical approach to leadership is proving to be less than effective in addressing change. Not only is higher education in need of a commitment to change, but there is a need for a new kind of leadership. Leadership is obviously central to transformational change. Furthermore, it is argued here that successful implementation of innovative approaches to teaching and learning is predicated on more effective collaboration. Collaborative leadership pulls together leaders at all levels of the institution. It means encouraging input and creating ownership through collaboratively developing a vision and plan as well as sharing responsibility for outcomes. Only through collaborative and systemic leadership can commitment be sustained.

We know the professed personal qualities of a leader—vision, integrity, openness and courage—but these individual qualities are no longer sufficient in times of rapid change. Leadership is not just about the exceptional characteristics of a leader as "more and more, people are beginning to view leadership as a way of working with others in a group rather than a set of personality traits that an individual needs to gain a position of authority" (Allen, 2004, p. 1). The charismatic leader who single-handedly transforms an organization is largely fictional. Perhaps the most important characteristic of today's leader is an authentic desire and ability to work collaboratively and constructively toward strategic goals. Effective leadership develops shared commitment and productive relationships in a culture of shared purpose and collaboration. In this way, leading collaboratively brings together groups to purposely explore ideas and test solutions in a climate of trust. Collaborative leadership mirrors a community of inquiry.

Much can be learned from the concepts associated with the Community of Inquiry (CoI) framework with regard to the dynamics of collaborative leadership. Collaborative leadership occurs in a community with the goal to create a sense of purpose and commitment in focusing on strategic change and finding solutions to pressing problems. This search for solutions is core to the process of inquiry. Inquiry provides the means for individuals to collaboratively contribute to addressing a problem and subsequently finding ownership in a solution to a problem. The objective here is to explore leadership through the lens of a community of inquiry and, specifically, the core elements of a community of inquiry.

It is the task of true leadership to create a sense of purpose and strategic cohesion through open communication and trust. These are the characteristics of social presence that have been shown to be essential to a community of inquiry. It is also the means for individuals to identify with change and create a safe environment to openly address challenges and share ideas. Only collaborative leadership that allows others to develop commitment and share responsibility will realize the concerted effort required to transform teaching and learning. As Weigel (2002) states, "Robust communities of inquiry that make education an exciting experience for both students and educators can hardly take root in organizational cultures marked by isolation, fear, territoriality, and power plays" (p. 127). Unfortunately, this is too often the case in many higher education institutions. Isolation and fear can only be overcome through open communication, cohesion and trusting relationships (i.e. social presence).

Collaboration to resolve a dilemma or problem is the means for organizational innovation.

> Developing a successful model for collaborative innovation—for innovating together—is thus the most sorely needed disruption in higher education .... The challenge for leaders in higher education, then, is to figure out how to incentivize collaborative behavior to drive innovation.
> (Burns, Crow & Becker, 2015, p. 12)

Inquiry is a collaborative process where new ideas can emerge and be tested. This is the workplace for collaborative leadership. Collaborative leadership is not about imposing a vision and dictating action plans. It is a new model where participants first come to understand the issues, clarify the facts, critically analyze solutions, develop a shared vision, and build consensus for action. However, agreement with regard to a vision and commitment to action is only the beginning. The inquiry process begins anew as participants address the task of creating a strategic action plan that is scalable and sustainable. This is where identifying with the goal and sustained support is essential. When it comes to change in teaching and learning, communication with the institutional community must be ongoing and expansive. In terms of a strategic action plan, there is a need to set strategic objectives, offer incentives, focus scarce resources, provide professional development and continue to promote the benefits of the initiative throughout the organization.

It is recognized that a community of inquiry must have strong leadership as reflected in the teaching presence construct. Teaching presence is leading collaboratively. It has been labeled teaching and not teacher presence because others also have the task to assume leadership responsibilities. All members of the community need to participate in the leadership function by facilitating and directing the process. It is explicitly recognized that there must be clear direction. This reflects the role of a strong leader—a leader who works collaboratively but recognizes his or her responsibility to take control when required to move the process forward, deal with emerging challenges, and ensure the goals are realized in an expeditious manner. The characteristics of teaching presence in a community of inquiry are those same features that shape collaborative leadership and that is so greatly needed if we are to address the need for transformative change in how we meaningfully engage students in an educational transaction.

Before concluding this section on leadership, it may be useful to remind ourselves of the challenge of significant change in institutions that have traditionally resisted change. It has famously been stated "that there is nothing more difficult to carry out, nor more doubtful of success, nor more dangerous to handle, than to initiate a new order of things" (Machiavelli, in Green, 1998, p. 396). This would surely be a fair comment about transforming teaching and learning in higher education. The point is that we need to recognize the challenges associated with the adoption of innovative approaches to learning and the courage required of our leaders to affect a "new order of things."

Significant change requires that participants come together and collaboratively assume the responsibilities of leadership. However, perhaps the greatest barrier to leading collaboratively is institutional bureaucracy. Unfortunately, too often bureaucracies reflect a diffusion of purpose, empire building and self-serving administration. While many modern organizations have flattened their organizational structures, higher education has expanded their administrative bureaucracy and layers (Ginsberg, 2011). This has resulted in greater emphasis on the "conspicuous activity" of the administrative bureaucracy with fewer resources directed to academic inquiry and the student experience (Garrison, 2016). This disconnect speaks directly to the need for strategic collaboration that goes beyond the rhetoric that senior administrators seem to be all too proficient. Unfortunately, the growth of administrative bureaucracy is disillusionment and withdrawal.

It is only realistic to expect that transformation associated with the adoption of online and blended learning needs to take an incremental approach. It would not be constructive to think that e-learning could somehow, overnight, magically transform teaching and learning in higher education. As important as collaborative leadership for change, it must also be sustainable. One of the realities in higher education is that leadership changes on a frequent basis. While it can be advantageous for new leaders to bring new ideas and energy to the process, too often it means shifting to new priorities with the loss of investment of time, resources and momentum, not to mention the risk of demoralizing faculty who committed to the previous process of change. Leaders must give innovation time before we can expect it to spread and become a contagion (Gladwell, 2002).

Faculty Development

From an online and blended learning perspective, we must be clear that innovation is a direct challenge to passive approaches to education and specifically the lecture. However, questioning the lecture is difficult for most professors when this is basically the only educational experience that they know. Moving away from the lecture is doubly troubling as it is also a move away from transmitting excessive amounts of content. Add on to this the reality of trying to cope with various new and emerging communication and information technologies essential for inquiry-based and engaged approaches to learning, e-learning may be an unacceptable confrontation for faculty. It is unrealistic to ask a professor to make these shifts in approach to teaching and learning while finding time to learn how to use new and emerging information and communication technologies. It is a nonstarter for most professors without sustained professional development support. On the other hand, faculty development initiatives are challenging the erosion of collegiality and community through collaborative approaches to leading and learning in course redesign initiatives.

The first step in providing constructive faculty development for online and blended learning design is to recognize that this is too complex to be successfully implemented without a coherent theoretical framework. In this regard, Pozzi and Persico (2013) categorically state, "Without theory, there is no solid grounding for learning designs and no generally applicable aspect to findings" (p. 11). To support faculty through the entire process of successfully designing, delivering and assessing e-learning experiences, there must be a commitment to a clear pedagogical approach and coherent framework that makes sustained faculty buy-in possible. This is where the CoI framework has been shown to be enormously useful in structuring work-shops and guiding faculty through the complexities of designing online and blended learning courses.

The effectiveness of the CoI framework to structure and guide faculty in redesigning their courses was demonstrated early in the development of blended learning approaches (Vaughan & Garrison, 2006). The idea was to create a community where faculty can be introduced to the key elements of a community of inquiry by experiencing the same trusting environment that they are tasked to create for their students. Through this process, a network of sustained faculty support is created. Instructional designers and technology support have to be there for them every step of the way. In this regard, it has also been noted that faculty learning communities "are less successful when there is a lack of dialog between meetings or when the facilitator does not provide adequate preparation for face-to-face meetings" (Wicks, Craft, Mason, Gritter & Bolding, 2015, p. 62).

A promising aspect of course and program design is the adoption of a team-based approach. When an institution or department is committed to a comprehensive course and program redesign, it makes imminent sense to take a team approach that can model a community of inquiry. Such teams are focused on a common design task as opposed to workshops supporting disparate disciplines and projects. That is, the team is focused on the design of a specific course or series of courses that will achieve the goal of engaging learners in communities of inquiry. Advantages include a greater openness to innovate and to consider new ideas to challenge students, engage them in critical discourse and design collaborate assignments. One example used a small team consisting of an instructor, instructional designer and administrator to redesign a large enrollment course using a blended approach (Freeman & Tremblay, 2013). The team consulted with all course instructors and its size provided the advantages of a team while expediting the progress of the redesign process. The initial design, however, was only the first phase. Implementation revealed a need to make adjustments that included specific instructor needs. The lesson here was the need to involve instructors "throughout the redesign process ... by encouraging a more integrated understanding of the course as it develops and provide instructors with the opportunity to reflect on their own teaching in light of the transition to online learning methods" (Freeman & Tremblay, 2013, p. 86).

To date, the CoI framework has been used to design and interpret research on a broad range of topics. The framework has been used to guide the implementation and assessment of collaborative constructivist approaches to teaching and learning (Swan, Day, Bogle & Matthews, 2014). In addition, case studies are emerging that use the CoI framework to guide faculty in the design of communities of inquiry at both the course and program levels. One successful initiative used professional development sessions to introduce faculty to the CoI framework as well as a curriculum design checklist based on the CoI framework (Jackson, Jackson & Chambers, 2013). Participants "were encouraged to discuss examples of where they might incorporate collaboration activities that would promote constructive meaning-making and trust between student participants in order to develop student collaboration and connectedness within the online environment" (Jackson et al., 2013, p.356). Moving beyond specific courses, the CoI framework has also been used to design programs of study that reflect engagement and collaboration (Kumar, Dawson, Black, Cavanaugh & Sessums, 2011).

Finally, going beyond pedagogical and technical support, faculty support must also be accompanied by incentives and scholarly recognition for those who take the risk and invest enormous amounts of time and energy in fundamentally redesigning their courses. This necessitates broader institutional support with regard to innovative teaching and learning approaches. Leadership and support must emanate from the senior levels of the institution (Garrison & Vaughan, 2008; Yamagata-Lynch et al., 2015). Focusing on institutional policy and adoption of blended learning, Graham, Woodfield and Harrison (2013) found that most innovations began at the faculty level but "barriers related to institutional policies, structures, and lack of support can prevent large-scale faculty adoption of BL [blended learning] and the accompanying institutional benefits" (p. 11). This is particularly true when innovation includes both new approaches and technologies. From the perspective of the use of technology to engage students, it has been found "that the greatest current impediment is probably undersupported faculty" (Brooks, Dahlstrom, Grajek & Reeves, 2015, p. 35). Faculty need sustained support understanding technology and how to use it effectively to improve the learning experience. It is not reasonable to expect faculty to become proficient with new and emerging learning technologies while learning to approach the educational experience in collaborative and transformational ways.

Organizationally, the core issues for innovation are strategy, structure and support. More specifically, qualitative interviews pointed to the importance of infrastructure, technical support and reducing teaching load (Porter, Graham, Bodily & Sandberg, 2016) for e-learning success. Successful e-learning requires investment in structural support, including institutional investment in teacher development and training (McGill et al., 2014). In particular, it is clear that e-teaching increases faculty workload considerably (Tynan, Ryan & Lamont-Mills, 2015) and this must be addressed for continuation of e-learning initiatives (McGill et al., 2014). The reasons for this are numerous but it comes down to the complexity and "sense of continuous engagement introduced by e-learning processes" (Martins & Nunes, 2016, p. 3). E-learning is extremely time-consuming in terms of both the design and implementation. As we have seen, e-learning responsibilities often extend over time and place and must be managed (see Chapter 9). This raises a very important consideration for the adoption of online and blended learning and faculty development. That is, providing release time for design and delivery as well as recognizing and rewarding faculty for the scholarly responsibilities associated with complex innovation. These challenges must be addressed to mitigate "longer and fragmented working days that make individuals constantly feel under time pressure" (Martins & Nunes, 2016, p. 12). In short, faculty support and incentives must recognize workload associated with e-learning.

Conclusion

To date, e-learning initiatives have a foothold in a broad range of educational institutions. The new challenge for many of these institutions will be to sustain these initiatives and ensure they move from incubation to mainstream. As important as teaching and learning factors are for the long-term success of the educational institution, factors such as financial and technology support will ultimately ensure the continuation of e-learning initiatives. This was the finding of a recent study of the factors that contributed to the continuation of e-learning initiatives (McGill et al., 2014). Somewhat surprisingly, the study also concluded "that it is not just the quality of the initiative that makes the difference" (p. 32) but the sustained support throughout the organization. That is, the relevance and superiority of the initiative by itself will not sustain an e-learning innovation. Sustainability is associated with ongoing institutional support felt at the local level that includes "gaining ongoing material support for the initiative and attracting others to become involved in the adoption and development" (McGill et al., 2014, 32). This means that senior leadership must be kept informed and onside.

A major factor in the inability to innovate and adopt new approaches to teaching and learning has to be visionary leadership and commitment. There is no excuse for indecision. The need and direction for change is apparent to those leaders who choose to see and comprehend. Leadership must get beyond rhetoric and address real change. The rhetoric is that the student is the most important stakeholder in higher education, but the reality often says something very different. The reality is that classes, or should we say lectures, has simply gotten larger with minimal accommodation to address engagement and communication with the professor. The time is now for collaborative leadership and a commitment to action with regard to collaboratively engaging learners.

In the coming together of the information era and knowledge society, institutions must be prepared to focus greater attention and resources on the strategic integration of online and blended learning. Institutions of higher education need to rediscover their roots and ideals. This will require constructing and communicating the vision and strategic plan often in the face of resistance. To be successful, leaders must understand the dynamics of change and be prepared to start small. This will require incubating e-learning as a disruptive technology while demonstrating how it can meet the challenges and demands of the future. From here e-learning innovation must be continually promoted and ongoing support attracted to the initiative.

Chapter 12

Future Directions

E-learning educators cannot afford to be seduced by the adoption of trivial social media masquerading as relevant and worthwhile educational experiences. Much of what we have experienced during the first decade of the 21st century is an infatuation with personal information and communication made possible by ubiquitous and inexpensive technologies. We have seen unimagined developments in interpersonal connections and the ability to express our opinions anytime and anywhere. However, the educational challenge is to understand how information and communication technologies can be used in the service of a worthwhile educational experience.

The reduced cost of storage and bandwidth were the significant technological advances at the beginning of this century. This provided instantaneous access to virtually unlimited information and the unprecedented sharing of personal information. However, these advances have largely been in the service of social communication and entertainment. While there were a select few who were using new communication technologies to reflect, share ideas and engage in discourse, most were not engaged in knowledge creation—they were largely consumers of selfies and titillating bits of information made possible by social networks. It was a period of turmoil as communication technologies were transforming society. As a result, the early part of this century has seen a period of confusion for educational institutions in terms of what to make of these technological developments.

From an educational perspective, the crucial insight is that society has come to accept the reality of being connected 24/7. Technology adoption no longer brings with it the resistance it once had. While many are frustrated by new technologies, we have come to accept their pervasive influence in society. This is certainly true in business and the home but its influence in the educational sector is only in its infancy. In the past, the problem was that educators focused too much on the technology and not enough on examining the quality of pedagogical practices in terms of deficiencies, limitations and learner dissatisfaction. The first task in this regard is an analysis of pressing educational needs and then an informed assessment of technological capabilities to achieve desired goals.

In the final analysis, e-learning is not about technology—it is about what we truly value as a worthwhile educational experience. As powerfully enabling as the new and emerging technologies are, it should always be about approaching the ideals of a deep and meaningful educational experience and developing practices that will develop the ability of individuals to adapt to a society based on creating and constructing knowledge. In this regard, in "today's world, higher-order thinking is not only a valuable skill, but necessary for understanding and solving complex, real world problems" (Johnson, Adams Becker, Estrada & Freeman, 2015, p. 28). As a result, educators are facing a significant transformational challenge and large undergraduate lectures are facing an existential crisis. Educators are recognizing the need to challenge the embedded information transmission model that has dominated education most of the 20th century.

A Quick Look Back

The first part of this century witnessed an intense exploration of e-learning. Consistent with an exploratory approach, the focus was on understanding the technology and its potential educational impact. This was a period of innovation and experimentation to understand how communications technology could be used to enhance educational environments through sustained connection. At the same time, e-learning was overhyped as new online learning enterprises proliferated. As a result, most of these new online learning operations did not survive and online learning had a limited influence on campus-based educational institutions. This was certainly true in the early part of the decade as we attempted to grasp the properties of information and communication technologies and their educational potential. As has inevitably occurred in the field of education, the technology got ahead of the pedagogy. As a result, we had to step back and reflect on these developments and consider the implications of the Internet and communications technology for the field of education.

A turning point in this exploration of e-learning in education was the idea of blended or hybrid educational designs. That is, the thoughtful integration of online and face-to-face approaches. The evidence of the potential of blended learning opened the eyes of many educators and the thought that we were not throwing out the many strengths of a face-to-face learning transaction provided the confidence to take e-learning to the next level (Garrison & Vaughan, 2008; Means, Toyama, Murphy, Bakia & Jones, 2009; Picciano, Dzuiban & Graham, 2014; Twigg, 2003). This did not mitigate, however, the challenges of integrating e-learning approaches in traditional educational institutions.

The result was that online and blended learning came of age during the early years of this century. E-learning evolved rapidly from experimentation with computer conferencing and the advent of the Internet. The publication of the Community of Inquiry (CoI) framework (Garrison, Anderson & Archer, 2000) marked the transition from a specific application of e-learning (computer conferencing) to the consideration of seemingly radical approaches that advocated sustained discourse and collaboration for educational purposes. E-learning in the 21st century marked a shift from an obsession with social presence in online learning environments to a comprehensive consideration of the dynamic interplay of social, cognitive and teaching presence in a collaborative constructivist educational environment. After nearly two decades of research using the CoI framework, we have seen a growing appreciation for the process of creating and sustaining collaborative thinking and learning in communities of inquiry.

The end of the first decade of this century was marked by the focus on the Web as a platform for thinking and learning collaboratively. While the Web opened the door for social networking, it also made possible the opportunity to create sustainable communities of inquiry. It is the realization of the educational possibilities associated with communities of learners that has been the catalyst for an exponential increase in e-learning research. The idea of creating and sustaining communities of inquiry for the purposes of thinking and learning collaboratively represents the conceptual transition to the second decade of e-learning in this century.

At the turn of the century, the predictions for fundamental change in higher education and even the demise of the university campus was prominent but did not materialize (Tapscott, 1996). This is an example of why it is so difficult to predict the impact of technological innovation. Katz (2010) reflects on the limits in predicting the future when he states that:

> the lens on the future has always been a cloudy one. We see through the glass darkly. Discovering later that we have understated the enormity of change wrought by existing or unimagined technologies while we have overstated the pace of change.
>
> (p. 44)

At best, we can extrapolate from the present in order to provide practical value in preparing for the future. The digital revolution did not reach into mainstream higher education at the turn of this century due largely to the excessive focus and infatuation with the technology. However, a more recent prediction is that the industrial model of pedagogy (visualize the large lecture hall) is becoming obsolete and the transformation of the university has become an imperative.

> Universities are losing their grip on higher learning as the Internet is, inexorably, becoming the dominant infrastructure for knowledge—both as a container and as a global platform for knowledge exchange

between people—and as a new generation of students requires a very different model of higher education.

(Tapscott & Williams, 2010, p. 16)

This statement better reflects the direction of e-learning in the near future than did the prediction of the demise of the university campus. We argue that attention must be focused on approaches to learning using technology and how faculty and students think and learn collaboratively. For example, beyond communication technologies, the Internet is a reservoir of information and an indirect form of teaching presence as it provides information in a timely manner and is in the control of the collaborators in a community of inquiry.

As a result of the openness of the information age classroom, higher education can no longer "survive on lectures alone" (Tapscott & Williams, 2010, p. 20). Unfortunately, educational institutions remain entrenched in a mass educational model of the industrial age. With the demands to educate more students and the facilities designed to deliver lectures to large numbers of students, there is an enormous structural and psychological constraint to adopt engaged and collaborative approaches to learning. The challenge is to critically analyze what are the organizational structures needed to provide collaborative constructive approaches to learning where participants can meet online or face-to-face depending on educational and sociological needs. The next and essential step is to convince others of the imperative nature to adopt collaborative approaches to thinking and learning.

The second decade of the 21st century is proving to be one where we are beginning to understand the enormous advantages of online and blended approaches to learning and concomitantly appreciate the potential of the Internet and communications technology to sustain collaborative thinking and learning. This decade is a time where the educational community is shifting to a vision for collaborative inquiry and blended approaches to learning. E-learning is being absorbed into the educational mainstream through blended learning by being seen as the means to realize sustainable learning communities. E-learning has become an essential aspect of academic life—both in the classroom and enhancing campus life more generally. Engagement online is contributing significantly to a new and richer academic and social life in educational institutions.

As we enter the age of technological adolescence in the field of education, educators are becoming more aware and responsible in applying technology with greater purpose. While technological advances will continue, providing educators with more (and less expensive) communication choices will see substantive educational improvements. This will certainly be the case educationally as we come to accept the need for change in how we design and deliver learning experiences that correspond to the needs of a connected knowledge society. Pressure has come to bear on the educational community to address concerns about quality and relevancy. The larger educational community (including students) will become increasingly restive as the need to turn away from passive information transmission models become apparent.

In the near future, we can see social media increasingly becoming the "university quad" where students can meet and create a sense of belonging and loyalty to the institution. This sense of community has been shown to be crucial for student satisfaction and persistence. This may well be the important contribution of social media. Social media may well become an essential element in creating an institutional environment that welcomes students, strengthens educational values, and grows relationships that support the academic goals of the students and the learning community. A connected campus life serves the academic and social aims for all members of the community. In general, e-learning will evolve into ever more sophisticated and powerful approaches to connecting learners that will enhance the educational experience cognitively and socially.

Future Research

The CoI framework has been the dominant theoretical perspective shaping online and blended learning research. For this reason, it is important to understand the CoI framework and how it can further e-learning research and practice. A good place to start is to reflect on a recent study that has provided a synthesis of CoI research and a roadmap for future research (Befus, 2016). The synthesis of CoI research associated with the seminal CoI article (Garrison et al., 2000) indicated "a continuous upward trend not only in citation counts, but in frequency of application of CoI-based concepts and protocols in a widening variety of contexts and populations" (Befus, 2016, p. 95). Citations have increased steadily and an increase in research validating the CoI theoretical framework was also revealed (Befus, 2016). Extrapolating from Befus' research, it would appear that the enduring use of the CoI framework can be attributed to interest in collaborative e-learning (i.e. community of inquiry approach), the methodological protocol to study e-learning environments, and the CoI questionnaire that has served as an important quantitative tool to analyze large populations and conduct experimental studies over a wide range of collaborative learning contexts and topics. The increasing interest in the CoI framework over a 15-year-period speaks to its enduring nature, theoretical relevance and methodology.

Perhaps the greatest testament to the popularity and usefulness of the CoI framework is that it has spawned so many important areas of research and questions associated with thinking and learning collaboratively—particularly in online and blended learning contexts. It has also helped reinvigorate research in traditional areas of study associated with critical thinking, regulation and metacognition among others. At the heart of this work is the goal of increasing our understanding of the composition and interaction of the three core presences in creating and sustaining a community of inquiry that will support deep and meaningful learning approaches and outcomes. While the CoI framework originally focused on online and blended learning approaches, it is a generic model and the core elements and principles are relevant to all educational environments and levels. Based on the results of CoI research, we identify achievements and areas for future research into thinking and learning collaboratively in the next sections.

The CoI Framework

Recently, there have been calls to add new presences to the CoI theoretical framework. For example, it has been suggested that there is a need to focus on self-regulation with the addition of a fourth presence—"learner" presence (Shea, Hayes, Smith, Vickers, Bidjerano, Picket, Gozza-Cohen, Wilde & Jian, 2012). It was argued that this proposed "enhancement" is without theoretical consideration of the CoI framework in terms of its basic premise of shared responsibilities and the need to consider the co-regulated environment of a community of inquiry (Garrison & Akyol, 2013). Apart from the fact that self-regulation and learner presence does not recognize the collaborative nature of the CoI framework, it also undermines the parsimony of a validated theoretical framework. Another example of a suggestion to add a fourth presence is the call for emotional presence (Cleveland-Innes & Campbell, 2012). The pervasive nature of emotional presence and its role in cognition does call for further reflection but the evidence does not reach the threshold for creating a distinct fourth presence (see Chapter 4).

Coming back to the suggestion to add "learner presence" as a fourth element of the CoI framework, it must also be noted that this is incongruent with the basic premise of the framework. Creating a learner presence (and by extension teacher presence) would fundamentally undermine the collaborative constructivist assumption and violate the unity principle central to Dewey's philosophy of an educational transaction (see Chapter 2), which speaks to the inseparability of private and public worlds. In a collaborative constructivist educational experience, teaching and learning can only be separated artificially—in reality they are one. A good example is metacognition. From the perspective of the CoI framework, we had to rethink individual metacognition if we were to retain the inseparability of the roles of teacher and learner in a collaborative learning environment. Metacognition was, therefore, reframed in terms of *shared* metacognition that unifies self- and co-regulation to monitor and manage a deep and meaningful collaborative learning experience (Garrison & Akyol, 2015a, 2015b).

The point is, as was briefly discussed in the third chapter, the focus of a community of inquiry must be on the collaborative dynamics of inquiry and how teaching and learning responsibilities shift among the participants as learning progresses. On the other hand, the mistake of focusing on individuals and discrete roles is to risk crystalizing these responsibilities as embodied in the teacher or learner. This undermines the distribution of teaching and learning responsibilities and the fusion of personal reflection and shared discourse. In reality, they simply cannot be separated which is the fundamental error of the lecture approach. Again, the logical conclusion of focusing on individual roles instead of the collaborative process and shared responsibilities is to risk creating a static and authoritarian structure where individuals have well-defined and largely immutable roles. To do so would be a very different framework that unfortunately does not shift us from the passive transmission approach to a collaborative educational experience.

While it is important to explore the dimensionality or structure of the presences (i.e. sub-elements, categories), we must be cognizant of the theoretical implications of expanding the number of core elements of the CoI framework. From a broader theoretical perspective, there is a fundamental principle of science, parsimony, which must not be dismissed. The principle of parsimony states that the simplest explanation or fewest entities postulated should prevail; at least until there is strong evidence and predictability to the contrary. That is, unless one explanation is clearly superior, the simplest explanation is preferred. It is the clear position here that the argument and evidence for new presences is not sufficient to move to a more complex explanation. Interpreting the interdependence (overlap) among four or five presences would be an exceedingly complex task and beyond the comprehension of most researchers let alone practitioners making sense of a community of inquiry. Notwithstanding the questionable rationale for increasing the number of presences in a community of inquiry, the current structure of three core elements is very likely the theoretical limit to making sense of the interdependence among the presences.

Recently my colleague Terry Anderson wrote a piece regarding the "search for the 'missing' element(s) in the COI" framework (sounds like a search for Big Foot). While in principle I am not opposed to such a search, to date there is little compelling evidence that we are missing an element. Instead, what may be missing is the integration of ideas and concepts such as shared metacognition that enriches the presences and community, but does not violate the premise and assumptions of the CoI framework. The challenge is to refine the existing presences and exploring the best conceptual fit for new ideas and processes that do not violate the fundamental principles of the framework. Unfortunately, the risk is eroding the importance of parsimony. Trying to make sense of all possible interactions of four elements immediately creates a level of complexity that is beyond intuitive comprehension. As a result, it would lose tremendous practical value and distort the core structure in a misguided attempt to be all inclusive.

At this point, we argue that the issues of regulation and emotion and related arguments for a fourth presence can be well accommodated in the current structure of the CoI framework. We argue that the simplest explanation and theory of online and blended approaches to learning that fits the preponderance of evidence is the three element CoI framework. The evidence would have to be sufficiently compelling to add a fourth presence and essentially create a new framework—keeping in mind that such a framework would have to demonstrate improved explanation and predictability along with greater simplicity. This would be an enormous challenge and likely to create more complicated theoretical explanations and predictability. The CoI framework has been a popular and successful catalyst and guide to a wide range of research into innovative educational approaches associated with thinking and learning collaboratively during the last two decades. It has proven to be invaluable in formulating relevant hypotheses and interpreting research findings. The conclusion at this point is that the basic structure of the CoI framework in terms of the three presences is sound. However, as with any other theoretical construct, it remains open to challenge, shown to be incorrect (disproven) and replaced.

Social Presence

Social presence has been the focus of research since the early adaptation of computer conferencing for learning purposes and has been shown to be an important mediating variable (Garrison, Cleveland-Innes & Fung, 2010; Shea & Bidjerano, 2009a). In particular, social presence is an important contextual variable that has considerable influence in establishing and sustaining a sense of community and is a predictor of persistence (Diaz, Swan, Ice & Kupczynski, 2010). That said, there is still work to be done to understand its importance in the dynamics of a community of inquiry and specifically its relationship to teaching and cognitive presence.

While there is evidence that the dimensionality of social presence is stable (Garrison, 2009b), there is a need to continue to explore and refine its dimensions. More specifically, there is a need to understand the focus and progressive nature of social presence. What are the differential effects or order of importance of each of the dimensions as a community of inquiry develops. For example, what should have precedence when creating a community of inquiry and establishing group cohesion—academic identity (course goals) or shared social identity (interpersonal relationships)? What is the social-emotional impact on learning and how does this evolve over time? There is an argument that academic or course identity may be more important at the beginning of a course (reason for attending), while social identity (sense of belonging) and emotion may help sustain a community of inquiry over time.

Cognitive Presence

An emerging challenge associated with cognitive presence is to explore the relationship between practical inquiry (phases of cognitive presence) and actual learning outcomes. While the CoI framework is first a process model, its goal is deep and meaningful learning outcomes. Beyond the strong theoretical arguments, there is a demonstrated link between inquiry and learning outcomes (Akyol & Garrison, 2010a; Yang, Quadir, Chen & Miao, 2016). Although the analysis and evidence suggest that the framework is congruent with achieving higher order learning outcomes (Akyol, Garrison & Ozden, 2009), this relationship needs to be explored further in a variety of learning environments. From another perspective, one of the most promising areas of cognitive presence research is that of shared metacognition and its relationship and role in learning outcomes in a community of inquiry. Successful inquiry learners must have a high degree of metacognitive awareness. In this regard, the inquiry process is greatly facilitated by metacognitive awareness of the inquiry cycle and outcome expectations. More specifically, shared metacognition research needs to be directed at understanding the interdependent roles of self- and co-regulation of the collaborative thinking and learning transaction. It is important to understand when and how self- and co-regulation emerge in a collaborative inquiry process.

A pressing area of research is to confirm the shared metacognition construct and the associated nascent instrument (Garrison & Akyol, 2015a, 2015b). To aide in the exploration of metacognition, the continued development of the shared metacognitive instrument is crucial. The development of a quantitative instrument to assess shared metacognition will open exciting and important areas to study the role of shared metacognition in terms of both process and outcome (see Appendix B). Such an instrument adds an efficient tool to rigorously explore the relationships metacognition has with monitoring the phases of inquiry (cognitive presence) as well as with teaching presence in terms of the development of management functions. There are many possibilities for studying shared metacognition when we consider disciplinary variations, educational levels, and the use of learning technologies. Considering the importance of shared metacognition in a truly collaborative community of inquiry needs to be identified as a key area for future research.

Teaching Presence

One consistent finding since the beginning of CoI research is the essential role that teaching presence plays in developing and sustaining a community of inquiry (Akyol & Garrison, 2008; Diaz et al., 2010; Garrison et al., 2010; Shea & Bidjerano, 2009a). It is the key to establishing and maintaining both social and cognitive presence and achieving worthwhile learning outcomes. For this reason, it is important to understand the role of each of the dimensions of teaching presence (design, facilitation and direction) and the complex dynamics of a community of inquiry.

An area of research that has raised an important question about teaching presence is associated with the dimensionality of the construct. While studies have validated a three-dimension teaching presence construct (Arbaugh & Hwang, 2006; Ke, 2010), other studies suggest teaching presence may be perceived by students as having two dimensions. Two different studies suggest conflation among the dimensions but with two different combinations among the three dimensions of teaching presence. In one study, students were not able to distinguish between facilitation and direct instruction (Shea et al., 2006), while in a second study there was a question whether students conflated design and direct instruction (Arbaugh, Cleveland-Innes Diaz, Garrison, Ice, Richardson, Shea & Swan, 2008). A similar issue with regard to the structure of teaching presence was raised in a third study that found bifurcated factor loadings of teaching presence categories (Diaz et al., 2010). While these findings can be explained in terms of the perspective of the student sample (see Chapter 6), we need to understand how different students in different contexts view teaching presence and why.

Another point with regard to the dimensionality of teaching presence is the structural and conceptual placement of assessment. It has been suggested that assessment should be an explicit component of teaching presence (Shea, Hayes & Vickers, 2010). While there is merit in explicitly including assessment as a component of teaching presence, theoretical and practical considerations suggest construct difficulties with this addition. Assessment has been identified as a distinct guiding principle because of its pervasive and crucial influence (Ramsden, 1988). The first challenge in creating assessment as a distinct category of teaching presence is that it is also an integral aspect of the other teaching presence categories. Design, facilitation and direct instruction are interdependent activities but they have conceptually distinguishable responsibilities. The same cannot be said of assessment. Assessment is integral to and dependent upon exercising each of the design, facilitation and direction responsibilities. There is a natural ebb and flow with the three teaching presence categories that is not paralleled by assessment. Assessment is pervasive and seldom fades to the background as naturally happens with the other teaching presence categories. Similarly, the second challenge is that assessment is integral to and sustained in the functions of social and cognitive presence. So the question is what might be gained or lost through the expeditious creation of an assessment category for teaching presence. It is argued here that assessment is better treated as a generalized discourse component that has a sustained influence across all presences.

Practically speaking, another worthwhile area of future research is to explore the dynamic balance between facilitation and direct instruction during a course of study. It is suggested here that too much direct instruction too early will discourage participation and learners from assuming increased responsibility for monitoring and managing the inquiry process. Moderating and shaping the direction of the discourse are important educational responsibilities that must be properly balanced to encourage shared metacognitive awareness and progression toward intended learning goals. Similarly, when should an instructor model critical discourse and metacognitive thinking and when is intervention necessary? While we understand the importance of ensuring a good balance between facilitation and direct instruction, contextual factors such as the discipline and student maturity will have a significant influence in practice.

Designing CoIs

An emerging area of study and practice is the use of the CoI theoretical framework to design and improve online and blended learning courses and programs. During the first decade, much research was focused on validating the structure and understanding of the CoI transactional dynamics. However, increased attention has now been directed to the use of the CoI framework in online and blended program and course design. A community of inquiry is a complex learning experience that is compounded when operating in e-learning environments. Designing a community of inquiry learning experience requires navigating a series of content and process decision points. To do this requires an understanding of the foundational assumptions that shape a collaborative learning experience, the dynamic relationships among the core elements/presences, and the principles and practical guidelines deduced from the CoI framework. Design decisions in collaborative learning environments can be exceedingly complex considering the range of disciplines, student levels and technology (all important but exogenous variables to the core social, cognitive and teaching presence dynamics of a community of inquiry).

A coherent framework is more than advantageous to assist faculty in designing flexible, collaborative approaches to teaching and learning in online and blended learning environments. One of the first initiatives to use the CoI for design purposes was conducted by Vaughan and Garrison (2006). Using the CoI framework as a development guide, they successfully created a blended environment for faculty development (Vaughan & Garrison, 2006). These workshops focused on designing blended approaches to teaching and learning that would engage participants in collaborative faculty development experiences. Faculty learned how to design blended learning environments by participating in blended learning workshops. More recently, the use of the CoI framework has been used to assess and enhance online learning experiences (Swan, Day, Bogle & Matthews, 2014). Specific to blended learning, it has been concluded that the "CoI provides a framework from which to educate faculty on issues relevant to teaching and facilitating blended courses, as well as providing a framework within which faculty can create blended courses" (Wicks, Craft, Mason, Gritter & Bolding, 2015, p. 53).

Using the CoI framework to design learning experiences is becoming more prevalent for those who wish to create collaborative constructivist learning experiences (Richardson, Arbaugh, Cleveland-Innes, Ice, Swan & Garrison, 2012). However, the complexity of designing an online or blended community of inquiry requires sharing more experience and conducting rigorous research before its full potential will be understood and realized. It is important that course and program designers understand and be consistent with the conceptual foundations of a community of inquiry. One example where greater design research is required is the study of faculty development in different disciplines (Wicks et al., 2015). Assessing the efficacy of design practices also need to be explored. Assessing the efficacy of designs is where the CoI survey instrument has shown promise (Richardson et al., 2012; Swan et al., 2014). It is important to empirically demonstrate the effectiveness and sustainability of a functional community of inquiry in terms of linking the process to intended learning outcomes.

K-12

The applicability of the community of inquiry approach for K-12 learners is grounded in the pioneering work of Matthew Lipman (2003). Using the community of inquiry approach to develop a wide range of thinking skills, Lipman (1985) has provided evidence for its effectiveness at the K-12 level and concludes that students exposed to this approach "are more reasonable and more thoughtful, and that their teachers are not merely better at teaching specific subjects, but also are more effective in developing general thinking skills" (p. 106). This suggests that the CoI framework could have significant benefit at the K-12 level.

Recent evidence of the community of inquiry's applicability and approach at the K-12 level was dramatically demonstrated in three studies designed to engage seventh grade students in structured discussions (Fair, Haas, Gardosik, Johnson, Price & Leipnik, 2015). Treatment had students work in pairs and then form a community of inquiry to present reasoned views, share agreement/disagreement, provide alternative viewpoints, and then encourage "the students to reflect on the discussion and how their thinking might have progressed" (Fair et al., 2015, p. 8). The one-hour-per-week treatment had a marked positive impact on the cognitive abilities of the students compared to the control group; however, the remarkable finding was the durability of the effects. Follow-up studies two and three years later showed the inquiry gains were maintained compared to the control groups.

Notwithstanding the applicability and potential to use a community of inquiry approach with secondary students, there currently exists a scarcity of K-12 research using the CoI framework. Befus (2016) in her synthesis of CoI research found eleven studies of K-12 populations that referenced the CoI framework but "with only two adopting CoI concepts on a research treatment level" (p. 103). On the other hand, Clark and Barbour (2015) have noted the emergence of blended learning in K-12 and estimated that 76 percent of schools in the USA offered at least one online or blended course. They also stated that there is "a tremendous need for research in the emerging field of K-12 distance, online and blended learning" (Clark & Barbour, 2015, p. 6). Considering this data, it would appear there is considerable potential for the CoI framework to shape online and blended learning in the K-12 environment.

Methodology

It is suggested that one of the reasons for the quick uptake and success of the CoI theoretical framework for research was the accompanying methodology (Garrison, Anderson & Archer, 2010). The methodology of the early studies focused on protocols to analyze transcripts of online communities of inquiry. Notwithstanding the issues around things such as unit of analysis and coding negotiation (Garrison, Cleveland-Innes, Koole & Kappelman, 2006), this methodology was instrumental in understanding the elements and dynamics of an online community of inquiry. The original qualitative transcript analysis phase could be described as the exploratory and descriptive phase of research into online communities of inquiry. There was, however, a need for a quantitative approach to expedite research and move toward a more rigorous study of the CoI framework and its validation as a comprehensive theoretical approach to online learning. This shift was marked by the development of the CoI survey and the initiation of large scale empirical studies that provided predictive analyses and increased explanatory power.

Significant progress has been achieved in developing a quantitative instrument that measures the presences of the CoI framework. As reviewed in the third chapter, studies across institutions have provided factor structure validation of the CoI framework and the CoI survey instrument (see Appendix A). The development of the CoI survey instrument addressed the need to mitigate the inherent limitations of transcript analysis in terms of time and reliability while offering increased methodological possibilities. The use of the CoI survey represented a significant enhancement and proliferation of CoI research through more efficient data analysis and by making possible large-scale studies across institutions, disciplines, demographic groups and technologies. In the interests of expanding this research, it has been suggested that disciplinary perspectives in particular hold considerable promise for further study in developing communities of inquiry (Richardson et al., 2012).

The CoI survey questionnaire could be a useful tool to study disciplinary differences. Arbaugh, Bangert and Cleveland-Innes (2010) have suggested that the CoI framework be used to study subject matter effects on student perceptions across the elements of a community of inquiry. One area of interest is using the CoI framework to explore direct instruction for "hard, pure disciplines" (Arbaugh et al., 2010, p. 43). We need to know whether cognitive presence effect is due to differences in discipline or subtler teaching presence effects such as design and leadership approaches (Garrison, et al., 2010). For example, disciplinary differences appeared to be due to teaching presence (Garrison & Cleveland-Innes, 2005). It would also be worthwhile to look at disciplines that approach their subject matter from an inductive or deductive perspective using the Practical Inquiry (PI) (cognitive presence) model. This would apply to the "soft social sciences" in making sense of ill-structured content and the applied, hard sciences in solving specific problems. Regardless, community of inquiry theory provides a coherent framework to explore disciplinary effects and opens up any number of research topics and hypotheses.

Another area of research using the CoI survey is blended learning. The CoI framework has been used to understand the properties of face-to-face and online learning approaches. The CoI survey could be an enormously valuable tool to study information and communication technologies across disciplines (Garrison & Vaughan, 2008). One broad question is when and with what subject matter is it advantageous to use direct (face-to-face) or mediated communication to create or sustain a community of inquiry? There are any number of practical questions associated with the design and delivery of blended approaches to teaching and learning. However, reliance should not be placed solely on quantitative measures. Qualitative measures may well provide insight and depth of understanding not possible with only quantitative instruments.

As noted previously, course design and the characteristics of the learning community do influence the respondents' ability to identify the specific components of teaching presence. Qualitative data may well be needed to get important insights into student perspectives associated with teaching presence (Diaz et al., 2010). Qualitative perspectives could also be useful to understand the role of social presence with regard to teaching and cognitive presence (Diaz et al., 2010). For example, why do students view social presence as largely a mediating variable (Garrison et al., 2010; Shea & Bidjerano, 2009a) and less important than the other presences (Diaz et al., 2010)? It is important to emphasize that we should not abandon qualitative approaches as we employ quantitative instruments such as the CoI survey in our quest to understand communities of inquiry. Qualitative approaches can provide insights and explanations not possible with objective instruments.

Therefore, there will always be a need for both quantitative and qualitative that can address breadth and depth of understanding that includes large and small sample sizes commensurate with the research question and hypotheses, theoretical and practical questions, and institutional contexts. We must also not lose sight of the need to continue to refine our research methodologies if we are to gain credibility. In this regard, an area of future research is refining the CoI survey items. For example, while the teaching presence construct remains strong, work may be needed to refine some of the items (Arbaugh et al., 2008; Diaz et al., 2010). An associated project is to construct a short version of the CoI survey that could be used for practical formative diagnostic purposes. Such an instrument could be of considerable value to practitioners to assess things such as group cohesion, inquiry progress and direction. Assessing the state of a community of inquiry over time through content analyses of the transcripts (data mining and learning analytics) for timely intervention is also a worthwhile long-term research project. As pragmatically valuable this would be, the difficulty of this challenge using content analytics cannot be underestimated (Joksimović, Gašević, Kovanović, Adesope & Hatala, 2014). The potential of automating content analysis of transcripts has been demonstrated in terms of classifying and predicting phases of cognitive presence (Kovanović, Joksimović, Waters, Gašević, Kitto, Hatala & Siemens, 2016). Finally, there is a need to document the literature and developments in CoI research that would address theoretical and practical interests. In this regard, meta-analyses of the research associated with the CoI framework would prove to be very useful to encourage and guide future research. Befus (2016) has provided direction in this area with her synthesis of research themes associated with the seminal CoI framework article (Garrison, 2000). However, there are many more CoI research articles and topics that did not fall within the purview of this particular study. Reviews of research and practice associated with the CoI framework will not only give us a good idea of what has been accomplished but provide direction for future research and potential pragmatic applications of the CoI framework.

In conclusion, there is little question about communities of inquiry as a promising area of research. The CoI survey instrument (see Appendix A) has provided the means and rigor to address "conceptual refinement of the relationships and interactions between/among the elements, both particularly and collectively" (Garrison & Arbaugh, 2007, p. 165). While much research is required to realize the full potential of the CoI theoretical framework to create and sustain online and blended learning environments, this does not take away from its current value and potential as an e-learning theoretical framework.

A Look Forward

The CoI framework represents an approach to thinking and learning that contrasts with the individual, passive model that was all too common to the educational enterprise in the 20th century. The collaborative constructivist approach of the CoI framework offers the possibility of moving beyond the transmission model and its emphasis on the assimilation of information to the deep and meaningful collaborative construction of knowledge that meets the needs of the evolving knowledge society. This 21st century transactional approach represents the process of practical inquiry where participants assume the responsibility of constructing personal meaning and shared understanding through critical reflection and discourse. Moreover, participants develop shared metacognitive awareness and ability that translate into successfully navigating a connected and rapidly changing society and knowledge based economy. The practicality of collaborative approaches to thinking and learning is growing as information and communication technologies evolve. This represents a move from competitive educational models to cooperative and shared approaches to learning and living. The interdependent nature of a community of inquiry mirrors the connective and collaborative developments for success in the evolving knowledge society.

A parallel to the CoI framework at the socio-economic level is the "collaborative commons" (Rifkin, 2014). Rifkin describes a new economic era where we are becoming more interdependent. He describes the collaborative commons as being "motivated by collaborative interests and driven by a deep desire to connect with others and share" (p. 22). From an educational perspective, knowledge is created collaboratively and "is treated as a publically shared good, available to all, mirroring the emerging definition of human behavior as deeply social and interactive in nature" (Rifkin, 2014, p. 135). The community of inquiry and collaborative commons replaces competition with collaboration in the educational and economic environments. While Rifkin describes the collaborative commons as the emerging model for economic organization, the educational parallel in the form of the community of inquiry is also in its ascendency. As a result of our connected world, the educational version of the collaborative commons is open to learners regardless of time and distance, connected to real communities (public commons), and ultimately is the practical means to successfully grow and live in a collaborative economy.

The educational significance is the potential of the technologically connected world to optimize its connective possibilities and the opportunities for unconstrained critical and creative discourse, that is, to think and learn collaboratively. The collaborative commons may ultimately create economic opportunities, but the complementary educational approach through the creation of sustainable communities of inquiry directed to the social good of creating deep and meaningful learning experiences provides the foundation for the collaborative economy, not to mention an open and democratic society. The CoI framework is the adaptation of the values of a collaborative commons to the evolving demands of a modern society. The Community of Inquiry approach is as disruptive to the vertically integrated educational structures as is the collaborative commons to the entrenched world-view of competitive economic institutions and markets.

The Community of Inquiry framework with an academic collaborative commons at its core has precipitated a rethinking of the educational experience that is consistent with a connected and dynamic knowledge society. At its essence, thinking and learning collaboratively is the same process of constructively sharing whether it is an economic or educational commons. The educational commons of a community of inquiry is the recognition that we all benefit from collaboration which has been recognized as the genesis of human evolution (Wilson, 2012). In the age of collaboration, competition only exists in the process of identifying new ideas and possible innovations through mutually beneficial, open discourse. The goal and benefit are to bring diverse and seemingly differing perspectives together to create new ideas and applications. Technological developments have rapidly shifted the economic and educational landscape and have been the catalyst in an era of creativity and innovation. As a result, it has been predicted that "in less than 15 years most academic institution[s] will have to change their learning strategy" (Editorial Board, 2015, p. 561).

Notwithstanding such predictions and the obvious signs of transformation, looking too far into the future is a mug's game. Prediction is grounded in unforeseeable or unpredictable forces. As a result, it has been noted that our accuracy of prediction only five years out is about ten percent (Ice, 2010). Mlodinow (2008) suggests that we should not necessarily abandon future scenarios but simply be more modest in considering the future.

> It is easy to concoct stories explaining the past or to become confident about dubious scenarios for the future. That there are traps in such endeavors doesn't mean we should not undertake them. ... We can learn to view both explanations and prophecies with skepticism.
>
> (p. 202)

What is less precarious and what we need to focus on is observing specific conditions and trends. Instead of trying to predict the future too far out, instead we must understand the underlying conditions. Brown (2015) argues that it is more practical to work with trajectories. He states:

> With a trajectory, we know where something is headed, but we cannot say ... where it will end. Working with trajectories is an admission that we cannot foresee the unanticipated factors and developments that might influence the trajectory, accelerating it or perhaps instead derailing it entirely. In this sense, working with trajectories is a more humble and realistic way of facing the future.
>
> (p. 17)

The trajectory is clear with regard to e-learning approaches. Thinking and learning collaboratively using information and communication technologies is the trajectory. How exactly and how quickly this will transform the educational sector is open to speculation but the trajectory is established. Societal exigencies make it very unlikely that this will be derailed. The challenge is to bring others onside through reasoned discoursed.

As we shift from a focus on the gee-whiz factor of technology and amusing but trivial applications, the resisters to educational change will come onside. Serious educators will recognize the potential of new and emerging communications technology and that education is about community and thinking and learning collaboratively. There is a growing consensus that a passive transmission of information is no longer relevant or acceptable. We are beginning to recognize that an educational commons based on new and emerging information and communications technology is the means to a more meaningful and worthwhile educational experience. For these reasons and based on research publications, the interest in the community of inquiry approach is growing exponentially (Befus, 2016).

The great contribution and potential of e-learning in higher education is the restoration of the educational commons as represented by the CoI framework. The significant contribution of online and blended approaches to learning is to integrate both the breadth of the Web and the depth of discourse into an accessible and collaborative educational experience. This is founded on a progression from our fixation on access to information, to the use of technology, to create communities of inquiry that support thinking and learning collaboratively. The emerging responsibility of educational institutions and educational leaders is to model and facilitate the development of learning communities that will restore the ideals of deep and meaningful learning experiences.

Conclusion

Interdependence and cooperation is the quintessential feature of human development and its prime mover in terms of evolution (Wilson, 2012). This places collaboration at the heart of most social human endeavors not the least of which is the educational enterprise. The educational impact of collaboration has moved to new levels with the emergence of modern information and communication networks. This has created an environment for the creation of learning communities that supports sustainable collaborative inquiry. At the heart of this environment is the dynamics of practical inquiry based on shared interests and leadership, an environment where creativity and innovation emerge through the connection and integration of diverse abilities and experiences. We cannot isolate creativity and innovation from a collaborative environment that nurtures such achievements.

Learning is cultivated in the complex dynamics of collaborative inquiry that support thinking and learning in critical and creative ways. Thinking and learning collaboratively is a necessity in the increasingly connected and complex knowledge society in which educators are tasked to develop the thinking and learning of students. However, collaboration is more than connecting students to information and each other. The benefits of collaboration come from identifying with the interests of a purposeful community of learners who are mutually committed to deep and meaningful approaches to thinking and learning. At the core is collaborative inquiry where open communication supports critical reflection and discourse. Collaborative inquiry is also essential to the development of shared metacognition that provides the means for continuous learning.

E-learning has gotten a foothold in higher education through the adoption of blended approaches to learning. E-learning in a blended context has come of age and is transforming higher education. Traditional higher education institutions are offering a range of e-learning choices using various forms of blended learning that capitalizes on integrating the individual strengths of face-to-face and online experiences. However, in the final analysis, techno-logical innovation can dazzle but does not directly reveal educationally worthwhile processes and outcomes. Higher education has reached the threshold of a new era driven by collaborative educational ideals and approaches. Educators are moving beyond the myth and hype of technology and are offering worthwhile and meaningful learning experiences uncon-strained by time and distance. What is needed now is to recognize the space-time shift that e-learning represents.

E-learning has the ability to eliminate boundaries and bring educational participants together in communities of inquiry. The nearly two decades of research associated with the multidimensional and dynamic elements of the CoI theoretical framework has shown a credible and transformational approach to thinking and learning that can meet the needs of a connected and evolving knowledge society. It is the intent of this book that it will serve as an inspiration and guide to advance thinking and learning collaboratively in purposeful communities of inquiry.

About the Author

D. Randy Garrison is Professor Emeritus at the University of Calgary. Dr. Garrison has published extensively on teaching and learning in adult, higher and distance education contexts. He has authored, co-authored or edited eleven books and well over 100 refereed articles/chapters. His recent books are *Blended Learning in Higher Education* (2008); *An Introduction to Distance Education: Understanding Teaching and Learning in a New Era* (2010); *Educational Communities of Inquiry: Theoretical Framework, Research and Practice* (2013); *Teaching in Blended Learning Environments: Creating and Sustaining Communities of Inquiry* (2013); and *Thinking Collaboratively: Learning in a Community of Inquiry* (2016).

Appendix A
Community of Inquiry Survey Instrument

Teaching Presence

Design and Organization

1 The instructor clearly communicated important course topics.
2 The instructor clearly communicated important course goals.
3 The instructor provided clear instructions on how to participate in course learning activities.
4 The instructor clearly communicated important due dates/time frames for learning activities.

Facilitation

1 The instructor was helpful in identifying areas of agreement and disagreement on course topics that helped me to learn.
2 The instructor was helpful in guiding the class towards understanding course topics in a way that helped me clarify my thinking.
3 The instructor helped to keep course participants engaged and participating in productive dialogue.
4 The instructor helped keep the course participants on task in a way that helped me to learn.
5 The instructor encouraged course participants to explore new concepts in this course.
6 Instructor actions reinforced the development of a sense of community among course participants.

Direct Instruction

1 The instructor helped to focus discussion on relevant issues in a way that helped me to learn.
2 The instructor provided feedback that helped me understand my strengths and weaknesses relative to the course's goals and objectives.
3 The instructor provided feedback in a timely fashion.

Social Presence

Affective expression

1   Getting to know other course participants gave me a sense of belonging in the course.
2   I was able to form distinct impressions of some course participants.
3   Online or Web-based communication is an excellent medium for social interaction.

Open communication

1   I felt comfortable conversing through the online medium.
2   I felt comfortable participating in the course discussions.
3   I felt comfortable interacting with other course participants.

Group cohesion

1   I felt comfortable disagreeing with other course participants while still maintaining a sense of trust.
2   I felt that my point of view was acknowledged by other course participants.
3   Online discussions help me to develop a sense of collaboration.

Cognitive Presence

Triggering event

1   Problems posed increased my interest in course issues.
2   Course activities piqued my curiosity.
3   I felt motivated to explore content related questions.

Exploration

1   I utilized a variety of information sources to explore problems posed in this course.
2   Brainstorming and finding relevant information helped me resolve content related questions.
3   Online discussions were valuable in helping me appreciate different perspectives.

Integration

1   Combining new information helped me answer questions raised in course activities.

2   Learning activities helped me construct explanations/solutions.
3   Reflection on course content and discussions helped me understand fundamental concepts in this class.

Resolution

1   I can describe ways to test and apply the knowledge created in this course.
2   I have developed solutions to course problems that can be applied in practice.
3   I can apply the knowledge created in this course to my work or other non-class related activities.

5-point Likert-type scale

1= strongly disagree, 2 = disagree, 3 = neutral, 4 = agree, 5 = strongly agree

References

Arbaugh, J. B., Cleveland-Innes, M., Diaz, S., Garrison, D. R., Ice, P., Richardson, J. Shea, P., & Swan, K. (2008). Developing a community of inquiry instrument: Testing a measure of the Community of Inquiry framework using a multi–institutional sample. *Internet and Higher Education*, 11, 133–136.

Appendix B
Shared Metacognition Questionnaire

When I am engaged in the learning process as an individual:
SELF-REGULATION

I am aware of my effort.
I am aware of my thinking.
I know my level of motivation.
I question my thoughts.
I make judgments about the difficulty of a problem.
I am aware of my existing knowledge.
I assess my understanding.
I change my strategy when I need to.
I am aware of my level of learning.
I search for new strategies when needed.
I apply strategies.
I assess how I approach the problem.
I assess my strategies.

When I am engaged in the learning process as a member of a group:
CO-REGULATION

I pay attention to the ideas of others.
I listen to the comments of others.
I consider the feedback of others.
I reflect upon the comments of others.
I observe the strategies of others.
I observe how others are doing.
I look for confirmation of my understanding from others.
I request information from others.
I respond to the contributions that others make.
I challenge the strategies of others.
I challenge the perspectives of others.
I help the learning of others.
I monitor the learning of others.

References

Garrison, D. R., & Akyol, Z. (2015a). Toward the development of a metacognition construct for the community of inquiry framework. (Developing a shared metacognition construct and instrument: Conceptualizing and assessing metacognition in a community of inquiry.) *Internet and Higher Education*, 24, 66–71.

Garrison, D. R., & Akyol, Z. (2015b). Corrigendum to 'Toward the development of a metacognition construct for communities of inquiry.' *Internet and Higher Education*, 26, 56.

References

Achenbach, J. (1999). The too-much-information age. *The Washington Post*, March 12, A23.

Akcaoglu, M., & Lee, E. (2016). Increasing social presence in online learning through small group discussions. *International Review of Research in Open and Distance Learning*, 17(3), 1–17.

Akyol, Z., & Garrison, D. R. (2008). The development of a community of inquiry over time in an online course: Understanding the progression and integration of social, cognitive and teaching presence. *Journal of Asynchronous Learning Networks*, 12(3), 3–22.

Akyol, Z., & Garrison, D. R. (2010a). Understanding cognitive presence in an online and blended community of inquiry: Assessing outcomes and processes for deep approaches to learning. *British Journal of Educational Technology*, 42(2), 233–250.

Akyol, Z., & Garrison, D. R. (2010b). Learning and satisfaction in online communities of inquiry. In S. Eom & J. B. Arbaugh (Eds.), *Student satisfaction and learning outcomes in e-learning: An introduction to empirical research* (pp. 23–35). Hershey, PA: IGI Global.

Akyol, Z., & Garrison, D. R. (2011a). Understanding cognitive presence in an online and blended community of inquiry: Assessing outcomes and processes for deep approaches to learning. *British Journal of Educational Technology*, 42(2), 233–250.

Akyol, Z., & Garrison, D. R. (2011b). Assessing metacognition in an online community of inquiry. *Internet & Higher Education*, 14(3), 183–190.

Akyol, Z., Arbaugh, J. B., Cleveland-Innes, M., Garrison, D. R., Ice, P., Richardson, J., & Swan, K. (2009). A response to the review of the community of inquiry framework. *Journal of Distance Education*, 23(2), 123–136.

Akyol, Z., Garrison, D. R., & Ozden, M. Y. (2009). Online and blended communities of inquiry: Exploring the developmental and perceptual differences. *International Review of Research in Open and Distance Learning*, 10(6), 65–83.

Akyol, Z., Ice, P., Garrison, D. R., & Mitchell, R. (2010). The relationship between course socio-epistemological orientations and student perceptions of community of inquiry. *The Internet and Higher Education*, 13(1–2), 66–68.

Alavi, S. M., & Taghizadeh, M. (2013). Cognitive presence in virtual learning community: An EFL case. *Journal of Distance Education*, 27(1). Retrieved December 4, 2014 from: www.ijede.ca/index.php/jde/article/view/818/1492.

Allen, I. E., Seaman, J., & Garrett, R. (2007). *Blending in: The extent and promise of blended education in the United States*. Newburyport, MA: Sloan Consortium.

Allen, K. (2004). An interview with Dr. Kathleen Allen on leading collaboratively. Retrieved May 24, 2016 from: http://www.kathleenallen.net/index.php/writings/lea dership-change/39-leading-collaborately-interview-with-kathleen-allen/file.

Amemado, D. J.-A. (2013). Pedagogical requirements in a university-context characterized by online and blended courses: Results from a study undertaken through fifteen Canadian universities (pp. 401–427). In Z. Akyol & D. R. Garrison (Eds.) (2013). *Educational communities of inquiry: Theoretical framework, research and practice*. Hershey, PA: IGI Global.

The American Heritage Dictionary of the English Language. (2000). Boston, MA: Houghton Mifflin.

An, H., Shin, S., & Lim, K. (2009). The effects of different instructor facilitation approaches on students' interactions during asynchronous online discussions. *Computers & Education*, 53, 749–760.

Anderson, T., Rourke, L., Garrison, D. R., & Archer, W. (2001). Assessing teacher presence in a computer conferencing context. *Journal of Asynchronous Learning Networks*, 5(2), 1–17.

Annisette, L. E., & Lafreniere, K. D. (in press). Social media, texting, and personality: A test of the shallowing hypothesis. *Personality and Individual Differences*. Retrieved March 3, 2016 from: http://dx.doi.org/10.1016/j.paid. 2016.02.043

Arbaugh, J. B. (2005). Is there an optimal design for on-line MBA courses? *Academy of Management Learning & Education*, 4(2), 135–149.

Arbaugh, J. B. (2008). Does the community of inquiry framework predict outcomes in online MBA courses? *International Review of Research in Open and Distance Learning*, 9, 1–21.

Arbaugh, J. B., & Benbunan-Fich, R. (2006). An investigation of epistemological and social dimensions of teaching in online learning environments. *Academy of Management Learning & Education*, 5(4), 435–447.

Arbaugh, J. B., & Hwang, A. (2006). Does "teaching presence" exist in online MBA courses? *The Internet and Higher Education*, 9(1), 9–21.

Arbaugh, J. B., Bangert, A., & Cleveland-Innes, M. (2010). Subject matter effects and the Community of Inquiry (CoI) framework: An exploratory study. *The Internet and Higher Education*, 13(1–2), 37–44.

Arbaugh, J. B., Cleveland-Innes, M., Diaz, S., Garrison, D. R., Ice, P., Richardson, J., Shea, P., & Swan, K. (2008). Developing a community of inquiry instrument: Testing a measure of the Community of Inquiry framework using a multi-institutional sample. *The Internet and Higher Education*, 11, 133–136.

Archer, W. (2010). Beyond online discussions: Extending the community of inquiry framework. *The Internet and Higher Education*, 1(1–2), 69.

Archer, W., Garrison, D. R., & Anderson, T. (1999). Adopting disruptive technologies in traditional universities: Continuing education as an incubator for innovation. *Canadian Journal of University Continuing Education*, 25(1), 13–30.

Archibald, D. (2010). Fostering the development of cognitive presence: Initial findings using the community of inquiry survey instrument. *The Internet and Higher Education*, 13(1–2): 73–74.

Are massive open online courses (MOOCs) enabling a new pedagogy? *Online Learning News*, May 20, 2015. Retrieved May 22, 2015 from: http://contactnorth.ca/trends-dir ections/are-massive-open-online-courses-moocs-enabling-new-pedagogy

Bai, H. (2009). Facilitating students' critical thinking in online discussion: An instructor's experience. *Journal of Interactive Online Learning*, 8(2), 156–164.

Baker, J. (2003). Instructor immediacy increases student enjoyment, perception of learning. *Online Classroom*, September.

Baker, J. D. (2004). An investigation of relationships among instructor immediacy and affective and cognitive learning in the online classroom. *The Internet and Higher Education*, 7(1), 1–13.

Bangert, A. (2008). The influence of social and teaching presence on the quality of online critical inquiry. *Journal of Computing in Higher Education*, 20(1), 34–61.

Bangert, A. W. (2009). Building a validity argument for the community of inquiry instrument. *The Internet and Higher Education*, 12, 104–111.

Befus, M. K. (2016). *A thematic synthesis of the community of inquiry framework: 2000 to 2014* (Doctoral Dissertation). Athabasca University, Athabasca, Alberta, Canada.

Benbunan-Fich, R., & Arbaugh, J. B. (2006). Separating the effects of knowledge construction and group collaboration in learning outcomes of web-based courses. *Information & Management*, 43(6), 778–793.

Bereiter, C. (1992). Referent-centred and problem-centred knowledge: Elements of an educational epistemology. *Interchange*, 23, 337–361.

Berge, Z. L. (1995). Facilitating computer conferencing: Recommendations from the field. *Educational Technology*, 15(1), 22–30.

Biggs, J .B. (1987). *Student approaches to learning and studying*. Melbourne, Australia: Australian Council for Educational Research.

Blanchette, J. (2001). Questions in the online learning environment. *Journal of Distance Education*, 16(2): 37–57.

Borokhovski, E., Bernard, R. M., Tamim, R. M., Schmid, R. F., & Sokolovskaya, A. (2016). Technology-supported student interaction in post-secondary education: A meta-analysis of designed versus contextual treatments. *Computers and Education*, 96, 15–28.

Borup, J., Graham, C. R., & Drysdale, J. S. (2014). The nature of teacher engagement at an online high school. *British Journal of Educational Technology*, 45(5), 793–806.

Boston, W., Diaz, S. R., Gibson, A., Ice, P., Richardson, J., & Swan, K. (2009). An exploration of the relationship between indicators of the community of inquiry framework and retention in online programs. *Journal of Asynchronous Learning Networks*, 13(3), 67–83.

Bozkurt, A., Akgun-Ozbek, E., Yilmazel, S., Erdogdu, E., Ucar, H., Guler, E., Sezgin, S., Karadeniz, A., Sen-Ersoy, N., Goksel-Canbek, N., Dincer, G. D., Ari, S., & Aydin, C. H. (2015). Trends in distance education research: A content analysis of journals 2009–2013. *International Review of Research in Open and Distance Learning*, 16(1), 330–363.

Brook, C., & Oliver, R. (2007). Exploring the influence of instructor actions on community development in online settings. In N. Lambropoulos & P. Zaphiris (Eds.), *User-centered design of online learning communities*. Hersey: Idea Group.

Brooks, D. C., Dahlstrom, E., Grajek, S., & Reeves, J. (2015). *ECAR study of students and information technology, 2015*. Research report. Louisville, CO: ECAR, December. Retrieved December 10, 2015 from: http://net.educause.edu/ir/library/pdf/ss15/ers1510ss.pdf

Brown, A. (1987). Metacognition, executive control, self-regulation and other more mysterious mechanisms. In F. E. Weinert, & R. H. Kluwer (Eds.), *Metacognition, motivation, and understanding* (pp. 65–116). Hillsdale, NJ: Lawrence Erlbaum Associates.

Brown, J. S., & Adler, R. P. (2008). Minds on fire: Open education, the long tail, and learning 2.0. *EDUCAUSE Review*, 43(1), 16–32.

Brown, M. (2015). Six trajectories for digital technology in higher education. *EDUCAUSE Review*, 50(4), 16–28.

Brown, M., Dehoney, J., & Millichap, N. (2015). The next generation digital learning environment: A report on research. *EDUCAUSE Learning Initiative Paper.*

Brown, M. B., & Diaz, V. (2010). Mobile learning: Context and prospects. A report on the ELI focus session. *EDUCAUSE Learning Initiative Paper.*

Brown, R. E. (2001). The process of community-building in distance learning classes. *Journal of Asynchronous Learning Networks*, 5(2), 18–35.

Brown, T. H., & Mbati, L. S. (2015). Mobile learning: Moving past the myths and embracing the opportunities. *International Review of Research in Open and Distributed Learning*, 16(2), 115–135.

Buraphadeja, V., & Dawson, K. (2008). Content analysis in computer-mediated communication: Analyzing models for assessing critical thinking through the lens of social constructivism. *American Journal of Distance Education*, 22(3), 130–145.

Burbules, N. (1993). *Dialogue in teaching: Theory and practice.* New York: Teachers College Press.

Burns, B., Crow, M., & Becker, M. (2015). Innovating together: Collaboration as a driving force to improve student success. *EDUCAUSE Review*, 50(2), 10–20.

Caspi, A., & Blau, I. (2008). Social presence in online discussion groups: Testing three conceptions and their relations to perceived learning. *Social Psychology of Education*, 11(3), 323–346.

Cecez-Kecmanovic, D., & Webb, C. (2000). Towards a communicative model of collaborative web-mediated learning. *Australian Journal of Educational Technology*, 16(1), 73–85.

Cho, M.-H., & Tobias, S. (2016). Should instructors require discussion in online courses? Effects of online discussion on community of inquiry, learner time, satisfaction, and achievement. *International Review of Research in Open and Distributed Learning*, 17(2), 123–140.

Choi, I., Land, S. M., & Turgeon, A. J. (2005). Scaffolding peer-questioning strategies to facilitate metacognition during online small group discussion. *Instructional Science*, 33(5–6), 483–511.

Christensen, C. (1997). *The Innovator's dilemma: When new technologies cause great firms to fail.* Boston: Harvard Business School Press.

Clark, R. E. (1983). Reconsidering research on learning from media. *Review of Educational Research*, 53, 445–459.

Clark, T., & Barbour, M. K. (2015). Online, blended, and distance education in schools. An introduction. In T. Clark & M. K. Barbour (Eds.), *Online, blended, and distance education in schools* (pp. 3–10). Virginia: Stylus Publishing.

Clarke, L. W., & Bartholomew, A. (2014). Digging beneath the surface: Analyzing the complexity of instructors' participation in asynchronous discussion. *Journal of Asynchronous Learning Networks*, 18(3). Retrieved from: http://olj.onlinelearning consortium.org/index.php/jaln/article/view/414/111

Cleveland-Innes, M., & Garrison, D. R. (Eds.) (2010). *An introduction to distance education: Understanding teaching and learning in a new era.* London: Routledge.

Cleveland-Innes, M., & Campbell, P. (2012). Emotional presence, learning, and the online learning environment. *International Review of Research in Open and Distance Learning,* 13(4), 269–292.

Cleveland-Innes, M., Garrison, D. R., & Kinsell, E. (2007). Role adjustment for learners in an online community of inquiry: Identifying the challenges of incoming online learners. *International Journal of Web-Based Learning and Teaching Technologies,* 2(1), 1–16.

Conrad, D. (2005). Building and maintaining community in cohort-based online learning. *Journal of Distance Education,* 20(1), 1–20.

Cotton, D., & Yorke, J. (2006). Analyzing online discussions: What are the students learning? In *Proceedings of the 23rd Annual Conference of the Australasian Society for Computers in Learning in Tertiary Education: "Who's learning? Whose technology?"* December, 2006, Sydney, Australia.

Dahlstrom, E., & Bichsel, J. (2014). ECAR study of undergraduate students and information technology, 2014. *EDUCAUSE Center for Analysis and Research* (ECAR). Retrieved November 8, 2015 from: http://net.educause.edu/ir/library/pdf/ss14/ERS1406.pdf

Dahlstrom, E., Walker, J. D., & Dzuiban, C. (2013). *ECAR study of undergraduate students and information technology* (Research Report). Louisville, CO: EDUCAUSE Center for Analysis and Research, September. Retrieved from: http://net.educause.edu/ir/library/pdf/ERS1302/ERS1302.pdf

Daniels, L. M., & Stupnisky, R. H. (2012). Not that different in theory: Discussing the control-value theory of emotions in online learning environments. *The Internet and Higher Education,* 15(3), 222–226.

Darabi, A., Arrastia, M. C., Nelson, D. W., Cornille, T., & Liang, X. (2011). Cognitive presence in asynchronous online learning: A comparison of four discussion strategies. *Journal of Computer Assisted Learning,* 27(3), 216–227.

Daspit, J. J., & D'Souza, D. E. (2012). Using the community of inquiry framework to introduce Wiki environments in blended-learning pedagogies: Evidence from a business capstone course. *Academy of Management Learning and Education,* 11 (4), 666–683.

Davie, L. (1989). Facilitation techniques for the online tutor. In R. Mason & A. Kaye (Eds.), *MindWeave* (pp. 74–85). Oxford: Pergamon Press.

de Leng, B. A., Dolmans, D. H. J. M., Jobsis, R., Muijtjens, A. M. M., & van der Vleuten, C. P. M. (2009). Exploration of an e-learning model to foster critical thinking on basic science concepts during work placements. *Computers & Education,* 53(1), 1–13.

Dewey, J. (1916). *Democracy and education.* New York: Macmillan.

Dewey, J. (1933). *How we think* (rev. ed.). Boston: D.C. Heath.

Dewey, J. (1938). *Experience and education.* New York: Collier Macmillan.

Dewey, J. (1967). Psychology. In J. A. Boydston (Ed.), *John Dewey: The early works, 1882–1898 Vol. 2* (pp. 204–213). Carbondale: Southern Illinois University Press. (Original work published 1887)

Dewey, J., & Childs, J. L. (1981). The underlying philosophy of education. In J. A. Boydston (Ed.), *John Dewey: The later works, 1925–1953, Vol. 8* (pp. 77–103). Carbondale: Southern Illinois University Press. (Original work published 1933)

Diaz, S. B., Swan, K., Ice, P., & Kupczynski, L. (2010). Student ratings of the importance of survey items, multiplicative factor analysis, and the validity of the community of inquiry survey. *The Internet and Higher Education*, 13(1–2), 22–30.

Dron, J., & Anderson, T. (in press). The distant crowd: Transactional distance and new social media literacies. *International Journal of Learning and Media*, 4(3–4).

Dubin, R. (1978). *Theory Building* (2nd ed.). New York: Free Press.

Duderstadt, J. J., Atkins, D. E., & Van Houweling, D. (2002). *Higher education in the digital age: Technology issues and strategies for American colleges and universities.* Westport, CT: Greenwood Press.

Dziuban, C., Hartman, J., Moskal, P., Sorg, S., & Truman, B. (2004). Three ALN modalities: An institutional perspective. In J. Bourne & J. C. Moore (Eds.), *Elements of quality online education: Into the mainstream* (pp. 127–148). Needham, MA: Sloan-C.

Dziuban, C. D., Hartman, J. L., & Mehaffy, G. L. (2014). Blending it all together. In A. G. Picciano, C. D. Dziuban & C. R. Graham (Eds.), *Blended learning research perspectives: Volume 2* (pp. 325–337). New York: Routledge.

Editorial. (2015). Promoting and researching adaptive regulation: New frontiers for CSCL research. *Computers in Human Behavior*, 52, 559–561.

Editorial Board. (2015). An emerging—Social and emerging computing enabled philosophical paradigm for collaborative learning systems: Toward high effective next generation learning systems for the knowledge society. *Computers in Human Behavior*, 51, 557–561.

ELI. (2010). 7 things you should know about mobile apps for learning. Retrieved May 14, 2010 from: www.educause.edu/Resources/7ThingsYouShouldKnowAboutMobil/204763

Entwistle, N. J., & Ramsden, P. (1983). *Understanding student learning*. London: Croom Helm.

Ertmer, P. A., & Koehler, A. A. (2015). Facilitated versus non-facilitated online case discussions: Comparing differences in problem space coverage. *Journal of Computing in Higher Education*, 27(2), 69–93.

Fabro, K. R., & Garrison, D. R. (1998). Computer conferencing and higher-order learning. *Indian Journal of Open Learning*, 7(1), 41–54.

Fair, F., Haas, L. E., Gardosik, C., Johnson, D., Price, D., & Leipnik, O. (2015). Socrates in the schools: Gains at three-year follow-up. *Journal of Philosophy in Schools*, 2(2), 5–17.

Feenberg, A. (1999). *Questioning technology*. London: Routledge.

Freeman, W., & Tremblay, T. (2013). Design considerations for supporting the reluctant adoption of blended learning. *Journal of Online Learning and Teaching*, 9(1), 80–88.

Flavell, J. H. (1979). Metacognition and cognitive monitoring: A new area of cognitive-developmental inquiry. *American Psychologist*, 34, 906–911.

Flavell, J. H. (1987). Speculations about the nature and development of metacognition. In F. Weinert and R. Kluwe (Eds.), *Metacognition, motivation and understanding* (pp. 21–29). Hillsdale, NJ: Erlbaum.

Gallego-Arrufat, M.-J., Gutiérrez-Santiustea, E., & Campaña-Jiménez, R.-L. (2015). Online distributed leadership: A content analysis of interaction and teacher reflections on computer-supported learning. *Technology, Pedagogy and Education*, 24(1), 81–99.

Garrison, D. R. (1987). Researching dropout in distance education: Some directional and methodological considerations. *Distance Education*, 8(1), 95–101.

Garrison, D. R. (1997). Computer conferencing: The post-industrial age of distance education. *Open Learning*, 12(2), 3–11.

Garrison, D. R. (2000). Theoretical challenges for distance education in the 21st Century: A shift from structural to transactional issues. *International Review of Research in Open and Distance Learning*, 1(1), 1–17.

Garrison, D. R. (2009a). Implications of online learning for the conceptual development and practice of distance education. *Journal of Distance Education*, 23(2), 93–104.

Garrison, D. R. (2009b). Communities of inquiry in online learning. In P. Rogers, G. Berg, J. Boettcher, C. Howard, L. Justice & K. Schenk et al. (Eds.), *Encyclopedia of distance learning* (2nd ed.) (pp. 352–355). Hershey, PA: IGI Global.

Garrison, D. R. (2013). Theoretical foundations and epistemological insights. In Z. Akyol & D. R. Garrison (Eds.), *Educational communities of inquiry: Theoretical framework, research and practice* (pp. 1–11). Hershey, PA: IGI Global.

Garrison, D. R. (2016). *Thinking collaboratively: Learning in a community of inquiry*. London: Routledge/Taylor and Francis.

Garrison, D. R., & Akyol, Z. (2013). Toward the development of a metacognition construct for the community of inquiry framework. *The Internet and Higher Education*, 17, 84–89.

Garrison, D. R., & Akyol, Z. (2015a). Toward the development of a metacognition construct for the community of inquiry framework. *Internet and Higher Education*, 24, 66–71.

Garrison, D. R., & Akyol, Z. (2015b). Corrigendum to 'Toward the development of a metacognition construct for communities of inquiry.' *The Internet and Higher Education*, 26, 56.

Garrison, D. R., & Arbaugh, J. B. (2007). Researching the community of inquiry framework: Review, issues, and future directions. *The Internet and Higher Education*, 10(3), 157–172.

Garrison, D. R., & Archer, W. (2000). *A transactional perspective on teaching and learning: A framework for adult and higher education*. Oxford, UK: Pergamon.

Garrison, D. R., & Cleveland-Innes, M. (2005). Facilitating cognitive presence in online learning: Interaction is not enough. *American Journal of Distance Education*, 19(3), 133–148.

Garrison, D. R., & Cleveland-Innes, M. F. (2010). Foundations of distance education. In M. F. Cleveland-Innes & D. R. Garrison (Eds.), *An introduction to distance education: Understanding teaching and learning in a new era* (pp. 13–25). London: Routledge.

Garrison, D. R., & Vaughan, N. (2008). *Blended learning in higher education*. San Francisco: Jossey-Bass.

Garrison, D. R., Anderson, T., & Archer, W. (2000). Critical inquiry in a text-based environment: Computer conferencing in higher education. *The Internet and Higher Education*, 2(2/3), 87–105.

Garrison, D. R., Anderson, T., & Archer, W. (2001). Critical thinking, cognitive presence and computer conferencing in distance education. *American Journal of Distance Education*, 15(1), 7–23.

Garrison, D. R., Anderson, T., & Archer, W. (2010). The first decade of the community of inquiry framework: A retrospective. *The Internet and Higher Education*, 13(1–2), 5–9.

Garrison, D. R., Cleveland-Innes, M. & Fung, T. S. (2010). Exploring causal relations among teaching, cognitive and social presence: A holistic view of the community of inquiry framework. *The Internet and Higher Education*, 13(1–2), 31–36.

Garrison, D. R., Cleveland-Innes, M., Koole, M., & Kappelman, J. (2006). Revisiting methodological issues in the analysis of transcripts: Negotiated coding and reliability. *The The Internet and Higher Education*, 9(1), 1–8.

Garrison, J. (1997). *Dewey and eros: Wisdom and desire in the art of teaching*. New York: Teachers College Press.

Gašević, D., Adesope, O., Joksimović, S., & Kovanović, V. (2015). Externally-facilitated regulation scaffolding and role assignment to develop cognitive presence in asynchronous online discussions. *The Internet and Higher Education*, 24, 53–65.

Ginsberg, B. (2011). *The fall of the faculty: The rise of the all-administrative university and why it matters*. Oxford: Oxford University Press.

Gladwell, M. (2002). *The tipping point: How little things can make a big difference*. New York: Little, Brown and Company.

Gorsky, P., Caspi, A., Antonovsky, A., Blau, I., & Mansur, A. (2010). The relationship between academic discipline and dialogic behaviour in open university course forums. *International Review of Research in Open and Distance Learning*, 11(2), 49–72.

Graham, C. R., Woodfield, W., & Harrison, J. B. (2013). A framework for institutional adoption and implementation of blended learning in higher education. *The Internet and Higher Education*, 18, 4–14.

Green, R. (1998). *The forty-eight laws of power*. New York: Viking Press.

Gunawardena, C. N. (1991). Collaborative learning and group dynamics in computer-mediated communication networks. *Research Monograph of the American Center for the Study of Distance Education*, 9, (pp. 14–24). University Park, Pennsylvania: The Pennsylvania State University.

Gunawardena, C. N. (1995). *Social presence theory and implications for interaction and collaborative learning in computer conferencing*. Paper presented at the Fourth International Conference on Computer Assisted Instruction, Hsinchu, Taiwan.

Gunawardena, C. N., & Zittle, F. J. (1997). Social presence as a predictor of satisfaction within a computer–mediated conferencing environment. *American Journal of Distance Education*, 11(3), 8–26.

Guri-Rosenblit, S. (2009). *Digital technologies in higher education: Sweeping expectations and actual effects*. New York: Nova Science Publishers.

Gutiérrez-Santiuste, E., & Gallego-Arrufat, M.-J. (in press). Type and degree of co-occurrence of the educational communication in a community of inquiry. *Interactive Learning Environments*. Retrieved January 7, 2016 from: www.tandfonline.com/doi/pdf/10.1080/10494820.2015.1114498.

Gutiérrez-Santiuste, E., Sabiote-Rodríguez, C., & Gallego-Arrufat, M.-J. (unpublished). Cognitive presence through social and teaching presence in communities of inquiry: A correlational-predictive study. Retrieved December 7, 2015 from: www.researchgate.net/publication/285593366_cognitive_presence_preprint.

Hadwin, A. F., & Oshige, M. (2011). Self-regulation, coregulation, and socially shared regulation: Exploring perspectives of social and self-regulated learning theory. *Teachers College Record*, 113(6), 240–264.

Halverson, L. R., Graham, C. R., Spring, K. J., & Drysdale, J. S., & Jeffery, S. (2012). An analysis of high impact scholarship and publication trends in blended learning. *Distance Education*, 33(3), 381–413.

Hampton, K., Rainie, L., Lu, W., Dwyer, M., Shin, I., & Purcell, K. (2014). *Social media and the 'spiral of silence.'* Retrieved September 8, 2015 from: www.pewin ternet.org/2014/08/26/social-media-and-the-spiral-of-silence/.

Harasim, L. (1987). Teaching and learning on-line: Issues in computer-mediated graduate courses. *Canadian Journal of Educational Communication*, 16, 117–135.

Harasim, L. M. (1989). On-line education: A new domain. In R. Mason & A. R. Kaye (Eds.), *Mindweave: Communication, computers, and distance education.* New York: Pergamon. pp. 50–62.

Hiltz, S. R., & Turoff, M. (1993). *The network nation: Human communication via computer.* Cambridge, MA: MIT Press.

Horzum, M. B., & Uyanik, G. K. (2015). An item response theory analysis of the Community of Inquiry scale. *International Review of Research in Open and Distance Learning*, 16(2), 206–225.

Huntsinger, J. R., & Ray, C. (2015). Emotion and decision making. In S. M. Kosslyn & R. A. Scott (Eds.), *Emerging trends in the social and behavioral sciences: An interdisciplinary, searchable, and linkable resource.* New York: Wiley.

Ice, P. (2009). Assessing the integration of new technologies in online courses with the Community of Inquiry framework survey. In *Society for Information Technology & Teacher Education International Conference (1902–1904).*

Ice, P. (2010). The future of learning technologies: Transformational developments. In M. F. Cleveland-Innes & D. R. Garrison (Eds.), *Teaching and learning in distance education: Enter a new era* (pp. 137–164). London: Routledge.

Ice, P., Curtis, R., Phillips, P., & Wells, J. (2007). Using asynchronous audio feedback to enhance teaching presence and students' sense of community. *Journal of Asynchronous Learning Networks*, 11(2), 3–25.

Ice, P., Gibson, A. M., Boston, W., & Becher, D. (2011). An exploration of differences between community of inquiry indicators in low and high disenrollment online courses. *Journal of Asynchronous Learning Networks*, 15(2), 44–69.

Iiskala, T., Vauras, M., Lehtinen, E., & Salonen, P. (2011). Socially shared metacognition of dyads of pupils in collaborative mathematical problem-solving processes. *Learning and Instruction*, 21, 379–393.

Ikenberry, S. O. (1999). The university and the information age. In W. Z. Hirsch & L. E. Weber (Eds.), *Challenges facing higher education at the millennium.* Phoenix, Arizona: Oryx Press.

Israel, M. J. (2015). Effectiveness of integrating MOOCs in traditional classrooms for undergraduate students. *International Review of Research in Open and Distributed Learning*, 16(5), 102–118.

Jackson, L. C., Jackson, A. C., & Chambers, D. (2013). Establishing an online community of inquiry at the Distance Education Centre, Victoria. *Distance Education*, 34(3), 353–367.

Jahng, N., Nielsen, W. S., & Chan, E. K. H. (2010). Collaborative learning in an online course: A comparison of communication patterns in small and whole group activities. *Journal of Distance Education*, 24(2), 39–58.

Janssen, J., Erkens, G., & Kirschner, P. A. (2012). Task-related and social regulation during online collaborative learning. *Metacognition Learning*, 7(1), 25–43.

Jiang, M., & Ting, E. (2000). A study of factors influencing students' perceived learning in a web-based course environment. *International Journal of Educational Telecommunications*, 6(4), 317–338.

Johansson, P., & Gardenfors, P. (2005). *Cognition, education, and communication technology*. Mahwah, NJ: Lawrence Erlbaum Associates.

Johnson, D. W., & Johnson, R. T. (2009). An educational psychology success story: Social interdependence theory and cooperative learning. *Educational Researcher*, 38(5), 365–379.

Johnson, L., Adams Becker, S., Estrada, V., & Freeman, A. (2015). *NMC Horizon Report: 2015 Higher Education Edition*. Austin, Texas: The New Media Consortium. Retrieved December 12, 2015 from: https://net.educause.edu/ir/library/pdf/HR2015.pdf

Joksimović, S., Gaševic, D., Kovanović, V., Adesope, O., & Hatala, M. (2014). Psychological characteristics in cognitive presence of communities of inquiry: A linguistic analysis of online discussions. *The Internet and Higher Education*, 22, 1–10.

Joksimović, S., Gaševic, D., Kovanović, V., Riecke, B. E., & Hatala, M. (2015). Social presence in online discussions as a process predictor of academic performance. *Journal of Computer Assisted Learning*, 31(6), 638–654.

Joo, Y. J., Lim, K. Y., & Kim, E. K. (2011). Online university students' satisfaction and persistence: Examining perceived level of presence, usefulness and ease of use as predictors in a structural model. *Computers and Education*, 57(2), 1654–1664.

Jordan, K. (2015). Massive open online course completion rates revisited: Assessment, length and attrition. *International Review of Research in Open and Distributed Learning*, 16(3), 341–358.

Kang, K. M., & Kim, M. J. (2006). Investigation of the relationship among perceived social presence, achievement, satisfaction and learning persistence in the blended learning environment. *Journal of Educational Technology*, 22(4), 1–27.

Katz, R. N. (2010). Scholars, scholarship, and the scholarly enterprise in the digital age. *EDUCAUSE Review*, 45(2), 44–56.

Kaye, T. (1987). Introducing computer-mediated communication into a distance education system. *Canadian Journal of Educational Communication*, 16, 153–166.

Ke, F. (2010). Examining online teaching, cognitive, and social presence for adult students. *Computers & Education*, 55, 808–820.

Kennedy, N., & Kennedy, D. (2010). Between chaos and entropy: Community of inquiry from a systems perspective. *Complicity: An International Journal of Complexity and Education*, 7(2), 1–15.

Kim, J. (2011). Developing an instrument to measure social presence in distance higher education. *British Journal of Educational Technology*, 42(5), 763–777.

Kim, Y., Glassman, M., & Williams, M. S. (2015). Connecting agents: Engagement and motivation in online collaboration. *Computers in Human Behavior*, 49, 333–342.

Kolowich, S. (2012). Online learning and liberal arts colleges. *Inside Higher Education*, June 29. Retrieved from: www.insidehighered.com/news/2012/06/29/liberal-arts-college-explore-uses-blended-online-learning#ixzz1zCWJTYw0

Koole, M., McQuilkin, J. L., & Ally, M. (2010). Mobile learning in distance education: Utility or futility? *Journal of Distance Education*, 24(2), 59–82.

Kovanović, V., Joksimović, S., Gaševic, D., & Hatala, M. (2014). What is the source of social capital? The association between social network position and social presence in communities of inquiry. In *Proceedings of the Graph-based Educational*

Data Mining Workshop at 2014 Educational Data Mining Conference, London, UK. Retrieved February 9, 2016 from: http://citeseerx.ist.psu.edu/viewdoc/summa ry?doi=10.1.1.664.4492

Kovanović, V., Joksimović, S., Waters, Z., Gaševic, D., Kitto, K., Hatala, M., & Siemens, G. (2016). Towards automated content analysis of discussion transcripts: A cognitive presence case. IEEE transactions on learning technologies. Retrieved May 14, 2016 from: www.researchgate.net/profile/Vitomir_Kovanovic/publication/283463126_Towards_Automated_Content_Analysis_of_Discussion_Transcripts_A_Cognitive_Presence_Case/links/5639185a08aed5314d221b01.pdf

Kozan, K., & Richardson, J. C. (2014). Interrelationships between and among social, teaching, and cognitive presence. *The Internet and Higher Education*, 21, 68–73.

Kozma, R. B. (1991). Learning with media. *Review of Educational Research*, 61(2), 179–211.

Kozma, R. (1994). Will media influence learning? Reframing the debate. *Educational Technology Research & Development*, 42(2), 7–19.

Kramarski, B., & Dudai, V. (2009). Group-metacognitive support for online inquiry in mathematics with differential self-questioning. *Journal of Educational Computing Research*, 40(4), 377–404.

Kumar, S., Dawson, K., Black, E. W., Cavanaugh, C., & Sessums, C. D. (2011). Applying the Community of Inquiry framework to an online professional practice doctoral program. *International Review of Research in Open and Distance Learning*, 12(6), 126–142.

Kupczynski, L., Ice, P., Wiesenmeyer, R., & McCluskey, F. (2010). Student perceptions of the relationship between indicators of teaching presence and success in online courses. *Journal of Interactive Online Learning*, 9(1), 23–43.

Lai, K. (2015). Knowledge construction in online learning communities: A case study of a doctoral course. *Studies in Higher Education*, 40(4), 561–579.

Lajoie, S. P., & Lu, J. (2012). Supporting collaboration with technology: Does shared cognition lead to co-regulation in medicine. *Metacognition and Learning*, 7(1), 45–62.

Lambert, J. L., & Fisher, J. L. (2013). Community of inquiry framework: Establishing community in an online course. *Journal of Interactive Online Learning*, 12(1), 1–16.

Larkin, S. (2009). Socially mediated metacognition and learning to write. *Thinking Skills and Creativity*. 4(3), 149–159.

Laumakis, M., Graham, C., & Dziuban, C. (2009). The Sloan-C pillars and boundary objects in framework for evaluating blended learning. *Journal of Asynchronous Learning Networks*, 13(1), 75–87.

Lee, C. D., & Smagorinsky, P. (2000). Introduction: Constructing meaning through collaborative inquiry. In C. D. Lee & P. Smagorinsky (Eds.), *Vygotskian perspectives on literacy research: Constructing meaning through collaborative inquiry* (pp. 1–15). New York: Cambridge University Press.

Lee, S-M. (2014). The relationships between higher order thinking skills, cognitive density, and social presence in online learning. *The Internet and Higher Education*, 21, 41–51.

LeMahieu, P. (2011). What we need in education is more integrity (and less fidelity) of implementation. *Carnegie Insight*. Retrieved February 12, 2016 from: www.ca rnegiefoundation.org/blog/what-we-need-in-education-is-more-integrity-and-less-fi delity-of-implementation/

Leong, P. (2011). Role of social presence and cognitive absorption in online learning environments. *Distance Education*, 32(1), 5–28.

Lim, D. H., Morris, M. L., & Kupritz, V. W. (2007). Online vs. blended learning: Differences in instructional outcomes and learner satisfaction. *Journal of Asynchronous Learning Networks*, 11(3), 27–42.

Lim, J., & Richardson, J. C. (2016). Exploring the effects of students' social networking experience on social presence and perceptions of using SNSs for educational purposes. *The Internet and Higher Education*, 29, 31–39.

Lipman, M. (1985). Thinking skills fostered by philosophy for children. In J. W. Segal, S. F. Chipman & R. Glaser (Eds.), *Thinking and learning skills: Volume I: Relating instruction to research* (pp. 83–108). New York: Routledge.

Lipman, M. (2003). *Thinking in education* (2nd Ed.). Cambridge: Cambridge University Press.

Liu, S., Gomez, J., & Yen, C. (2009). Community college online course retention and final grade: Predictability of social presence. *Journal of Interactive Online Learning*, 8(2), 165–182.

Lombardi, M. M. (2008). Making the grade: The role of assessment in authentic learning. ELI Paper 1, EDUCAUSE. Retrieved April 16, 2016 from: www.educause.edu/ELI/MakingtheGradeTheRoleofAssessm/162389

Ma, J., Han, X., Yang, J., & Cheng, J. (2015). Examining the necessary condition for engagement in an online learning environment based on learning analytics approach: The role of the instructor. *The Internet and Higher Education*, 24, 26–34.

McCarthy, J. W., Smith, J. L., & DeLuca, D. (2010). Using online discussion boards with large and small groups to enhance learning of assistive technology. *Journal of Computing in Higher Education*, 22, 95–113.

McGill, T. J., Klobas, J. E., & Renzi, S. (2014). Critical success factors for the continuation of e-learning initiatives. *The Internet and Higher Education*, 22, 24–36.

Malmberg, J., Järvelä, S., Järvenoja, H., & Panadero, E. (2015). Promoting socially shared regulation of learning in CSCL: Progress of socially shared regulation among high- and low-performing groups. *Computers in Human Behavior*, 52, 562–572.

Martins, J., & Nunes, M. B. (2016). The temporal properties of e-learning: An exploratory study of academics' conceptions. *International Journal of Educational Management*, 30(1), 2–19.

Marton, F. (1988). Describing and improving teaching. In R. R. Schmeck (Ed.), *Learning strategies and learning styles*. New York: Plenum.

Marton, F., & Saljo, R. (1976). On qualitative differences in learning: I – Outcome and process. *British Journal of Educational Psychology*, 46, 4–11.

Mason, R. (1991). Moderating educational computer conferencing. DEOSNEWS, 1(19).

Means, B., Toyama, Y., Murphy, R., Bakia, M., & Jones, K. (2009). Evaluation of evidence-based practices in online learning: A meta-analysis and review of online learning studies. U.S. Department of Education. Retrieved January 29, 2010 from: www2.ed.gov/rschstat/eval/tech/evidence-based-practices/finalreport.pdf

Meyer, K. (2003). Face-to-face versus threaded discussions: The role of time and higher-order thinking. *Journal of Asynchronous Learning Networks*, 7(3), 55–65.

Meyer, K. (2004). Evaluating online discussions: Four difference frames of analysis. *Journal of Asynchronous Learning Networks*, 8(2), 101–114.

Mlodinow, L. (2008). *The drunkard's walk: How randomness rules our lives*. New York: Pantheon.

Moore, J. C., & Shelton, K. (2013). Social and student engagement and support: The Sloan-C Quality Scorecard for the Administration of Online Programs. *Journal of Asynchronous Learning Networks*, 17(1), 53–72.

Nagel, L., & Kotze, T. G. (2010). Supersizing e-learning: What a CoI survey reveals about teaching presence in a large online class. *The Internet and Higher Education*, 13(1–2), 45–51.

Nickerson, R. S. (1998). Confirmation bias: A ubiquitous phenomenon in many guises. *Review of General Psychology*, 2(2), 175–220.

Nippard, E., & Murphy, E. (2007). Social presence in the web-based synchronous secondary classroom. *Canadian Journal of Learning and Technology*, 33(1). Retrieved March 24, 2010 from: www.cjlt.ca/index.php/cjlt/article/view/24/22

O'Donnell, A. M., & Kelly, J. O. (1994). Learning from peers: Beyond the rhetoric of positive results. *Educational Psychology Review*, 6, 321–349.

Olson, D. K. (1994). *The world on paper: The conceptual and cognitive implications of reading and writing*. New York: Cambridge University Press.

Ong, W. (1982). *Orality and literacy*. New York: Routledge.

Paechter, M., Maier, B., & Macher, D. (2010). Students' expectations of, and experiences in e-learning: Their relation to learning achievements and course satisfaction. *Computers and Education*, 54(1), 222–229.

Palloff, R. M., & Pratt, K. (2005). *Collaborating online: Learning together in community*. San Francisco: Jossey-Bass.

Palloff, R. M., & Pratt, K. (2009). *Assessing the online learner*. San Francisco: Jossey-Bass.

Paulsen, M. (1995). Moderating educational computer conferences. In Z. Berge & M. Collins (Eds.), *Computer mediated communication and the online classroom* (pp. 81–90). Cresskill, NJ: Hampton Press, Inc.

Pawan, F., Paulus, T. M., Yalcin, S., & Chang, C. F. (2003). Online learning: Patterns of engagement and interaction among in-service teachers. *Language Learning and Technology*, 7(3), 119–140.

Perry, B., & Edwards, M. (2005). Exemplary online educators: Creating a community of inquiry. *Turkish Online Journal of Distance Education*, 6(2), 46–54.

Peters, O. (2000). Digital learning environments: New possibilities and opportunities. *International Review of Research in Open and Distance Learning*, 1(1).

Peters, O. (2007). The most industrialized form of education. In M. G. Moore (Ed.), *Handbook of distance education* (pp. 57–68). Mahwah, NJ: Lawrence Erlbaum.

Phan, H. (2009). Reflective thinking, effort, persistence, disorganization, and academic performance: A mediational approach. *Electronic Journal of Research in Educational Psychology*, 7(3), 927–952.

Picciano, A. G., Dzuiban, C. D., & Graham, C. R. (Eds.). (2014). *Blended learning research perspectives: Volume 2*. New York: Routledge.

Pisutova-Gerber, K., & Malovicova, J. (2009). Critical and higher order thinking in online threaded discussions in the Slovak context. *International Review of Research in Open and Distance Learning*, 10(1).

Porter, W. W., Graham, C. R., Bodily, R. G., & Sandberg, D. S. (2016). A qualitative analysis of institutional drivers and barriers to blended learning adoption in higher education. *The Internet and Higher Education*, 28, 17–27.

Power, M., & Vaughan, N. (2010). Redesigning online learning for international graduate seminar delivery. *Journal of Distance Education*, 24(2), 19–38.

Pozzi, F., & Persico, D. (2013). Sustaining learning design and pedagogical planning in CSCL. *Research in Learning Technology*, 21. Retrieved Oct 7, 2013 from: www.researchinlearningtechnology.net/index.php/rlt/article/view/17585

Pratt, D. D. (1981). The dynamics of continuing education learning groups. *Canadian Journal of University Continuing Education*, 8(1), 26–32.

Privateer, P. M. (1999). Academic technology and the future of higher education. *The Journal of Higher Education*, 70(1), 60–79.

Puzzi, F., Ceregini, A., Ferlino, L., & Persico, D. (2016). Dyads versus groups: Using different social structures in peer review to enhance online collaborative learning processes. *International Review of Research in Open and Distributed Learning*, 17(2), 85–106.

Ramsden, P. (1988). Context and strategy: Situational influences on learning. In R. R. Schmeck (Ed.), *Learning strategies and learning styles* (pp. 159–184). New York: Plenum.

Ramsden, P. (2003). *Learning to teach in higher education* (2nd Ed.). London: Routledge.

Report of a University of Illinois Faculty Seminar (1999). *Teaching at an Internet distance: The pedagogy of online teaching and learning*. Chicago: University of Illinois.

Resnick, L. B. (1987). *Education and learning to think*. Washington, DC: National Academy Press.

Reychav, I., Dunaway, M., & Kobayashi, M. (2015). Understanding mobile technology-fit behaviors outside the classroom. *Computers and Education*, 87, 142–150.

Richard, G. (2005). *E-learning in tertiary education: Where do we stand*. Paris: Centre for Education Research and Innovation.

Richardson, J. C., & Ice, P. (2010). Investigating students' level of critical thinking across instructional strategies in online discussions. *The Internet and Higher Education*, 13(1–2), 52–59.

Richardson, J. C., & Swan, K. (2003). Examining social presence in online courses in relation to students' perceived learning and satisfaction. *Journal of Asynchronous Learning Networks*, 7(1), 68–88.

Richardson, J., Arbaugh, J. B., Cleveland-Innes, M., Ice, P., Swan, K., & Garrison, D. R. (2012). Using the Community of Inquiry framework to inform effective instructional design. In L. Moller & J. B. Huett (Eds.), *The next generation of distance education: Unconstrained learning* (pp. 97–125). New York: Springer.

Richardson, J. C., Besser, E., Koehler, A., Lim, J., & Strait, M. (2016). Instructors' perceptions of instructor presence in online learning environments. *International Review of Research in Open and Distributed Learning*, 17(4), 82–103.

Richardson, J. C., Ice, P., Boston, W., Powell, K., & Gibson, A. (2011). Using the community of inquiry framework survey for multi-level institutional evaluation and continuous quality improvement. *World Conference on Educational Multimedia, Hypermedia and Telecommunications*, 2011(1), 1968–1977. Retrieved February 9, 2016 from: www.editlib.org/noaccess/38131/

Rienties, B., Giesbers, B., Tempelaar, D. T., & Lygo-Baker, S. (2013). Redesigning teaching presence in order to enhance cognitive presence, a longitudinal analysis. In Z. Akyol & D. R. Garrison (Eds.), *Educational Communities of Inquiry: Theoretical framework, research and practice* (pp. 109–132). Hershey, PA: IGI Global.

Rifkin, J. (2014). *The zero marginal cost society*. New York: Palgrave Macmillan.

Roblyer, M. D., Freeman, J., Donaldson, M. B., & Maddox, M. (2007). A comparison of outcomes of virtual school courses offered in synchronous and asynchronous formats. *The Internet and Higher Education*, 10(4), 261–268.

Roblyer, M. D., McDaniel, M., Webb, M., Herman, J., & Witty, J. V. (2010). Findings on Facebook in higher education: A comparison of college faculty and student uses and perceptions of social networking sites. *The Internet and Higher Education*, 13, 134–140.

Rockinson-Szapkiw, A. J., Wendt, J., Wighting, M., & Nisbet, D. (2016). The predictive relationship among the community of inquiry framework, perceived learning and online, and graduate students' course grades in online synchronous and asynchronous courses. *International Review of Research in Open and Distance Learning*, 17(3), 18–34.

Rogers, P., & Lea, M. (2005). Social presence in distributed group environments: The role of social identity. *Behavior & Information Technology*, 24(2), 151–158.

Rosenberg, M. J. (2001). *E-Learning: Strategies for delivering knowledge in the digital age*. New York: McGraw-Hill.

Rourke, L., & Anderson, T. (2002). Exploring social communication in computer conferencing. *Journal of Interactive Learning Research*, 13(3), 259–275.

Rourke, L., & Kanuka, H. (2007). Barriers to online discourse. *Computer Supported Collaborative Learning*, 2, 105–126.

Rourke, L., & Kanuka, H. (2009). Learning in communities of inquiry: A review of the literature. *Journal of Distance Education*, 23(1), 19–48.

Rourke, L., Anderson, T., Archer, W., & Garrison, D. R. (1999). Assessing social presence in asynchronous, text-based computer conferences. *Journal of Distance Education*, 14(3), 51–70.

Rovai, A. P., & Jordan, H. M. (2004). Blended learning and sense of community: A comparative analysis with traditional and fully online graduate courses. *International Review of Research in Open and Distance Learning*, 5(2).

Rowntree, D. (1977). *Assessing students*. London: Harper & Row.

Rubin, B., & Fernandes, R. (2013). The teacher as leader: Effect of teaching behaviors on class community and agreement. *International Review of Research in Open and Distance Learning*, 14(5).

Rubin, B., Fernandes, R., & Avgerinou, M. D. (2013). The effects of technology on the Community of Inquiry and satisfaction with online courses. *The Internet and Higher Education*, 17, 48–57.

Saab, N., van Joolingen, W., & van Hout-Wolters, B. (2012). Support of the collaborative inquiry learning process: Influence of support on task and team regulation. *Metacognition and Learning*, 7, 7–23.

Saade, R. G., Morin, D., & Thomas, J. D. E. (2012). Critical thinking in e-learning environments. *Computers in Human Behavior*, 28, 1608–1617.

Sanger, L. (2010). Individual knowledge in the Internet age. *EDUCAUSE Review*, 45(2), 14–24.

Saritas, T. (2008). The construction of knowledge through social interaction via computer-mediated communication. *The Quarterly Review of Distance Education*, 9(1), 35–49.

Savvidou, C. (2013). "Thanks for sharing your story": The role of the teacher in facilitating social presence in online discussion. *Technology, Pedagogy and Education*, 22(2), 193–211.

Sawyer, R. K. (2008). Optimising learning: Implications of learning sciences research. In *Innovating to learn: Learning to innovate*. OECD.

Schellens, T., Van Keer, H., De Wever, B., & Valcke, M. (2009). Tagging thinking types in asynchronous discussion groups: Effects on critical thinking. *Interactive Learning Environments*, 17(1), 77–94.

Schrage, M. (1989). *No more teams! Mastering the dynamics of creative collaboration*. New York: Currency Doubleday.

Schraw, G. (2001). Promoting general metacognitive awareness. In H. J. Hartman (Ed.), *Metacognition in learning and instruction: Theory, research and practice* (pp. 3–16). Boston: Kluwer.

Schreiner, L. A. (2009). Linking student satisfaction with retention. Retrieved January 19, 2010 from: https://www.noellevitz.com/NR/rdonlyres/A22786EF-65FF-4053-A15 A-BE145B0C708/0/LinkingStudentSatis0809.pdf

Schrire, S. (2004). Interaction and cognition in asynchronous computer conferencing. *Instructional Science*, 32, 475–502.

Schrire, S. (2006). Knowledge building in asynchronous discussion groups: Going beyond quantitative analysis. *Computers & Education*, 46(1), 49–70.

Shea, P., & Bidjerano, T. (2009a). Community of inquiry as a theoretical framework to foster "epistemic engagement" and "cognitive presence" in online education. *Computers and Education*, 52(3), 543–553.

Shea, P., & Bidjerano, T. (2009b). Cognitive presence and online learner engagement: A cluster analysis of the community of inquiry framework. *Journal of Computing in Higher Education*, 21, 199–217.

Shea, P., Li, C. S., & Pickett, A. (2006). A study of teaching presence and student sense of learning community in fully online and web-enhanced college courses. *The Internet and Higher Education*, 9(3), 175–190.

Shea, P., Hayes, S., & Vickers, J. (2010). Online instructional effort measured through the lens of teaching presence in the community of inquiry framework: A re-examination of measures and approach. *The International Review of Research in Open and Distance Learning*, 11(3), 127–154.

Shea, P., Hayes, S., Vickers, J., Gozza-Cohen, M., Uzner, S., Mehta, R., Valchova, A., & Rangan, P. (2010). A re-examination of the community of inquiry framework: Social network and content analysis. *The Internet and Higher Education*, 13(1–2), 10–21.

Shea, P., Hayes, S., Smith, S. U., Vickers, J., Bidjerano, T., Picket, A., Gozza-Cohen, M., Wilde, J., & Jian, S. (2012). Learning presence: Additional research on a new conceptual element within the Community of Inquiry (CoI) framework. *The Internet and Higher Education*, 15(2), 89–95.

Shea, P., Hayes, S., Uzuner-Smith, S., Gozza-Cohen, M., Vickers, J., & Bidjerano, T. (2014). Reconceptualizing the community of inquiry framework: Exploratory and confirmatory analysis. *The Internet and Higher Education*, 23, 9–17.

Sheridan, K., & Kelly, M. A. (2010). The indicators of instructor presence that are important to students in online courses. *Journal of Online Learning and Teaching*, 6(4), 767–778.

Sheridan, K., Kelly, M. A., & Bentz, D. T. (2013). A follow-up study of the indicators of teaching presence critical to students in online courses. In Z. Akyol & D. R. Garrison (Eds.), *Educational communities of inquiry: Theoretical framework, research and practice* (pp. 67–83). Hershey, PA: IGI Global.

Shin, W. S., & Kang, M. (2015). The use of a mobile learning management system at an online university and its effect on learning satisfaction and achievement. *International Review of Research in Open and Distributed Learning*, 16(3), 110–130.

Short, J., Williams, E., & Christie, B. (1976). *The Social Psychology of Telecommunications*. Toronto: John Wiley and Sons.

Sims, R. (2001). From art to alchemy: Achieving success with online learning. *IT Forum*, 55. Retrieved June 6, 2002 from: http://itforum.coe.uga.edu/AECT_ITF_PDFS/paper55.pdf

So, H., & Brush, T. A. (2008). Student perceptions of collaborative learning, social presence and satisfaction in a blended learning environment: Relationships and critical factors. *Computers & Education*, 51(1), 318–336.

Sobel-Lojeski, K. (2015). The subtle ways our screens are pushing us apart. *Harvard Business Review*, April 8, 2015. Retrieved February 9, 2016 from: https://hbr.org/2015/04/the-subtle-ways-our-screens-are-pushing-us-apart

Song, H., Kim, J., & Luo, W. (2016). Teacher–student relationship in online classes: A role of teacher self-disclosure. *Computers in Human Behavior*, 54, 436–443.

Staley, J., & Ice, P. (2009). Instructional design project management 2.0: A model of development and practice. Paper presented at the 25th Annual Conference on Distance Teaching and Learning, Madison, WI, August.

Stein, D. (1992). (Ed.). *Cooperating with written texts: The pragmatics and comprehension of written texts*. Berlin: Mouton de Gruyter.

Stein, D. S., Wanstreet, C. E., Glazer, H. R., Engle, C. L., Harris, R. A., Johnston, S. M., Simons, M. R., & Trinko, L. A. (2007). Creating shared understanding through chats in a community of inquiry. *The Internet and Higher Education*, 10, 103–115.

Stein, D. S., Wanstreet, C. E., Slagle, P., Trinko, L. A., & Lutz, M. (2013). From 'hello' to higher-order thinking: The effect of coaching and feedback on online chats. *The Internet and Higher Education*, 16, 78–84.

Stenbom, S. (2015). *Online coaching as a relationship of inquiry: Exploring one-to-one online education* (Doctoral Thesis). KTH Royal Institute of Technology, Stockholm: Sweden.

Stewart, P. W., Cooper, S. S., & Moulding, L. R. (2007). Metacognitive development in professional educators. *The Researcher*, 21(1), 32–40.

Sun, C.-Y., & Wu, Y.-T. (2016). Analysis of learning achievement and teacher-student interactions in flipped and conventional classrooms. *International Review of Research in Open & Distance Learning*, 17(1), 79–99.

Sun, Y., Franklin, T., & Gao, F. (2015). Learning outside of classroom: Exploring the active part of an informal online English learning community in China. *British Journal of Educational Technology*. Retrieved May 24, 2016 from: http://onlinelibrary.wiley.com/doi/10.1111/bjet.12340/epdf.

Swan, K., & Richardson, J. C. (2003). Examining social presence in online courses in relation to students' perceived learning and satisfaction. *Journal of Asynchronous Learning Networks*, 7, 68–82.

Swan, K., & Shih, L. F. (2005). On the nature and development of social presence in online course discussions. *Journal of Asynchronous Learning Networks*, 9(3), 115–136.

Swan, K., Day, S. L., Bogle, L. R., & Matthews, D. B. (2014). A collaborative, design-based approach to improving an online program. *The Internet and Higher Education*, 21, 74–81.

Swan, K., Schenker, J., Arnold, S., & Kuo, C-L. (2007). Shaping online discussion: Assessment matters. *e-Mentor*, 1(18), 78–82.

Swan, K., Shen, J., & Hiltz, R. (2006). Assessment and collaboration in online learning. *Journal of Asynchronous Learning Networks*, 10(1), 45–62.

Sweller, J. (2016). Story of a Research Program. *Education Review*, 23, 1–17. Retrieved February 12, 2016 from: http://edrev.asu.edu/edrev/index.php/ER/article/viewFile/2025/545.

Szeto, E. (2015). Community of Inquiry as an instructional approach: What effects of teaching, social and cognitive presences are there in blended synchronous learning and teaching? *Computers and Education*, 81, 191–201.

Tapscott, D. (1996). *The digital economy: Promise and peril in the age of networked intelligence.* New York: McGraw-Hill.

Tapscott, D., & Williams, A. D. (2010). Innovating the 21st-century university: It's time! *EDUCAUSE Review*, 45(1), 16–29.

Tarricone, P. (2011). *The taxonomy of metacognition.* New York: Psychology Press.

Tayebinik, M., & Puteh, M. (2012). Sense of community: How important is this quality in blended courses. *Proceeding of the International Conference on Education and Management Innovation, Singapore.*

Thaler, R. H., & Sunstein, C. R. (2008). *Nudge: Improving decisions about health, wealth, and happiness.* New Haven, CT: Yale University Press.

Toven-Lindsey, B., Rhoads, R. A., & Lozano, J. B. (2015). Virtually unlimited classrooms: Pedagogical practices in massive open online courses. *The Internet and Higher Education*, 24, 1–12.

Tsiotakis, P., & Jimoyiannis, A. (2016). Critical factors towards analysing teachers' presence in on-line learning communities. *The Internet and Higher Education*, 28, 45–58.

Twigg, C. A. (2003). Improving learning and reducing costs: New models for online learning. *EDUCAUSE Review*, 38(5), 29–38.

Tynan, B., Ryan, Y., & Lamont-Mills, A. (2015). Examining workload models in online and blended learning. *British Journal of Educational Technology*, 46(1), 5–15.

Unwin, A. (2015). Developing new teacher inquiry and criticality: The role of online discussions. *British Journal of Educational Technology*, 46(6), 1214–1222.

Valcke, M., De Wever, B., Zhu, C., & Deed, C. (2009). Supporting active cognitive processing in collaborative groups: Potential of Bloom's taxonomy as a labelling tool. *The Internet and Higher Education*, 12, 165–172.

Van Kleef, G. A., De Dreu, C. K. W., & Manstead, A. S. R. (2010). Chapter 2 – An interpersonal approach to emotion in social decision making: The emotions as social information model. *Advances in Experimental Social Psychology*, 42, 45–96.

Vaughan, N., & Garrison, D. R. (2005). Creating cognitive presence in a blended faculty development community. *The Internet and Higher Education*, 8(1), 1–12.

Vaughan, N., & Garrison, D. R. (2006). How blended learning can support a faculty community of inquiry. *Journal of Asynchronous Learning Networks*, 10(4), 139–152.

Vaughan, N. D., Cleveland-Innes, M., & Garrison, D. R. (2013). *Teaching in blended learning environments: Creating and sustaining communities of inquiry.* Athabasca, Alberta, Canada: Athabasca University Press.

Volet, S., Vauras, M., & Salonen, P. (2009). Self- and social regulation in learning contexts: An integrative perspective. *Educational Psychologist*, 44(4), 215–226.

Vygotsky, L. S. (1978). *Mind in society: The development of higher psychological processes*. Cambridge MA: Harvard University Press.

Wade, S. E., & Fauske, J. R. (2004). Dialogue online: Prospective teachers' discourse strategies in computer-mediated discussions. *Reading Research Quarterly*, 39(2), 134–160.

Walther, J. (1992). Interpersonal effects in computer mediated interaction: A relational perspective. *Communication Research*, 19(1), 52–90.

Warner, A. G. (2016). Developing a community of inquiry in a face-to-face class: How an online learning framework can enrich traditional classroom practice. *Journal of Management Education*, 40(4), 432–452.

Wasson, C. (2013). "It was like a little community": An ethnographic study of online learning and its implications for MOOCs. *Ethnographic Praxis in Industry Conference Proceedings*. Retrieved November 10, 2014 from: http://epiconference.com/2013/sites/default/files/EPIC-Proceedings.pdf#page=180.

Weigel, M., Straughn, C., & Gardner, H. (2010). New digital media and their potential cognitive impact on youth learning. In M. S. Khine & I. M. Saleh (Eds.), *New science of learning: Cognition, computers and collaboration in education* (pp. 2–22). New York: Springer.

Weigel, V. B. (2002). *Deep learning for a digital age: Technology's untapped potential to enrich higher education*. San Francisco: Jossey-Bass.

Wells, G. (2000). Dialogic inquiry in education: Building on the legacy of Vygotsky. In Lee, C. D., & Smagorinsky, P. (Eds.), *Vygotskian perspectives on literacy research: Constructing meaning through collaborative inquiry* (pp. 51–85). New York: Cambridge University Press.

White, B. Y., Frederiksen, J. R., & Collins, A. (2009). The interplay of scientific inquiry and metacognition: More than a marriage of convenience. In D. Hacker, J. Dunlosky & A. Graesser (Eds.), *Handbook of metacognition in education* (pp. 175–205). New York: Routledge.

Wicks, D. A., Craft, B. B., Mason, G. N., Gritter, K., & Bolding, K. (2015). An investigation into the community of inquiry of blended classrooms by a faculty learning community. *The Internet and Higher Education*, 25, 53–62.

Wilson, E. O. (2012). *The social conquest of earth*. New York: W. W. Norton.

Winne, P. H. (2015). What is the state of the art in self-, co- and socially shared regulation in CSCL? *Computers in Human Behavior*, 52, 628–631.

Wisneski, J. E., Ozogul, G., & Bichelmeyer, B. A. (2015). Does teaching presence transfer between MBA teaching environments? A comparative investigation of instructional design practices associated with teaching presence. *The Internet and Higher Education*, 25, 18–27.

Wright, P. (2015). Comparing e-tivities, e-moderation and the five stage model to the Community of Inquiry model for online learning design. *The Online Journal of Distance Education and e-Learning*, 3(2), 17–30.

Wu, D., & Hiltz, S. R. (2004). Predicting learning from asynchronous online discussions. *Journal of Asynchronous Learning Networks*, 8(2), 139–152.

Yamagata-Lynch, L. C., Cowan, J., & Luetkehans, L. M. (2015). Transforming disruptive technology into sustainable technology: Understanding the front-end design of an online program at a brick-and-mortar university. *The Internet and Higher Education*, 26, 10–18.

Yang, J. C., Quadir, B., Chen, N-S., & Miao, Q. (2016). Effects of online presence on learning performance in a blog-based online course. *The Internet and Higher Education*, 30, 11–20.

Yeh, S. S. (2009). The cost-effectiveness of raising teacher quality. *Educational Research Review*, 4(3), 220–232.

Young, A., & Fry, J. D. (2008). Metacognitive awareness and academic achievement in college students. *Journal of the Scholarship of Teaching and Learning*, 8(2), 1–10.

Zawacki-Richter, O., & Anderson, T. (2014). Introduction: Research areas in online distance education (pp. 1–35). In O. Zawacki-Richter & T. Anderson (Eds.). *Online distance education: Towards a research agenda.* AU Press.

Zhan, Z., & Mei, H. (2013). Academic self-concept and social presence in face-to-face and online learning: Perceptions and effects on students' learning achievement and satisfaction across environments. *Computers and Education*, 69, 131–138.

Zhao, H., & Sullivan, K. P. H. (2016). Teaching presence in computer conferencing learning environments: Effects on interaction, cognition and learning uptake. *British Journal of Educational Technology*, 47. Retrieved May 24, 2016 from: http://onlinelibrary.wiley.com.ezproxy.lib.ucalgary.ca/doi/10.1111/bjet.12383/pdf

Zhao, H., Sullivan, K. P. H., & Mellenius, I. (2014). Participation, interaction and social presence: An exploratory study of collaboration in online peer review groups. *British Journal of Educational Technology*, 45(5), 807–819.

Index

Page numbers in italics refer to figures. Page numbers in bold refer to tables.